Warren Beatty

Also by John Parker

King of Fools: A Biography of the Duke of Windsor
Five for Hollywood
The Princess Royal
The Trial of Rock Hudson
Prince Philip: A Critical Biography
The Joker's Wild: The Biography of Jack Nicholson
The Queen: The New Biography
At the Heart of Darkness
Sean Connery
Elvis: The Secret Files

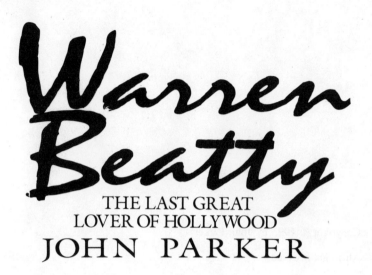

Warren Beatty

THE LAST GREAT
LOVER OF HOLLYWOOD

JOHN PARKER

Carroll & Graf Publishers, Inc.
New York

Copyright © 1993 by John Parker

Published by arrangement with Headline Book Publishing PLC.

First Carroll & Graf edition April 1994

Carroll & Graf Publishers, Inc.
260 Fifth Avenue
New York, NY 10001

Library of Congress Cataloging-in-Publication Data

Parker, John, 1938 Aug. 5–
    Warren Beatty : the last great lover of Hollywood / John Parker.—
1st Carroll & Graf Publishers ed.
        p.   cm.
    ISBN 0-7867-0072-6 : $21.00
    1. Beatty, Warren, 1937–   . 2. Motion pictures actors and
actresses—United States—Biography.   I. Title.
PN2287.B394P37   1994
791.43'028'092—dc20
    [B]   94-141
                                                                                        CIP

Manufactured in the United States of America

Contents

	Acknowledgements	vii
	Snapshots	1
1	The Kid	9
2	A Brief Apprenticeship	25
3	Fame Before Stardom	37
4	Natalie, Susan and Vivien	53
5	Whirlwind	69
6	Wanted	85
7	In Swinging London	97
8	Promise Her . . .	111
9	Achieving the Impossible	127
10	Just Julie	143
11	Elizabeth's Game	157
12	Meeting Jack	173
13	McGovern's Man	187
14	Shampoo	199
15	Michelle, Briefly	215
16	Heavenly Bodies	229
17	Reds	241
18	Enter Gary Hart	259
19	A Song and Dance	273
20	Dick and Madonna	289
21	Madonna Takes All	303
22	Bugsy and Bening	315
	Filmography	331
	Select Bibliography	337
	Index	339

Acknowledgements

The author records his thanks and appreciation to the many people on both sides of the Atlantic who assisted in the compilation of this biography through personal interviews, telephone conversations and correspondence. I am especially grateful to Leslie Caron for her patience, David Puttnam for reading a section of the manuscript, Charlton Heston for his recall of fifties Hollywood, and as ever to Maureen Stapleton, a font of memories of the American film and theatre communities; to Joan Collins and Britt Ekland for permission to quote briefly from the following: *Past Imperfect, the autobiography of Joan Collins*, now published by Virgin Publishing Ltd, London; and *True Britt, the autobiography of Britt Ekland*, published originally by Sphere, now Little, Brown of London.

Snapshots

LESLIE CARON, Paris, March 1993: Leslie Caron first met Warren Beatty in 1963 at a party given by her press agents Rogers and Cowan at the fashionable restaurant, the Bistro, in Beverly Hills. The party was to promote Leslie for the forthcoming Academy awards for her part in *The L-Shaped Room* (for which she received an Oscar nomination) and to announce her starring role in a new film with Cary Grant. Leslie wrote for the author:

'I was struck by his appearance and his personality. He had star quality – very good looks, a great smile, he was tall and athletic; seduction was his greatest asset.

'Once he was interested in a woman, he would never let go. He enveloped her with his every thought; he wanted total control of her, her clothes, her make-up, her work; he took notice of everything.

'And he sent every one of us to a psychoanalyst.

'He believed the experience was beneficial. He was right. It was a great experience. My analyst was extremely well read. I felt I was having a private university course. Very enlightening. Everyone should have it if they can afford it. Warren went as well, of course, to his own. He was so fond of his analyst – a brilliant and witty man – that he never stopped going.

'Warren had great dynamism, will power, and as I got to know him better I realised he had talents far above acting. He was a born leader which was eventually demonstrated when he became a producer. He could have been the head of a studio had he wanted to.

'I found Warren very conscientious about his work and career – obsessionally so. He was always very particular about what he did. He was offered everything, every major male part and turned down most of them. He refused more scripts than he accepted. That did not seem to affect his position in Hollywood.

'I think, in some way, he was unsure of himself in those days. He wanted desperately to be taken seriously as an actor and would not accept anything unless he considered that the film had Academy awards potential. He only wanted to do prestigious material – author-films based upon the works of writers such as Tennessee Williams, William Inge and that group of American writers who created post-war American film dramas. Warren would only go with authors and directors who were of that intellectual level. He was uncompromising about quality.

'He was to some extent influenced by the Method. I don't think that any actor, at that time, could avoid the overwhelming novelty and success of that style of acting. Marlon Brando, James Dean and Montgomery Clift were the most famous exponents of it. Warren did not set out to imitate any of them; that was just the style of the moment.

'The phenomenon happened as with the Impressionists who all have a common denominator in their painting. So it happened with acting. This school of acting was first created by Stanislavski, director of the Moscow Arts Theatre, and Lee Strasberg developed his own interpretation of it [in New York]. This fad, with its inevitable abuse, hit the American film and the theatre of the fifties.

'The Method was an open challenge to the somewhat facile acting that was practised previously – the "just look beautiful and speak your lines fast" school of acting. Those trained in the Method were told among other things to think their lines before speaking them ... to take their time and only speak when the thought was ripe. Strangely enough this thinking process was something new. Of course, this did not affect English actors playing Shakespeare, for instance, where rhythm is essential.

'Warren trained in New York with Stella Adler who also taught the Method, but I think that the actor who influenced

2

him most was Spencer Tracy who never heard of Stanislavski, except perhaps late in his career. Spencer Tracy developed his own style of acting, playing in a modern way. He invented something which was also an important part of Stanislavski's training: he knew how to listen. Warren had noticed that and incorporated it in his own work.

'Warren and I worked on one film only: *Promise Her Anything*. He chose the script. He had been looking for a film that would suit us both and settled on this American comedy. It was, for me, totally different from *The L-Shaped Room*, an English film and a social statement on unwed mothers, and a departure for Warren, too. His previous films were social dramas, but American comedies were extremely popular at the time with the likes of Cary Grant, Doris Day and Rock Hudson.

'Then, looking for another project we went to Paris. Warren greatly admired the French director François Truffaut who was preparing *Fahrenheit 451*. We were in Paris, indeed I would vouchsafe to say that Warren decided we should go to Paris so that he could meet Truffaut to talk to him about doing the film with him.

'I knew Truffaut and so we arranged a lunch together. Warren decided he would only come for coffee. He could not speak French and so feared that his presence during the whole meal would make for laborious conversation.

'When he expressed his desire to play the lead in *Fahrenheit*, François said, "No I can't have you for this part. I have already given it to Oskar Werner [the German actor] to co-star with the British actress Julie Christie. But if you are looking to do something with Leslie, there is a property that was offered to me by two American writers and which should really be done by an American. It is extremely good ... it is called *Bonnie and Clyde*."

'It was arranged that a copy of the script should be handed over; we both read it and thought it was excellent. However, Warren had serious doubts because he thought at that time Westerns were not doing at all well. Also the film version of Truman Capote's *In Cold Blood* was just being done and he worried that the two films would clash. I told Warren that Bonnie and Clyde did not seem to me to be a Western,

3

although set in Texas, and as for *In Cold Blood*, by the time *Bonnie and Clyde* was out, it would be forgotten; no one would see any resemblance.

'I strongly advised him to buy the property. Warren went to New York, met Robert Benton [one of the writers] and bought it. At first it was intended that I would play Bonnie but on second thoughts, Warren wondered whether it was a good idea. Bonnie should be played by an American; she was a Texas girl. Of course, he was right. He approached Natalie Wood but she turned him down; eventually he got Faye Dunaway.

'He also had the courage to ask Arthur Penn to direct. Arthur was primarily a stage director from New York who had never had a hit in films. I thought the result was wonderful. The film created a great deal of controversy. The violent killings shook the world. Furthermore, the heroes are utterly amoral and utterly seductive. They killed one and all with charming nonchalance.

'I think *Bonnie and Clyde* split us up. Warren was away working on location in Texas for months, then he was in post-production in Hollywood, whereas I was in England.

'But I kept a wonderful souvenir of our years together. Our life was what you would call glamorous. To an excess. A front page kind of life which isn't me.

'Warren knew everyone and he had a subtle way of getting to know people. Like a detective, he would discover all about them. He never made any secret of the fact that he wanted the world. He loved power, and he went for it.'

SUSANNAH YORK, London, January 1993: Susannah found herself playing opposite Warren Beatty in the film *Kaleidoscope*, not long after she had finished making *Freud* for John Huston, in which she co-starred with Montgomery Clift whom she adored, though she was rather less enamoured with Beatty:

'The movie Warren and I made together was very much a sixties showcase; pure froth with a thriller embedded in the comedy. Warren seemed the right actor for it, though it wasn't a many-layered piece, and the characters weren't deep or intense. He appeared to me first and foremost a ladies' man and as I was happily married, I found myself smacking his hand as he went to pinch my bum, saying "stop it Warren". He is a very spontaneous actor but the script did not call for either of us to be much more than gay and full of fun. And he was certainly that.

'He was very pretty and in acting if your looks are very striking, as Warren's were, people find that they are loath to give you credit for your acting ability. They assume that you are there because you are pretty and don't investigate the fact that you are there because you are jolly good. I'm sure Warren wasn't taken as seriously then as he could have been but it could also have been of his own doing.

'I did not become intimately friendly with him. We had fun but I did not mix with the same swinging London crowd. Leslie Caron was also around quite a lot, and came to the set often, and she was quite jealous, not just of me but possibly any woman – and probably quite rightly so. Warren loves women, and he's rather babylike. Or was then. He had a naughty little boy way of acting and thought it was quite fun to pinch people's bottoms. On one level, you laughed, and on another you would get annoyed. I felt cross with him some-times, but never got into a rage. He was never offensive.

'He did have an irrepressibly good opinion of himself and of his charm and way with women. All of which was quite clearly merited, but it could be irritating – particularly if you weren't going down that route. He was quite persistent and you just had to laugh it off. It was a problem in a way because it precluded you from being friends. I also felt he believed it was expected of him.

'I would have liked to get closer as a friend, but I could not go beyond that. I still feel a nice warm glow for him; he was very intelligent and bright and had a sense of humour. I think the answer to his so-called secret with women is his boyish charm and particularly his sense of humour.

SALLY OGLE DAVIS, Los Angeles, March 1993: Ms Davis is a Hollywood writer and has been involved in the film world for many years. She first met Warren Beatty in the sixties, and for reasons which she now explains, began observing his progress:

'I once watched Warren Beatty make love. Imagine, if you can, a party at the mansion of Bernie Cornfeld who was, at that time in the late sixties, a financial wheeler-dealer riding high on the Beverly Hills social waves, later to be incarcerated for an international fiddle to be known as the IOS (International Overseas Services) scandal. The party, nevertheless, was a very dull affair.

'I became tired of trying to make conversation with stoned-out, emaciated starlets and plump, balding tycoons anxious for more non-verbal forms of communication and I took myself to a deserted screening room and sat down in the third row to watch a thoroughly undistinguished British thriller. Twenty minutes or so into the movie, Beatty walked in with a giggling young woman. Despite all the empty seats around me, they sat down in the row directly in front of me and proceeded to make out.

'While Beatty was busily engaged in the activity for which he had become renowned he kept winking at me over the young lady's shoulder as if to say, "How am I doing?" He appeared to be doing very well indeed.

'Such naked narcissism is rare even in Hollywood and so, not surprisingly, I have been fascinated with Warren Beatty ever since.'

MAUREEN STAPLETON, Massachusetts, December 1992: Doyenne of the New York Method acting scene in the fifties, Ms Stapleton was a close friend of many emerging stars, and especially Marlon Brando and Montgomery Clift with whom she trained at the Actors Studio. She became one of the most sought-after character actresses in major movies for forty years. She vaguely remembered Beatty in New York in the late fifties. Her pal William Inge, the playwright (*Bus Stop, Come Back Little Sheba*, etc.), who was Beatty's mentor in those days, had written a play (*A Loss of Roses*) in which his young protégé would make his debut on Broadway, though it was short lived. She recalls:

'I remember they talked about Warren back then; he was a beautiful kid and apparently very intense. He was very much into the New York scene, trained with Stella Adler, herself a disciple of Stanislavski, and subsequently he first made his name in work by Bill Inge and Tennessee. But he was just a boy then ... Jesus, so long ago. I did not get to work with him until probably twenty years later, in 1980 when he had become a power in the land. He cast me in *Reds*, which was his big movie, his ten-year obsession [and in which Maureen won an Oscar for best supporting actress].

'At the time, he was with Diane Keaton who was also his co-star in the movie, along with myself and Jack [Nicholson], of course, was his big buddy. But the film was Warren's in every respect – he was producer, director, co-writer and star and he was such a goddamned perfectionist. I'm not knocking that, but there were some heady moments, classic Warren. We were filming in England and a lot of work had been done by the time I arrived, and Warren had gotten into the habit of doing a lot of re-takes.

'Well, one big scene was being filmed in Manchester. I was supposed to be addressing a crowd of people, standing there in the pouring rain. It was an atrocious day, which was a coincidence because it was the same when I last filmed in Manchester (for a TV version of *Cat On A Hot Tin Roof*), and on that occasion I was so depressed that Larry Olivier and Robert Wagner had to help me to my room, but that's another story.

'This particular scene in *Reds* involved about six hundred extras. And we had done eight or nine takes, perhaps ten or eleven, I don't know how many. I couldn't see anything wrong with it – they all looked the same to me. Anyway, he was way down the other end of the block and shouted for the umpteenth time through his bullhorn, "One more time, sweetheart". So I took the bullhorn from Simon, one of the unit directors, and I shouted back, "Warren, are you out of your fucking mind?" And the whole crowd of extras cheered and clapped. So he comes back on the bullhorn: "I may be, darling, but do it again, anyway." So we did it again. That's my abiding memory of Warren Beatty, and I love him.'

BRITT EKLAND, Los Angeles, 1980: Star of more than thirty films and equally famous as ex-wife of Peter Sellers and for her association with Rod Stewart, Britt Ekland experienced a brief interlude with Beatty during his long affair with Julie

Christie, whom Ekland observed was temporarily and 'foolishly absent' from his life when they met:

'He could handle women as smoothly as operating an elevator. He knew exactly where to locate the top button. One flick and we were on the way. He had never sacrificed his good looks: the dark hair neatly combed, the innocently sensual eyes constantly inquiring. He exudes charm, wit and intelligence.

'I first met him years earlier, when he was with Leslie Caron. Sellers and I joined them for dinner. We met again at a dinner party for Roman Polanski, and his gaze descended upon me. My affair with Warren fell into a kind of category I had never experienced before, where fantasy became reality. He was the most divine lover of all, his libido was as lethal as high octane gas. I had never known such pleasure or passion in my life.

'For a long spell, I lied to myself. I was convinced that Warren might abandon all his other women for me, but of course he did not. There were always the whispered telephone calls he made to Julie. No man had made me happier, and I fought hard to keep him, but he was always apprehensive about our affair in case Julie found out. I believed that then Warren was incapable of lasting love.'

The above recollections are an intriguing but small cross-section of reminiscences from friends and associates which have been drawn upon for this biography. As the story of Warren Beatty is revealed, there is always the danger that the aspect for which he perhaps became most famous – his legion liaisons – might overshadow the underlying story of one man's steadfast determination and single-minded pursuit of his goals. There is more, much more, to the man than this superficial image.

And so let us begin, and attempt at the outset to put this whole question of Warren Beatty versus the female of the species into some sort of perspective.

1
The Kid

A quotation by Woody Allen may be familiar but it is the only one with which to start a biography of Warren Beatty. Allen said that if he ever came back in another life, he wanted to be Warren Beatty's fingertips. The very association of Beatty and sex, sexual endeavour, sexual activity, sexual potency and sexual inventiveness has become synonymous with his public persona. Whereas most actors who inscribe a character upon modern society do so through their screen image, Warren Beatty is Warren Beatty.

His reputation, acquired over more than three decades prior to his marriage to Annette Bening in 1992, portrayed him as a jet-setting, quicksilver Casanova star of 1001 bedroom scenes around the world. This portrayal early in his career extended to a level of fame well beyond that merited by his intermittent screen appearances. He became famous for his conquests. He became famous for having sex with famous people, a list which if true is a veritable Who's Who of prominent females of the past three decades.

In a very wide circle of showbusiness, everyone knows someone who claims to have had sex with Warren Beatty. It angers him, but he admits nothing and refutes little, so the legend is self-feeding.

To the media which projected this sexuality and this fame he eventually became elusive and reclusive, evasive and deliberately enigmatic, monosyllabic and intense. He gives nothing away. He has shown a general and long-standing reluctance to indulge in self-discussion. He turns down most requests for interviews, and those he does grant are cautious and usually unrevealing. He has become so skilled at it that famous writers can spend four hours with him and then play back their tape to find he has said nothing. He believes that by saying nothing, he will neither be misunderstood or misquoted.

His long silences are deafening.

The enigma feeds the mythology. Stardom has become real life, lived in actuality, apparently populated for the most part with hell-bent women, steamy Hollywood libidos, played out in 3D, larger than life itself, completely divorced from his screen roles. This life, after a few initial shocks during the pre-permissive age, has been hyperactive but largely free of scandal. He is his own dramatist, and had produced for public consumption a character unmatched by any he has portrayed. He stands above the Hollywood hoi polloi because he possesses a personal image which puts his screen image, however vibrant it may have been at the peaks of his career, in the shade. It is this character, the one he uses for day-to-day life, that makes his well-spaced on-screen performances fascinating.

Here, in a nutshell, is what divides Beatty from his contemporaries. His best friend Jack Nicholson, for example, had been around Hollywood for fourteen years before he became an overnight star in *Easy Rider*. Robert Redford and Paul Newman emerged from the shadows in the guise of major screen characters, as did Dustin Hoffman, Clint Eastwood and any one of the actors or actresses who were coming through the mill at the same time. Go back further, or move forward in screen history, and the pattern is repeated – the all-important screen image is the one which eventually decides the success or failure, the staying power of any star. It usually has something to do with ability too, because a characterisation created for cinema audiences has to be forceful and memorable.

Name any star and audiences are most likely to identify him/her with a particular role. Each new role merely tops up the acclaim, keeps the impetus moving onwards and upwards to ensure that the star remains a star and does not fade into oblivion on the dark side of the moon. That is the general pattern. It never happened with Beatty. He walked into instant stardom as a movie actor, never ever had to be a bit-part player to gain a foothold in a precarious profession, and he assumed the aura of a star as if it were a custom-tailored suit before his first film was released.

Everything was present, everything was running for him. He had good connections, he was adopted as a protégé by a famous writer, he was darkly handsome, he was acclaimed in New York as the next young actor in the mould of James Dean or Montgomery Clift and he gave out the vibrations and body language of a man very much in demand even before anyone knew his name. Warren Beatty was created almost by sleight of hand, and eventually he became so highly publi-cised that he actually did not need the support of screen appearances, otherwise he might have found it necessary to provide his audiences with a rather more intensive demon-stration of his talents than is apparent from his sparse CV of films – twenty movies in thirty years compared, for example, with Nicholson's fifty.

His many critics have cited this lack of activity as demon-strating not a reluctance to work but a fear of it; a fear which, in the early days, made him unsure of his ability to undertake many roles which might otherwise have brought him to the screen in comparable quantitative terms to other actors in his age group. He has been accused of having a rather small repertoire of acting technique, of having a career that has been moderate and without severe challenge, built purely on the sexual chemistry, which is why he never knocks it. But can that really be all there is?

'Definitely not,' said director George Stevens. 'He is an ice-berg in the sense that what you see of him on the surface is no part of him at all. He is not lighthearted and frivolous. He is scholarly, headstrong and tough, very tough.'

He is not stupid either. The whole act is a part of the theatre of Hollywood in which he is the star player. Because sex is the running theme, and he teases and tantalises his public and the media bedroom voyeurs who feast on the rumours but cannot get past his almost impenetrable fence of intellectual deflection.

Henry Warren Beaty – with one 't' – born on 31 March 1937 in Richmond, Virginia, at the very heart of the southern influence that became integral to the United States of America, is the living legend who could today provide a class of psychology students with material for a full term of study. They would begin their research, just as a biographer does, at the roots of his life, and there discover the conflicts and contrasts that would present themselves in later years, when a boy from the gentility and strictness of middle-class America would confront the razzmatazz of Hollywood.

The maternal influence which seems ever-present in the lives of movie stars is always a good starting point. It is a curious truth that mothers invariably figure in the beginnings of any such story, not necessarily for pushing the child towards acting. Montgomery Clift, to whom Warren Beatty the movie star would be compared in his early work, had an overbearing mother who never let him out of her sight, wanted him to be a doctor and was horrified when he chose acting.

Two more of Warren's Hollywood friends, Elizabeth Taylor and Natalie Wood, on the other hand, were both hawked around the studios in early childhood. It is likely in star biographies that mothers are noted for being there as the most important of the two parents during formative years when traits of character are taking shape. The exception was James Dean, whose mother died when he was nine, but he had a fixation about her, curiously blaming himself for her death from cancer. So mothers seem to be there, always.

Warren's mother, born Kathlyn MacLean, was a school-teacher who had also taught acting. Her personal involvement in the performing arts was apparent to both her children, Henry Warren and his older sister, Shirley, but she does not appear to have been the inspiration for their eventual arrival on Sunset Boulevard in the City of Dreams, whose lifestyle such a woman as she would doubtless have frowned upon. She was teaching drama at Maryland College, Baltimore, when she met and married Ira Owens Beaty, a professor of psychology who had given up a promising talent as a violinist in favour of the more secure profession of teaching and wondered for the rest of his life whether he had made the right decision.

They set up home in Richmond, where Ira became a prominent figure in local circles of the heartland of the old Confederacy, where white-haired southerners still ran up the Confederate flag to commemorate the Civil War. It was a city of statues to men like Robert E. Lee, of old conservatism and strict family values.

Ira rose to be superintendent of Richmond High School, and perhaps it was to be expected that a man who was called upon to deal with the well-being of a large number of children every day of his working life could not switch off the instant he walked through his front door. He was always the headmaster. He was overprotective and overbearing, and an insight into the Beaty childhood comes directly from sister Shirley who, in later years, became as open and forthright in her communications with the outside world and her audience as her brother was secretive.

Ira was autocratic, Shirley MacLaine wrote in her autobiography *Don't Fall Off the Mountain*. He was a portly man, stern and full of suspicion. He was the censor of all he surveyed and the guardian of his children's safety, for fear they should fall into the bad habits which he knew abounded among the children in his greater care. His own believed he knew about the bad things they were going to do even before they had done them. Ira had feelings, certainly, but he preferred, said Shirley, to keep everything on a strictly intellectual rather than emotional level.

Mother was tall and slender, almost ethereal. She hated any kind of unpleasantness or family squabbles. She was of such a romantic inclination that she could not accept that unpleasantness even existed, and would turn away from it and pretend it was not there. Even so, when ultimately Shirley showed the first signs of rebellious attitude and there were arguments between father and daughter, the mother would eventually step in and say, 'All right Ira, that's enough.' And Ira was quelled. He had no stomach for a fight just as he had found no courage to pursue a musical career.

Warren Beatty has been characteristically sparse in his recollections of his childhood. He did, however, recall in one interview that his father could be distant and unapproachable, an aspect of his early life which seems to have affected his own calculations on how to handle himself in public. He said his childhood was very strongly and positively affected by the women who surrounded him – his mother, sister, aunts, great-aunts and his cousins, all women. They did not smother him, but by his own admission he came to trust women more than he ever could his men friends.

Later, when Jack Nicholson became his friend, the two of them used to compare notes about their upbringing, and the influence that women had had on their early lives. Warren was fascinated by Nicholson's own remarkable beginnings, brought up as he was by three women whom he believed were his mother and two elder sisters. He was thirty-two years old before he discovered he was illegitimate, and that one of his 'sisters' was really his mother. By the time he found out, she had died from cancer and had never called him 'son'.

In comparison Beatty's formative life was conformity itself, though never dull. The family moved to Arlington, Virginia when Warren was still an infant. Home was redbrick, leafy-lined suburbia, and a house filled with furnishings and collectibles which children must not touch. There was an air of slightly phoney formality, inspired not least by Warren's maternal grandmother, who had been Dean of Women at Acadia University, Wolfville, Nova Scotia, and with whom Warren had a rather special relationship. She was meticulous about her appearance, always dressing for dinner and upholding the standard of the family's social graces and linen napkins.

Both parents, and other members of the family, had an expressive interest in the arts. Shirley was encouraged towards the usual avenues of self-expression suitable for young girls of her age. Warren was directed towards the piano and became an accomplished pianist before he had entered his teens. He had a secret passion for Al Jolson, and played his records in the basement. When no one was at home, he would lip-synch the words and act out the songs. Eugene O'Neill was another boyhood hero, and if anyone had ever challenged him in his youth, he could have recited lines and meanings of any one of O'Neill's plays.

He has said he never had visions of becoming an actor, however, and certainly those heroes of the silver screen appearing at the local cinemas in his youth were not on his list of idols. It would have to be a special kind of movie to secure both his interest and his parents' permission to view it. He has said that he used the piano as a sort of therapy to work out his problems, running his fingers over the keys as he mused over his troubles. Both O'Neill and the piano were to figure quite strongly in his later developments.

Shirley reckoned the parental penchant for the performing arts had both a positive and a negative influence on the young Beatys. On the one hand, their father had a domineering talent for securing the attention in any room with his story-telling. Their mother, meanwhile, reacted to him in an intense way, and the pair were like a high-class vaudeville act. Shirley reminisced that she and Warren – or Little Henry, as he was then known within the family – would watch with shy apprehension.

Shirley overcame the shyness fairly promptly with her own outgoing soul, but it remained a lingering problem for Warren, who was reluctant to step into the limelight on any occasion. He could not bring himself to perform as the centre of atten-tion, like his father. And so he sought seclusion and privacy in the basement.

The impression gained by those inquiring into his past is that he was a loner, constrained by two strong and strident parental figures who barely gave him the chance to seek his own destiny. There was a snapshot of him doing the rounds when he became famous which showed him as a wistful child whose good looks were already very evident. Shirley said she was always aware that he was 'prettier' than herself.

In later years, their childhood was recalled by Shirley pub-licly when she became a star and faced the barrage of ques-tions that confront all new stars. Fan magazines in those days sought the minutiae of the past, of the upbringing and influences that all contributed to the arrival of this exciting young woman. Beatty was confounded by the knock-on effect when his turn came.

There were to be periodic rumours, once he had himself arrived in the maelstrom of Hollywood, that he had become estranged from his parents and his sister, allegedly through irreconcilable differences emanating from his childhood. His anger, for once, was apparent. There were differences but they were not serious enough to drive a wedge between himself and his parents or his sister. He was old-fashioned enough, he said in his early twenties, when he was newly arrived and these questions first began to emerge, to state publicly that he loved his parents. Family affection had been at the centre of his life. Each respected the other, and though disagreements occurred, there was no question of any gulf in the family.

This experience so early in his Hollywood days led Beatty to a certain reticence in discussing his family and childhood, and then any personal matters, and he pretty well stuck to it. This was compounded when a writer from one of the big glossy magazines was preparing a cover story on Shirley, who had entered what was commonly assessed as 'the big time'. Warren was approached to fill in some childhood gaps and give his own impressions of the success of his sister. He was cautious, not knowing how the article would eventually turn out, and refused to discuss his sister, a fact duly recorded and repeated to imply that the family ties had been disconnected.

It was probably to be expected that when they both became stars the media would attempt to play one off against the other. Studio pressures to give interviews were ever-present, and perhaps they were both swayed in those days, in the early sixties, by the need to feed some lines to an important writer wheeled in by the film publicists. Shirley was recorded as saying that they rarely saw each other and that he 'just doesn't seem to want to communicate with me'. When Warren was approached he refused to be cajoled into a family slanging match. He was, however, coaxed into talking about his own earliest memories of ambition. Politics figured strongly and his interest remained and expanded in later life. The interest was natural enough; at the time the family was living in Arlington, close to the hub of political life in Washington.

The war was ending as Warren's boyhood blossomed into a more adventurous era as he gained confidence and grew physically. The period and location provided the next natural influences on a young mind. The National Cemetery at Arlington was a focus for pilgrims and grieving relatives of fallen heroes, and he was there at the heart of the triumphal celebrations and the sadness. His tutorial parents were inclined to press upon their son the importance of these events as soon as he was adjudged capable of taking in the news. In his earliest memories of future ambition, he talked about becoming a politician, a governor or even President.

Shirley was moving away from him as girls of that age do. She had been his best friend and roustabout companion. She had been a tomboy who played the boys' games, was a big hitter in softball, and was his guardian from bullies. Then, suddenly, she was a lady and it was time for her to enter the socially expected routine that faced all such girls from middle-class families: the ballet class, the dances, the elocution lessons taught by her grandmother. He, too, became caught up in the cause of self-improvement, although for the son of two educators his school grades were relatively unimpressive, in spite of the fact that he voluntarily buried his young head in books as he sat on the window ledge of his bedroom.

He now attended the Washington-Lee High School, where a tutor provided him with a glimpse of the future, and of the need to apply himself to his best abilities. That tutor believed the answer lay in sport. Warren was a fine but reluctant athlete and had been chided not long before for his lack of enthusiasm for field events. The switch from bookworm to school sporting hero was completed almost overnight. He put away his books and his beloved O'Neill plays and spent every living hour that the curriculum permitted on the sports field. He became a star at football, baseball and on the track.

His parents, meanwhile, would surely have preferred their only son to have shown interest in a career in one of the professions, perhaps as a teacher, a doctor or a lawyer. If any such hopes were harboured, they were swept aside. The last four years of his stay at Washington-Lee were devoted to sport.

By seventeen, the wistful, retiring child had grown into a strapping youth, six foot one tall and weighing 205 lb, the heaviest he has ever been in his entire life. He had the close-cropped Army-style crewcut that was the fashion with all sports players and he could have adorned any sports magazine cover. He was confident and popular with his school-friends, who appointed him class president, and was the favoured pupil of several tutors, especially those who scouted for footballing colleges. And so, when he came to do *Heaven Can Wait* (1977), in which he played a footballer, it was a real skill, and not acted.

One step further at that impressionable point in his life, when teenage boys normally dream of becoming a great sporting hero, would have taken him down the road to a football career. But as suddenly as he had taken it up, he swung round again and rejected the career as a sporting star that his school tutors said was available to him. He stopped dead in his tracks and reconsidered his position at a time when his sister's dedication and good fortune must have had some bearing on his thoughts.

Shirley had already set sail for the bright city lights in search of fame and fortune as a dancer, much to the chagrin of her father. Just as soon as she graduated from high school she announced that she wanted to become a professional dancer. Ira tried to talk her out of it, of course, and put forward several reasons why it was not a good idea, which basically amounted to the same fears that he had expressed to himself a quarter of a century earlier when he had decided against becoming a professional musician.

The headstrong Shirley could not be dissuaded and very quickly proved she possessed enough talent and ambition to reach for the celestial plane. She went to New York in 1952, shared an apartment at 116th Street and Broadway with a group of other hopefuls and spent half her life standing in line for auditions for parts she never got. She was flat broke, living on biscuits and had lowered her sights considerably by the time she was finally offered a job in the Servel Ice-Tea Travelling Trade Show. The folks back home never knew how close she was to starvation. In 1954, when Warren was seventeen, she progressed from the back row of the chorus to understudy Carol Haney, one of the leads in *The Pajama Game*. As in all good showbusiness stories, Carol broke her ankle and Shirley was presented with her chance. She never looked back.

The success of his sister apparently had a deep effect on Warren. During the summer of 1954, with Shirley set for stardom, he began hanging around the National Theatre in Washington, looking for part-time work. Well, as it happened, the National management was looking for a strong youth, though sadly not for internal duties: the theatre had been recently invaded by rats and a couple of actors had been attacked and bitten in the dressing-rooms. Helen Hayes had arrived to appear in Thornton Wilder's *The Skin of Our Teeth*, the Pulitzer prize-winning play that was an amusing yet profound fable of humanity's struggle to survive. It was the play, coincidentally, in which twenty-two-year-old Montgomery Clift made his name when it first opened in New York in 1942, under the direction of Elia Kazan, who discovered Beatty for the movies when he cast him in *Splendor in the Grass* with Natalie Wood in 1959.

Back in 1954, Warren's role was strictly anonymous. Miss Hayes decided that if she were to survive on the stage of the Washington National, there could be no rats running wild in the building. The very sight of one, she proclaimed, would send her into a dead faint. So it was that the 200 lb youth, armed with sticks and stones and a strong shouting voice, was hired to patrol the alleys and corridors of the theatre to scare them all away.

Miss Hayes was thankful for this robust performance and had an idea then that the boy who had saved her from the rodents' bite would turn up later in Hollywood and become rather more famous than herself. This encounter, and Shirley's success in New York, was the sum total of his theatrical involvement up to the time he graduated in 1955. When the time came for graduation from Washington-Lee, he faced the decision of accepting a football scholarship or changing direction completely. Sporting tutors at high school were telling him to go for a sporting scholarship, the scouts were lining up to secure him and he had no fewer than ten football scholarships on offer.

His decision, like Shirley's, surprised everyone. He decided he was going to take a Bachelor of Science degree in speech and talked vaguely about doubling up with law, which was a drastic turnaround from the football field. Warren explained that he did not believe he was good enough for any lasting success in football, just as his father had not believed he was good enough to become a solo violinist. He argued that he did not think he would do as well as the college people thought

19

he would; worse, he was fed up with football. He couldn't see himself enjoying it, and he persisted with reasoning that football was the type of occupation that you had to enjoy to do. He did not think he would enjoy it for long.

His father detected that Warren had been brooding about the future since Shirley had gone to New York and was anxious to steer his son towards one of the professions. Law would be very good, he said. Warren secured a place at Northwestern University in Evanston, Illinois, which was famed for its output of stars, including Charlton Heston who was, that year, appearing as Moses in *The Ten Commandments*. Others who made the grade from Northwestern include Patricia Neal, Paula Prentiss and Ann-Margret – all destined to meet Warren in the future.

He arrived there in September 1955, taking up his place in the School of Speech, located in the centre of the campus. It was the focal point for drama majors, although the freshmen who were devoted to the dramatic arts found that while the college pursued a strong and liberal arts policy, it was linked proportionally to general studies. As each month went by, the young Beaty became more and more disillusioned with university life.

Having secretly set his mind on acting as a career, he was disappointed to discover that the tutorial programme expected him to devote more time to the basic fundamentals of academic life, such as studies in mathematics, social sciences and languages, than to his dramatic intentions. For a young man in a hurry, it was a disaster. He had a vision of his future, and the rudiments of higher education had little relevance to his plans. The novelty of leaving home and breaking out, that explosion of freedom that grips every college student, soon wore off. He began to wrestle with the university system, well-established and factory-like in its production of intellectual minds.

When his hopes for a more intense study of the dramatic arts failed to materialise, he began to view his course as a waste of his time. He enjoyed the jolly hysteria among kids who, like himself, had escaped from middle-class homes which had denied them some of the worldly experiences that those in the less privileged parts of the system had long ago experienced. He did all the things that new students do: he shared a dorm, dated girls, stayed out late, went to classes, skipped classes he did not like, had a small singing role in a show, dated more girls.

Gradually the disdain welled up. He had no time for the periphery. James Dean was already dead, killed in a car crash on 30 September 1955, aged twenty-four. The carefree life and the unhindered exploitation of illicit sex, booze and other previously unknown areas of social intercourse were, and still are, part of the preparation process. Yet Warren found them unappealing and distracting. He related an occasion towards the end of his first year when one of his friends, a large hulk of a boy from Ohio who eventually became an All-American, was found lying drunk in the men's room, asking for his pal, Beaty. Warren went to help, and found him lying in a mess of vomit. 'Man, I'm too sensitive for this,' Beaty said. And he decided there and then to quit university life for good.

He returned home from the spring semester of 1956 complaining that he had spent most of his time on general course work and barely had time to expand his studies in the art of drama. He had been brooding over his plight for weeks and had apparently discussed his position with friendly tutors.

They argued that whether he was studying law or drama, the underlying need of essential learning was the same. He could bring far more to the acting craft, if that was his eventual destiny, if he knew the history and geography of it. They said that he would be a much better actor if he had studied the origins of the Greek plays, the historical effects of Restoration Comedy and the psychology of Shakespeare. One told him that acting was like being an artist. He would have to paint a living portrait on screen, and while it was one thing to know the subject subliminally, it was quite another to know him intellectually.

Beaty could see the point, but it made no difference. An actor needed to get out and do it. The research and the learning could come later. Anyway, he had read of and discussed with his university drama group the great explosion of acting talent emerging from the Actors Studio of New York, where the techniques used were based on the idea that acting was of an innate nature, coming from within and not from without.

21

So what case was there for a traditional education? New York was where it was happening. Brando, Clift, Dean and a galaxy of other names had all graduated from Broadway and the New York acting classes, notably those teaching variations of Stanislavski's Method.

His decision to drop out must have come as a great shock to his parents, who still hoped that he would abandon these ideas about becoming an actor and pick up his law studies. The paradox confronting the two professional educators was that both their children had failed to progress into the realms of higher learning. Both had turned their backs on all that their parents had worked for themselves, and had discarded the parental ambition like an old pair of shoes.

The Beatys continued to advise caution, just as they had to Shirley when she left home. They tried to build Warren's confidence by telling him he had the potential to be whatever he wanted to be and it would be far better to obtain a degree that would guide him towards the legal profession. Get that under his belt first, said his father, and he would always have a career to fall back on. They warned him about the pitfalls of an actor's life, that the theatre seemed romantic and glamorous but was in reality a very hard life in which only a few enjoyed what might be considered a decent standard of living. They reminded him that half his life might be spent trudging from one audition to another in the hope of finding work, and that even if he made it, the future would always be uncertain.

Even Shirley was enlisted to back up their fears, but to her brother she had become the shining example of what could be achieved in a mere three years. In 1955, she had been whisked away to Hollywood to appear in Alfred Hitchcock's *The Trouble With Harry*. She quickly followed that with a smallish role in Frank Tashlin's *Artists and Models* and then telephoned home excitedly with the news that she had been offered a place in the all-star cast of Mike Todd's *Around the World in Eighty Days*, in which everybody who was anybody was appearing. Shirley was hardly a model for the cautious approach being recommended to Warren.

His parents wanted to take him upstairs and lock him in his bedroom until the moment had passed. But they were educators and they knew that a young mind would only rebel against a forced situation. They might even lose him forever. And so the Beatys gave him their reluctant support. That summer, he left Arlington, Virginia, and headed, full of hope, for New York, bright lights and excitement.

2

A Brief Apprenticeship

Warren had been spirited away by his teenage dreams. Shirley's escape from the mundane expectations of Virginian life had obviously had some effect on his aspirations, too: that alone must have provided some sort of spur for her brother, but it was more than either of those things that set Warren Beatty on his own journey towards Hollywood.

He dropped out of college before dropping out became fashionable, against the background of a whole new social order which was in its infancy but emerging strongly in the fifties American boom years, when the new affluent society had money to burn. Big cars, Cadillacs and Chevies, and Oldsmobiles and Fords; television sets – two sets – electronic gadgetry galore; sell, sell, spend spend.

Even in the last days of high school, when he was playing football and living out the final months of his middle-class teenage existence, the stirrings were beginning on a much wider front than the mere facets of home life. Youth itself was stirring from its slumbers and a great, meandering movement of post-war rebellion and protest was dawning. New icons, new dreams, new fears were on the immediate horizon, dead ahead. The social order established among Eisenhower's children, and then followed elsewhere in the world, was on the brink of dramatic, even catastrophic change.

The Cold War had begun. The threat of nuclear annihilation was, for the first time, being discussed in terms of when, rather than if. The effect on young people was to raise the question, 'What's the point? Live life today, and enjoy it.

Tomorrow may be too late.' Politicians were tub-thumping and concern over the expansion of the Soviet Union had produced a frantic reaction of hysteria within the United States which had led to war on communism and un-American activities. On the campuses and in the colleges the debates were wide-ranging and exciting. Attention turned towards the new leaders, new heroes on the silver screen, new writers and poets, and off in the distance, the first faint sounds were heard of a raucous new music which became known as rock 'n' roll.

All of these things came together in a loud crescendo as Henry Warren Beaty anguished over his future during the last months of his brief stay at Northwestern. It is worth just reminding ourselves about the developments of that era, because they had a deep effect upon his thoughts and certainly provided the role models to whom he would later be compared. The positive influence upon his own emergence as a star becomes clear when we divert from his story momentarily to draw a route map for his career.

It began, really, with Montgomery Clift, who was an early leader as youth searched for icons when he starred with Elizabeth Taylor in George Stevens' *A Place in the Sun* in 1950. Although Clift was already an established star in the theatre, the movie brought incredible fan reaction, boys and girls mobbing him wherever he went and forming a permanent crowd outside the entrance to his apartment in New York. Clift was a sensitive, gentle soul, representing perhaps a classier image than those who would follow him in impressing themselves upon the youth of the day. His own upbringing had been, like Beatty's especially genteel and middle-class.

He came to prominence at the same time as Marlon Brando, who had been a more intense student of the Stanislavski Method school of acting at the Actors Studio, where they both studied intermittently in the late forties and early fifties with the likes of Maureen Stapleton, James Dean, Karl Malden, Shelley Winters, and Marilyn Monroe who came into the 1954–5 season. Both Clift and Brando were appearing in New York theatre when they were discovered by Hollywood, which gave them a wider audience, and ultimately presented them as role models.

26

Brando stamped his mark on the embryo youth movement in 1951 with far greater force than Clift with his riveting performance in *A Streetcar Named Desire*, and he became the absolute hero of youth in his 1953 appearance in *The Wild One*, a film which was banned for a time in Britain for fear it would incite gang riots. Arriving leather-clad on a motorcycle in a small American town, he is asked, 'What are you rebelling against?' and growls back, 'Whaddya got!'

Between them, in the early fifties, Clift and Brando provided the disorientated youth movement in search of idols with a whole new repertoire of sayings and postures, stances and gestures and they also opened the door for a whole new genre of movies and actors.

Youth appeal in the movies at a time when the industry was facing its greatest threat from television was at its lowest ebb and ready for an invasion of young talent. Audiences were evaporating, box-office takings slumping. Picture after picture went wrong. The golden age was done for and the old studio system that had nurtured and cared for more stars than there were in heaven was in its death throes. It seems hardly feasible, looking back through the list of big names available to the major studios in the fifties, that there weren't enough names in Hollywood to make films with which the young people who paid to see them could identify. The years had taken their toll and the talents of Gable, Bogart, Flynn, Cooper, Stewart, Turner, Garland, Swanson and Bergman had been used and abused to the point of excess. Even their collective charisma could not sustain the fans' interest. The need for new actors, which would eventually become a lifeline for the career-minded young Warren Beatty, was highlighted in an article in *The New York Times* in 1954:

'The reality is that time has caught up with most of the front-line stars; middle-age paunches, disappearing or greying hair, sagging facial tissues have blunted the romantic appeal of too many top-rated stars ... the rapport between stars in their forties and fifties and the broad mass of film audiences, which ranges from fifteen to twenty-five, isn't as close as it should be.'

However, Elia Kazan, one of the leaders of the new wave of film and theatrical directors, who had brought Brando to

27

Hollywood, also plucked James Dean from relative obscurity. Dean had just had his first big break on Broadway in a play called *The Immoralist*. Kazan saw him and against all odds selected him to star as Cal Trask in the screen adaptation of John Steinbeck's *East of Eden*, a role which made him an instant star.

Even before it was released, he was signed for another youth film, *Rebel Without a Cause*, which Warner had nervously backed. In both films he portrayed characters who were supposedly crying out for parental love. The films were statements of parental attitudes and their consequences rather than about youth rebellion itself. Dean caught the mood of it when he told Dennis Hopper, his friend and co-star in *Rebel*, 'Y'know I've got to make it because on this hand I'm holding Marlon Brando, saying fuck you! and in this hand I'm holding Monty Clift saying please forgive me! So it goes: fuck you, please forgive. Fuck you, please forgive. And somewhere in the middle is James Dean . . .'

When *East of Eden* was released, Dean was hailed as the kind of new talent the film industry needed – an actor in touch with his audience – although many established actors who came to know him neither applauded his work nor liked him as a person. That never worried Jimmy, whose antagonism towards the Hollywood gloss grew as each week passed. By the time he died, Dean had crystallised that vague, ill-defined mood of youth and turned it into a positive force which provided the opening through which others would follow.

Five years later, Kazan repeated the operation with similar success with another unknown called Warren Beatty, even down to matching him with Dean's co-star in *Rebel*, Natalie Wood. As *The New York Times* had prophetically pointed out, the need for vibrant new talent brought stardom for young newcomers emigrating from New York, like Beatty, Steve McQueen, Paul Newman, Dustin Hoffman, Anthony Perkins, George Peppard, Robert Duvall and others.

So Dean was dead and fans around the world wailed and mourned his passing. His image, those sad eyes, moist from the stinging effect of marijuana smoke, peered down from hoardings and screens and on the campuses and in the drama groups young people debated his impact and imitated his style. In the first few months of 1956, when *Rebel Without a Cause* was doing record business and giving the sagging cinema finances a fantastic boost, millions of words and hundreds of newspaper articles were being written about him.

Warren Beatty never admits to having been influenced by Dean, or by anyone, or even by the events of the era; he was even refusing to admit that he wanted to be an actor. But there was the Great White Way, a yawning chasm ahead of him, waiting for him to try his luck. In many respects, his route to fame was identical to Dean's, although far less tortuous. In 1952, after three years of struggling to get noticed in Hollywood, Dean had turned up in New York looking for work. The city was a veritable melting pot of burgeoning new talent, of writers, directors and actors who were yet to become famous. They all took spare-time, or often full-time, jobs washing dishes and parking cars while eking out their pay on acting lessons and sitting over a coffee and a slice of toast shared between two or three at a time.

Beatty, like Dean, took a stinking hovel of an apartment because it was cheap, eight dollars a week. It was in West Sixty-eighth Street, in one of the old run-down tenements that were eventually demolished to make way for the Lincoln Center. It had a view of Broadway, but it was a 'junk-heap', he admitted, and smelled awful. The previous inhabitant was a junkie, and there remained a lingering stench of smouldering grass and other substances.

Had he asked Shirley for advice, a pointer for where to start? We can only assume that he had, because neither has talked of these early years. Perhaps it was she who said, 'Find Stella Adler.' Any actor, or budding actor, in New York knew Stella. She was one of the original importers of the Stanislavski Method into the American acting system, and was loved and hated in equal measure for doing so. The daughter of a famous Jewish actor, Jacob Adler, Stella rose to prominence herself in the 1930s and became an integral member of the group of young theatrical revolutionaries who formed the Group Theater Company. A photograph in the archives of the Actors Studio shows her with a host of luminaries who were at the core of the New York acting scene for the next three decades, including Elia Kazan, fresh from Yale, the writer Clifford Odets, Cheryl Crawford, Paula Miller (later Strasberg, and Marilyn Monroe's mentor), Bobby Lewis, Harold Clurman and Lee Strasberg.

The group was in part financed by a $1,000 donation from Beatty's boyhood hero, the playwright Eugene O'Neill. The company was heavily into the study techniques of acting improvisation devised and recommended by the Russian director Constantin Stanislavski, whom Adler met in Paris in 1934. When Stella returned from Paris, she brought with her a chart system which she had devised after consultation with Stanislavski and which was to be the basis of her own studies for years to come. This caused a stand-up row between her and Lee Strasberg, a leading figure in the translation of the Stanislavski Method on to the American stage. He accused her of totally misinterpreting what the great director had meant. This was in part confirmed later by the Russian himself, who remembered Adler as a 'panic-stricken young woman clutching at his arm and begging him to save her from the effects of his system.'

The upshot of all this, for the New York theatre, was an ongoing controversy about the 'Method', not least among the teachers of it, who included Kazan, Lewis, Strasberg and Adler, when the Method became the most debated topic among actors in post-war New York. The basic fundamentals were the same, that of improvisation and seeking inspiration from within oneself rather than from the normal, conventional acting school techniques of projection, and especially in thinking the lines. The Actors Studio, formed in New York in 1947 by Bobby Lewis and Cheryl Crawford, became the Mecca of actors wishing to get to grips with the Stanislavski system. Many famous names passed through the tutorials.

By the time Beatty arrived, Lee Strasberg was virtually running the studio and Stella Adler had formed her own school. The kid from Virginia stepped straight into a mêlée of controversy which had reached its peak in the mid-fifties when an internecine struggle had developed among the Method-ists, most notably between its two leading tutors, Lee Strasberg and Stella, whose differences flared up both in public and privately.

The Method, in simple terms, was based upon experimentation and exercises to help an actor draw upon his own emotions, from inside his mind and body, to create the character he was portraying. The exercises involved long and deep periods of concentration, sometimes ending with an explosion of physical acts which could be violent or sexual. Many established actors dismissed it as worthless mumbo-jumbo, propagating tricks and stunts which got in the way of serious acting. Charlton Heston described it to me as 'like masturbation – a lot of fun but it gets you nowhere.'

What was a nineteen-year-old youth, with no insight into acting other than what he had gleaned from reading and his limited studies at Northwestern, to make of it all? He was certainly to be confronted by a diversity of opinions in New York, which would alter yet again when he eventually arrived in Hollywood. But it was in New York, during four years of scratching around for parts and studying with Adler in between washing dishes to earn a crust, that he began forging his working abilities, his style and general demeanour which could mean the difference between developing into a busy star player or one relegated permanently to the small print in the credits. The fact that he had, through the actors' starvation diet, slimmed down to 170 lbs and grown into a remarkably handsome young man, would also have some bearing on the situation.

Maureen Stapleton, who was in the thick of this confusing controversy that surrounded Beatty and other newcomers, explained the scene for me: 'I suppose by the mid-fifties, when Warren arrived in New York, there was a diversity of teachers. There had been a lot of rows and fallings-out over whose teachings were correct. Lee Strasberg emerged as the driving force at the studio, but you could not say he was the only leading light. As Bobby Lewis said to me, it was down to the teacher. Lewis taught the Lewis Method. Strasberg taught his system and Stella Adler taught the Stella Adler Method. Basically it didn't matter who was right or who was wrong. I mean, you did not even have to study Method to become a good actor; dozens who did not became big stars. But to those of us involved at the time, it was a very intense and studious form of tuition. The Method was supposed to help you learn your craft, bring your inner self to the surface and improvise on all your feelings and senses, as opposed to just standing there and bellowing your lines with no more thought than to make sure your voice could be heard in the back row of the gods. Marlon never did talk loud, but that was Marlon. If he boomed clear and precise like Lord Sir God [Laurence Olivier], he wouldn't be Marlon. Monty, similarly, was quiet and sensitive, though filled with private demons. His talent in those days was breathtaking. They had developed their own style, even before they came to classes, and the studio encouraged people to develop these styles. But Bobby Lewis always warned you not to overdo it. If you went nuts about the Method, you were in trouble. Dean did that ... Warren was much quieter, more like Monty, though we were never allowed to compare anyone with anyone.'

Personal styles were of paramount importance and encouraged by tutors like Strasberg and Adler. Stella would impress upon her pupils that there was no point in trying to be someone else. Dean was heavily censured, perhaps unfairly in hindsight, for trying to emulate Brando. Any form of copying was frowned upon. Ben Gazzara, who was himself accused of the same crime, said: 'People who imitate Marlon are just punks. Lee would not let anyone get away with it. It would destroy an actor's integrity.'

It certainly irritated Brando. When *East of Eden* opened, Brando remarked that Dean was 'wearing my last year's wardrobe and using my last year's talent.' Such comments merely contributed to the conflict and controversy surrounding the Method, but although it was a fashionable subject, vividly represented by publicity about some of the forms of actor training, like pretending to be a tree or acting out sexual potency, it was little understood.

However, Walter Kerr, influential critic on the *New York Herald Tribune*, was to write: 'Like it or lump it, the Actors Studio has given birth to the clearest, most carefully defined, most virile approach to the player's craft that the American theatre has yet produced ... if it has partial roots in the Stanislavski-born and Group Theater-nourished techniques, it has gone well beyond them, from low-keyed naturalism to open fire ... it has evolved the right pattern for the plays of Tennessee Williams, Arthur Miller and William Inge who are, after all, our best young playwrights.'

Although only on the periphery of these startling events through his contact with Stella Adler, Beatty was nonetheless to be greatly influenced by all of them and his career would involve help from many of the names mentioned. There were to be other early guiding influences to fashion a young mind caught in this maelstrom of debate on the performing arts. The Method was just one part, one element in the fundamental upheaval in the theatre, television and film as Beatty came through.

Charlton Heston, who stayed at Northwestern rather longer than Beatty, recalled that many established actors treated exponents of the Method with open derision. There was almost a division between the New York crowd and established Hollywood actors, many of whom had come through the studio system which, in its heyday, taught its young actors the conventional skills, with speech therapy, dance lessons, even ballet and tap. 'They all went through that in the system and everybody got a chance to bat.' That 'system' was already in decline, along with the fortunes of the big studios, when Heston arrived in Hollywood in 1950. By the time Beatty made tracks for California it was all but dead, and Hollywood was an uneasy place to be.

Heston recalled: 'A Supreme Court ruling that the studios should divest themselves on their monopoly interest in the cinema chains was one nail in the coffin because it virtually finished the production of B movies in which many young actors had their first try-out. Another was the upsurge of television. But in fact, though the studio moguls would have nothing to do with it, television provided an opportunity in the fifties for a whole new generation of actors, writers and directors to come through. The studios would not allow their contract players anywhere near television, so a whole new medium was left to a bunch of twenty-four-year-olds whose basic qualification was that they were unemployed. Here we were, racketing around inventing a medium because the networks did not know how to do it either. They were presenting a wide range of drama from *Julius Caesar* to *Jane Eyre*, which went out live after a week's rehearsal. An actor doesn't draw breath who isn't going to be good in any one of those parts.

All that happened because of the studio system ... it was a brief and very rewarding time for new people.'

Thus, it was television that offered Warren Beatty his first breaks. Even so, like everything in his life so far, it was merely a glancing involvement, peripheral, even incidental, as if he had no real heart for what he had thrown himself into. Or, if he did have the heart, and was truly set on an acting career, then it was going to be at his own pace, with his own decisions and his own selection of work.

In fact, the months since his arrival in New York had passed with little event and often depressing gloom. He had the usual variety of jobs, ranging from washing dishes to carting sand for builders of the third tube of the Lincoln Tunnel. Sometimes, he would be lucky and get temporary work playing piano in a cocktail lounge. He met some future familiar faces doing the rounds of the shows and auditions, dated a few young budding actresses, including Diane Ladd, who found him exceedingly attractive but aggressively ambitious to the point that she felt intimidated in his company. She recalled that when they came home from their date he would kiss her on the threshold and then come inside and kiss all her flatmates goodnight too.

One setback occurred when he was invalided back to Arlington with an attack of hepatitis. He soon recovered with parental attention and returned to the city just as soon as he was strong enough. He resumed his search for artistic employment which, apart from playing the piano, had so far eluded him. This was not entirely due to lack of offers. He was already getting something of a reputation as a young actor who did not, indeed would not, accept just any part just for the experience, as did many of his contemporaries. He admitted that Stella Adler, in her strident control of her students, had equipped him with a certain arrogant self-confidence which provided him with the ability to say no when everyone else was saying yes. He would, as one of his contemporaries put it, 'take no shit'.

If he did not like a casting director, did not like the part, did not even like the atmosphere, he would walk away and say no thanks. This, in some quarters, has been interpreted as a blind, masking a fear of the work and of his ability to succeed in any particular part. When one director criticised him for having a low voice, of mumbling like Brando, he simply handed back the script and walked out. And so his acting work was, to say the least, sparse.

Beatty's most intense period of continual employment in New York can be discussed and dismissed quite briefly: between the spring of 1957 and early 1959, he appeared in a number of small roles in television drama productions of the kind mentioned by Charlton Heston. He was seen on the CBS network, Studio One and on NBC's *Playhouse 90*. He won a starring role in another television production, *The Curly-Headed Kid*, for the Kraft Theater. He did a summer season at the Gateway Theater, Long Island, appeared in numerous stock productions, was signed for winter stock at the North Jersey Playhouse, playing a selection of roles in numerous plays. In total he appeared in more than forty separate productions in pleasant obscurity way off Broadway and largely out of sight of the big time. As things turned out, this run of work and his classes with Stella Adler would prove to be the sum total of his 'training' to be an actor. The life of a struggling actor, with all its uncertainty, starvation diets, depressing auditions and directors he did not like, was all but over.

It was by chance that his moment arrived when, like all good Hollywood success stories, he was 'discovered'. Two men, a famous director and a famous playwright, simultaneously found this young man and decided to make him a star. Joshua Logan, the director and writer, and William Inge, writer of such hits as *Come Back Little Sheba, Bus Stop, Picnic* and *The Dark at the Top of the Stairs*, dropped into New Jersey to watch the production of Meyer Levin's *Compulsion*. Inge was immensely impressed with the young actor and decided instantly to write a play especially for him.

Logan's plans were more immediate. A past associate of Stella Adler, he had taught for a brief period at the Actors Studio. He used to relate to students how he had been exposed to the Method very early in his career when he made a trip to the Soviet Union in 1931 and met Stanislavski. He had been part of that burgeoning New York scene during the rise of some of America's great writers and actors of the era.

He started in pictures in 1930 and came back to Broadway

as a director, staging the original production of *Annie Get Your Gun, South Pacific, Mister Roberts*, which he co-wrote, and Bill Inge's *Picnic*. He returned to the movies in the fifties to make the screen versions of his Broadway successes. He cast Marilyn Monroe in Inge's *Bus Stop*, discovered Kim Novak for *Picnic*, and among his most notable works was the film of *Mister Roberts*, which won an Academy award nomination and an Oscar for Jack Lemmon. Then fifty-nine years old, he was an influential contact for any young actor. Now, he sat back in his seat in the stalls, looking at the young man named Beatty who possessed a certain magnetism, exuded charm and had good stage presence. He was not overtly Method in his acting, but Logan spotted the mark of Stella Adler, liked his style and was especially struck by the intensity of his eyes when he spoke his lines.

Logan called Beatty for an interview and after they had talked for a while, offered him a screen test. He was about to bring a new movie into production. Beatty was invited to fly to California. He was not yet twenty-two years old, but this was graduation day.

3

Fame Before Stardom

Warren Beatty became the absolute example of the well-worn expression 'overnight star' even before he appeared in a picture. There were to be no mundane flicks of dubious quality, no trawling around the studios waiting for a sympathetic casting director to give him a break, no B movies, where countless contemporaries learned their craft, nor, as we have seen, a long and painful dalliance in the lower regions of theatrical apprenticeship. What actually made him suddenly bloom into a star baffled even the hard-nosed seen-it-all-before brigade of Hollywood commentators. He was suddenly there, a handsome, alluring young man who was to be seen in all the right places with all the right people as if he had been born to it. His very appearance in Hollywood invited producers and studios to court him with scripts and offers, and that is no exaggeration.

He had arrived in Hollywood early in 1959 at the behest of Joshua Logan, who had been signed to direct a new Warner Bros film called *Parrish*. Logan had also brought along a suggested co-star, Jane, the young and talented daughter of his old friend Henry Fonda, who, like Beatty, was scouting for her first movie. Logan set up the screen test and it involved a passionate kiss which they had rehearsed several times. If they had decided in advance to make an impact with the test, then they succeeded. The embrace was so long and intense that the director shouted 'Cut!' three times before they parted. 'We kissed until we had practically eaten each other's heads off,' Fonda related.

Afterwards, Warren invited Jane out to dinner while they hung around to await the outcome of their endeavours. They treated themselves by going to the fashionable Hollywood restaurant La Scala. At a nearby table, Joan Collins was wrestling with an oversized bite of cannelloni and brooding over whether 20th Century-Fox would call her for the lead in *Cleopatra* or give Elizabeth Taylor the queen's ransom she was asking, when suddenly she noticed him. She asked a companion if she knew the identity of the young man over on a far table whom she was sure was giving her the eye. 'That boy,' said Joan's friend, 'is Shirley MacLaine's brother, Warren something or other...' Joan studied him covertly, and their eyes met several times, unnoticed by Fonda who was, according to Miss Collins, hanging on his every word. Joan observed him long enough to recall twenty years later exactly what he was wearing at the time, a blue Brooks Brothers shirt and a tweed jacket, and that he looked appealing and vulnerable.

Beatty and Fonda left the restaurant and waited for the news of their test. The test was good, said Logan, and he was impressed by both, as was Jack Warner, although the studio mogul did have trouble with Beatty's name, introducing him to the press as 'one of our brightest new stars, Mr Warner Beaker.' In the event, *Parrish* did not get made – at least not by Logan and his new discoveries, although it was made later on, starring Troy Donahue, Claudette Colbert and Connie Stevens. Logan did not like the script for *Parrish* when it finally arrived from Warner, in fact he hated it, and asked to be relieved of the task of directing.

The studio agreed and immediately offered him another project, *Tall Story*, a youth film about a young basketball player who marries a cheerleader and runs into problems. Fonda and Beatty were again placed at the top of Logan's list but by then the director's short-term contract with Warren had expired and he was being wooed by MGM. Warner wanted Logan to cast another startling young newcomer, Anthony Perkins, opposite Fonda, which he did.

Beatty had been in Hollywood for a matter of weeks and had had offers of two films which he would not make. A third was already on the horizon. The playwright William Inge, who had seen him in *Compulsion*, had two projects in store, a film based on his story *Splendor in the Grass*, which Elia Kazan was going to make, but which had been delayed, and a new play, *A Loss of Roses*, which was being prepared for a provincial try-out prior to a Broadway production. Inge had already said he would try to get Warren the lead in both, but could promise nothing. They were months away from coming to fruition. The play was nowhere near actual production and the film was put on hold because Kazan was still working on two other projects, directing a Broadway production of the Tennessee Williams play *Sweet Bird of Youth* and then flying directly to Hollywood for a new picture.

Kazan was the most sought-after director in town after *On the Waterfront* with Brando and *East of Eden* with Dean. He was currently working with Montgomery Clift, the third of the leading New York iconoclasts from his days at the Actors Studio, whom he cast in *Wild River*, an interesting sociological drama set in 1939. Kazan had first discovered Monty in 1942 for the Broadway production of Thornton Wilder's *The Skin of Our Teeth*. It was coincidentally at a revival of the same play in Washington that Warren Beatty had had his first theatrical experience, serving as the ratcatcher. Now, in 1959, Kazan found Monty to be a shadow of his former self, a wreck. He was, said Kazan, a 'tenderhearted shell, shaky and wobbly' from his constant intake of orange juice mixed with vodka and Demerol, and his handsome features were badly scarred and misshapen after a terrible car crash one night as he was driving home from Elizabeth Taylor's house.

Monty Clift, once the stylist of youth and the darling of the New York theatre scene, was already heading to his demise, which arrived with his sudden death within half a dozen years. Susannah York, then a young actress who appeared with him in his penultimate film, said: 'I loved Monty, everyone loved Monty. He was an absolute dear to all of us, but his drinking and his drugs would madden and frustrate any director.'

So that was the scene: Dean was gone, Monty was fading and Brando was being Brando, reclusive and turning down most of the scripts that were sent to him. Directors like Kazan whose work veered towards the intellectual, or at least came out of an intellectual stable, were searching for new talent.

Without a trace of modesty, Kazan said that by 1959, when he was filming *Wild River* and standing by to do *Splendor in the Grass*, he had personally become 'one of the most respected men in my profession and I would choose among unlimited opportunities. I'd appear at the yearly judging of young actors applying for membership of the Actors Studio, a position of great power at the time.'

Beatty, meanwhile, was waiting for someone to offer him work. Between visits to New York, he became a familiar figure around the night-spots of Los Angeles and would soon be sought by studio scouts looking for young stars to go with their new-wave directors and their powerful scripts by writers like Tennessee Williams, Thornton Wilder, Arthur Miller and William Inge in the hot new Hollywood era when realism was all the rage. Beatty was in awe of this huge talent of the American playwrights and literary giants and deliberately sought them out for conversation, gleaning and learning. One night, he gatecrashed his first Hollywood party. It was at Romanoffs, and he was working the floor – 'I couldn't dance that well' – when his eyes fell upon Rita Hayworth, who was dancing with a man whose strangely misshapen shoes caught Beatty's eye. Beatty began inadvertently to stare, first at the shoes and then at Hayworth until eye contact was sustained. She turned and looked at him inquiringly, as if she should know him.

'I'm sorry,' said Beatty, 'but I just can't help it – looking at you, I mean.'

'Forget it,' said the goddess. 'What's your name?'

'Warren Beatty.'

'I'm Rita Hayworth.'

'Yes, I know that.'

'Come and join us.'

'Thanks.'

'This is Clifford Odets.'

Beatty had never met Odets, but knew that name. Playwright, actor and film writer, he had been a major force in the New York theatre and one of the founders of the Group Theater, which had eventually spawned the Actors Studio. He was considered one of the most important American playwrights of the thirties, and his works were strong in social conscience arising from the Depression, with such plays as *Waiting For Lefty, Awake and Sing* and *Till the Day I Die*. His most recent success in film was *The Big Knife*, starring Jack Palance, a vitriolic, if overheated, melodrama about a fading Hollywood star.

Beatty's interest in Hayworth quickly subsided and he devoted his whole attention to Odets, whom he regarded as a demigod. Odets noticed Beatty was looking at his shoes.

'I'm sorry,' said Beatty, apologising again. 'I did not mean to be rude.'

'That's all right,' said Odets. 'I have to wear these bloody awful shoes now because my father never bought me shoes that were big enough when I was a boy, and they damaged my feet. So I had to have these corrective things made.'

They talked until Hayworth began yawning and Beatty ended up at Odets' house, where they continued their discussions until 4.00 a.m. It was the first of numerous chats, and one of many important acquaintances made.

One night at a drinks party, Beatty inquired of Odets, 'Who is that heavy guy standing by the window?'

'That,' said Odets, 'is Jean Renoir. Come and meet him.'

Beatty did not know who Renoir was. 'Is he related to the painter?'

'Yes,' said Odets, 'but he is also a rather good director. He did a little picture called *Grand Illusion* and another called *Rules of the Game*.'

'Are they good?' asked Beatty.

'I think you should see them as soon as possible,' said Odets.

The word about young Beatty was not long in passing through the grapevine. An executive from MGM eventually arrived bearing a contract for five years at a weekly salary of $400, a meagre figure compared with star salaries but a princely sum to an undiscovered talent. In fact, Beatty was among the last long-term players to be signed by Metro, whose fortunes were no less parlous than most of the big studios. And they, more than most, needed the new young actors to replace their collection of ageing stars who had earned them millions in the previous two decades.

The star system had been a particular feature of an actor's

life with MGM, who nurtured, cared for and guided the careers of their contract players, for good, bad or perhaps evil. But as Charlton Heston had predicted, it was virtually at an end. They had done the religious epics and period pieces, they had done the big, expensive musicals, and still television was biting into the cinema audiences. In recent years, the MGM studio had taken the quite dramatic step of disposing of some of its once brightest stars, like Judy Garland, Clark Gable, Gene Kelly and Lana Turner, who said her last day on the set of Metro, which had been her home for seventeen years, was 'like standing amid ruins'. Where once there were 'more stars than in heaven', there were dark clouds.

Clark Gable, before he was finally let go, had been bitterly critical of the studio system and those who ran it. 'They're absolute bastards,' he said. 'They encourage us to be larger than life, give actors anything they want, take any crap provided they interest the public, but the moment they slip – oh brother! They'll ruin us all.' Elizabeth Taylor also wanted out, fed up with the scripts she was being offered. But Elizabeth was 'hot' again, as the scandalous headlines raged over her affair with Eddie Fisher, the best friend of her recently departed husband Mike Todd. MGM would refuse to let her go until she had completed *Butterfield 8*, a film verging on the pornographic in which she appeared as a nymphomaniac who becomes a prostitute but does not charge for her services. She vowed she would never do it but was finally forced to when MGM refused to release her for *Cleopatra* unless she signed. In the event, she won an Oscar.

Beatty, yet to make Miss Taylor's acquaintance, viewed the mass of press coverage of the star's new romance and studio rows with a mixture of horror and unabated voyeurism as Elizabeth was branded the scarlet woman who had stolen Debbie Reynolds' husband. A closer relationship between Beatty and Taylor lay in the future.

In terms of the first step in his career, Beatty fared no better than some of the recent evacuees, but he was not about to fall into the same trap. He read the script of the first film MGM offered him, with the uninspiring title of *Strike Heaven in the Face*. He took one look, decided he was not going to do the film, and furthermore that if that was the kind of material

42

that MGM was going to offer him, there was no point in staying.

If there was one thing that had already impressed him it was to go for quality, not quantity, and to try to walk that tightrope between becoming a popular actor and appearing only in work that appealed to him as a person. Beatty realised he had made a huge mistake in signing with MGM and courageously asked to be released from his contract, borrowed some money to pay back his advance and went looking elsewhere.

There was solace and encouragement on hand. Joan Collins, who had not been given the role of Cleopatra, 20th Century-Fox producer Walter Wanger having succumbed to the demands of Miss Taylor and stumped up the first guaranteed million-dollar fee in Hollywood history, was bumping and grinding on Stage Six in the Fox studios, rehearsing her role as a stripper in *Seven Thieves*, co-starring Edward G. Robinson and Rod Steiger. Miss Collins, twenty-five-ish, was a $2,000 a week contract player for Fox and even then a permanent fixture in the gossip columns after a spectacular divorce, some high-profile romances and some rebellious bust-ups with her studio bosses. A Rank starlet at sixteen, she had arrived in Hollywood before she was twenty and had had her first major international role in Howard Hawks' *Land of the Pharaohs*. She was married early, to the British actor Maxwell Reed, who created history and headlines by suing her for $1,250 a month in maintenance when they parted. Collins refused and the judge upheld her decision, although she had to make a once-and-for-all payment of $6,000 to the departing husband.

After that, there were various headlined affairs, some real, others imagined by the gossips, and she had a long-standing relationship with Arthur Loew Jr, the celebrated Hollywood millionaire producer and knight errant known for his alacrity in assisting damsel stars in distress. Collins found him a charming, elegant and rich escort to fill the void and help smooth away the trauma of her divorce. She had a brief encounter with Marlon Brando and a longer affair with Sydney Chaplin. Mr Loew meanwhile had offered a calm haven to Elizabeth Taylor during the turbulent period after

Mike Todd was killed in an air crash, before she suddenly ran off with Eddie Fisher. Loew then found himself offering companionship to Debbie Power, the widow of Tyrone, who had died from a heart-attack. Well, Collins and Taylor could have been knocked down with a feather when they heard that Arthur and Debbie were to marry.

A pre-wedding party was planned at the Power mansion in Beverly Hills and Joan was naturally invited. Come party time, a Saturday evening, she was tired and fed up after a long day bumping and grinding and smarting from having been named in gossip columnist Louella Parsons' list of the ten worst-dressed women. She decided to live up to the title by dressing for the occasion in a pair of men's grey Bermuda shorts, long grey socks, sneakers and a man's shirt, in the days when such clothing was considered eccentric to say the least. It had the desired effect of shocking the rest of the party crowd who were more suitably and elegantly attired.

Joan, in carefree style, stood sipping champagne and picking at passing vol-au-vents, allowing herself to be soothed by a pianist player out of sight somewhere in the far corner, and giving, she thought, superb imitations of George Shearing, Oscar Peterson and Errol Garner. 'Who is that boy playing the piano?' she inquired of her companion for the evening, John Foreman.

'Oh, don't you know?' he said. 'That's Shirley MacLaine's little brother, Warren.'

Joan, craning her neck above the crowd to take her first look, said, 'So it is . . . hmmm.'

Beatty saw her looking. Eyes met once again although they did not have the opportunity to speak to each other the entire evening. When Collins left, they still had not met.

The following day, she went to the beach to get some sun and when she came home to her apartment at Shoreham Drive, just off Sunset Strip, to prepare for a cocktail party for songwriter Jimmy McHugh, her answering service informed her that there had been six telephone calls from a Mr Warren Beatty, who requested that she call him at the Chateau Marmont without delay. The Chateau was a slightly run down but fashionable apartment hotel often used and recommended by visiting thespians from New York when they arrived looking for employment, and by Los Angelians seeking privacy. It was also very reasonable.

Collins wondered whether or not to call. She did, and he picked up the phone and said, 'Ah . . . you've called. I wondered whether you would.' They arranged to meet that evening for dinner. Joan threw on a pair of jeans and restyled her hair so as not to emphasise the age difference between them. When they finally met for the first time, she was struck by his youthful features. He looked seventeen, and had spots.

Joan's own account of the romance was filled with passion and sex. They became inseparable. They spent the night 'exploring each other's minds and bodies' and while she was at work on her new film, he would telephone almost hourly. 'We could not bear to be apart,' she wrote in her autobiography, *Past Imperfect*. She also spoke highly of Beatty's sexual prowess, adding that now famous line that he had an insatiable appetite for lovemaking, three, four, sometimes five times a night. He also possessed the unique capacity to take telephone calls while in the act of sexual endeavour which made for a rather interesting reversal of the heavy-breathing syndrome. Joan would turn up at Studio Six to bump and grind with saggy, bloodshot eyes and had difficulty in stifling the occasional yawn.

As these hot summer nights in the Collins household cooled with the onset of autumn, the first of Beatty's ambitions to appear in a Bill Inge play was finally realised. He was calling Inge daily in New York, sometimes two or three times. They had long conversations about the new play and the film, which Inge hoped that Elia Kazan would soon be ready to work on.

Inge, forty-six in 1959, was to become a major influence on Beatty's entry into mainstream theatre and Hollywood and would launch him in his career. He was undoubtedly infatuated with this young man, whom he considered his protégé.

Maureen Stapleton, who knew Inge, was among those who remained a friend later in life when the inner torments that were so common among writers and actors of his group finally began to take hold of his personality. These led him towards the same fate of drink and barbiturate addiction that had become the plight of the likes of Montgomery Clift, tortured

45

by their homosexuality and insecurities. Stapleton recalled that Inge was gentle and kind, with a temperate goodness. He was a quiet and peaceful man, so different from some of the emotionally overheated contemporaries with whom he ran, like Tennessee Williams and Arthur Miller. Born in Independence, Kansas, he had graduated as a teacher, and taught and wrote art criticism for the *St Louis Star-Times* before heading for New York. Although outside of the mainstream of American theatre, he was nevertheless an important writer of the period. His work was less fiery than that of some of his friends, and more akin to the romanticism of the American heartlands, invariably running with the theme of the need to escape from the ordinariness and daily drudge of life, to seek love and happiness and new opportunities.

Inge had four smash hit plays in a row: *Come Back Little Sheba* (1950), *Picnic* (1953), *Bus Stop* (1955) and *The Dark at the Top of the Stairs*, first produced in 1947 and revised in 1957, in which he transformed the lives of people living in drab surroundings into significant dramas of human experience. He was awarded a Pulitzer prize in 1953. The Actors Studio often delved into his work and Elia Kazan directed the revised version of *Dark*, which received unanimous acclaim when it opened in New York. Hollywood snapped up all four plays for the big screen, with equal success. Shirley Booth won an Oscar in *Come Back Little Sheba, Picnic*, which starred Kim Novak and William Holden, received an Academy nomination for best picture and *Bus Stop* provided Marilyn Monroe with one of her best roles.

Kazan developed a great fondness for Inge: 'His telephone calls were long and quiet, but in fact, ardent reaches for companionship – a meal, a stroll, a talk. I sensed some mystery in his past.' Later, Kazan discovered Inge had been a patient in a mental institution. His work, the director added, provided actors with exceptional opportunities for good performances, climaxing in moments that revealed their best gifts, not least in the poignancy of his dialogue, which had insight and tenderness.

By the end of September, his play *A Loss of Roses*, partly inspired by his desire to write something for Beatty, was ready for casting. Daniel Mann, a strong manipulator of talent

who had a string of successes including Inge's *Come Back
Little Sheba* to his name was appointed director. Inge suggested that he should consider Warren Beatty for the lead,
the part of twenty-one-year-old Kenny, who falls for an older
woman, and is described in the play as 'a nice-looking boy
who wears a mysterious look of misgiving on his face as
though he bears some secret resentment that he has never
divulged and has perhaps never admitted to his conscious-
ness.' It sounded tailor-made for Beatty, as indeed it was.

Inge, incidentally, had more clout over the staging of this
play than with any of his previous works. Against the advice
of his friend Tennessee Williams, he sank $100,000 of his own
money into the production, which meant that when he spoke
people actually listened, a novel experience for an author.
Beatty, nervous and excited, flew to New York at the beginning of October for rehearsals. The play was due to open for
a trial run in the National in Washington DC – coincidence
again, a return to the old rat-stamping ground of his youth.

Rehearsals were tempestuous and argumentative. Beatty's
co-star, Shirley Booth, from *Come Back Little Sheba* and
specially chosen by Inge, felt uncomfortable about her role,
and was less than happy about the interventionist attitude of
Beatty, who was intense and frequently wanted to stop to
debate the meaning of his lines and her responses. She quit
the show before it reached Washington for its try-out and
was replaced by Betty Field. Director Danny Mann was also
troubled. Later he was to say: 'In my forty-year career, I've
directed some of our finest actors – Brando, Vanessa Redgrave, Anna Magnani, Elizabeth Taylor – but I have to say,
Warren was one of the few to give me a problem. He would
not listen to me. He plays upon his sex appeal and charm
and then goes and does something on stage that we do not
even know about.'

This kind of reaction is not unusual for conventional actors
and directors when they first run up against young blood,
fresh from being taught confidence verging on arrogance and
improvisation techniques at the Stella Adler School, or from
the Actors Studio. The tricks, the unscripted pauses, the
nuances pulled up from within, the psyching-out before cur-
tain-up, can be debilitating for other actors not party to them.

A Method actor in the midst of a more conventional group often appeared to be taking control, even usurping the director. Ann Doran, who played James Dean's mother in *Rebel Without a Cause*, best summed up the effect: 'On the first day, Jim Backus [Dean's screen father] and I couldn't believe it. We were watching Jimmy do his scene and someone said, "Quiet, we're going to shoot now." Jimmy went down in the foetal position, gave this funny kind of soft whistle, which was a signal, and the director said, "Action!" Jimmy let out this scream of expletives then stood up and went into his scene. Jim Backus was hysterical with laughter. Jimmy pulled the scene into himself, and because of that he was doing the directing, too. He dominated the entire thing and I think that is why in the picture things did not lock together. It was the strangest thing I ever saw . . .'

Even actors experienced in the teachings of the New York Method-inspired tutors occasionally found it difficult. 'Everyone was like it from time to time, even Marlon,' said Maureen Stapleton. She recalled a moment when they were filming *The Fugitive Kind*. The actors – herself, Brando, Joanne Woodward and Anna Magnani – sat around a table for a reading. Everyone was talking low and quiet, taking the lead from Brando. Eventually Stapleton, an old friend who used to live in the apartment below Brando's in New York, felt it incumbent upon her to say something. ' "What the fuck are you doing, Marlon? I can't hear a word anyone is saying. Have I gone deaf or what?" Now he didn't want the part in the first place, but they were paying him a fortune. So I said, for all the money he was getting he ought at least to let everyone hear what he was saying. Well, Marlon fell about. Anna kissed me, so did Joanne. And Tennessee Williams, who wrote it, and was sitting off somewhere, said, "Thank God, darling. I haven't heard a bloody thing all week." '

The point of these examples was that the teachings of Lee Strasberg, Stella Adler and the rest could simply not be laid selfishly over a production by an actor without thought for his colleagues. On stage, more so than in film, the actor had to be an integral part of the whole team, bending and moulding his own work to fit like a jigsaw with the others. Beatty had much to prove. He was, first and foremost, a perfectionist and wanted his first major dramatic role to be right. The result was that he kept changing the way he performed his part.

Some thought he was also trying to impress Joan Collins, who had finished her commitment on *Seven Thieves* and had flown into Washington to join him, and was a regular observer at rehearsals. There was trouble with the play itself, too. Inge agreed to carry out a fair amount of rewriting and reconstruction, building up some parts and cutting back others. 'It is the pressure of the theatre today,' Inge said in 1960. 'People become excited and mistrust their best instincts.' He also defended his protégé, who he said was a young colt out in new green pastures. He possessed a self-protective quality; he was reluctant to trust people in charge and sometimes Inge wanted to say to him, 'Oh, shut up and get on with your part.' But basically, he said, Beatty was a very fine kid who would eventually learn a way of working with people.

In the autumn of 1959, he had not achieved that ability. Carol Haney, who played the older woman, was reduced to tears on occasions and the problems had not been smoothed out by the time the play opened, coincidentally at the charming and cosy Eugene O'Neill Theater on 28 November 1959.

It was received with as much warmth as the biting temperatures outside on Broadway, although Beatty himself fared better than the play. Walter Kerr of the *New York Herald Tribune* said: 'Mr Beatty's performance is mercurial, sensitive, excellent,' and Kenneth Tynan, the British critic giving his verdict in the *New Yorker*, wrote in such gushing praise of Beatty that no one could possibly fail to sit up and take notice. 'Mr Beatty, sensual around the lips and pensive around the brow, is excellent as the boy.' His co-stars Carol Haney and Betty Field were also warmly applauded, but the praise for individual performances was insufficient to sustain the play and *A Loss of Roses* was retired after only twenty-five performances.

While the play was trying out in Washington, Joan Collins shared Beatty's room at the Willard Hotel. They managed to drive out to Arlington to meet his parents and then when the company moved to New York, she followed. They stayed at the Blackstone Hotel, where she was reading the long-awaited final script for what was supposed to be her next movie, the screen adaptation of D. H. Lawrence's *Sons and Lovers*, which was being produced for 20th Century-Fox by Jerry Wald. It was the most prestigious and demanding role she had been offered, although it did not appeal to Joan herself. Wald had promised alterations to the script, and while she still did not like it, she might have decided to do it had it not been for her own lover.

Warren, she said, encouraged her not to accept. Joan argued that she had no choice; it was not an offer, but an instruction. She was a contract player and if she turned it down, she would be suspended. She recognised that Beatty's advice was 'not entirely selfless'. It would have meant going immediately to England for the location work, since the story was set in Nottingham, and he did not want her to leave him. 'Don't go, butterfly,' he said. 'Don't leave your bee.'

Joan said no to *Sons and Lovers*, which was probably not the best career move she ever made. She was immediately placed on a month's suspension by Fox, losing $8,000 in salary, but more importantly the film was highly rated. Mary Ure, who took over her role, won an Academy award nomination, as did her co-star, Trevor Howard.

Warren and Joan lingered in New York after the closure of *A Loss of Roses*, and were photographed together in fashionable night-spots. Joan made the headlines once her suspension became known and the added attraction for the gossip writers was her involvement with Shirley MacLaine's brother.

No one would have said then that it would be the last time Warren Beatty would appear in the New York theatre.

For his mentor, Bill Inge, the experience had been more hurtful, and his friends later identified it as the beginning of his decline into sad oblivion. With *A Loss of Roses* and the novelette which formed the basis for the upcoming *Splendor in the Grass* added to his list of more successful plays, Inge had already written the works for which he would be best remembered. Thereafter began his slide into mental torment and we cannot pass without a mention of his eventual demise. Tennessee Williams said of him: 'I think of Bill Inge . . . as a tragic person. Tragic. The critics treated him cruelly. When he came to visit me in Key West, I was using drugs to lift my depression. Bill was abusing them because he could not bear life. He drank all the time. He would sleep with barbiturates under the bed.'

Near the end of Inge's life, Maureen Stapleton had met Williams in New York. They were discussing Inge, who would commit himself to hospital, but then would walk out the following day. Maureen called Inge's sister and warned her that he was desperately ill. Tennessee was blunt about it. Bill was on a suicide course unless he was committed for a longer, compulsory stay in hospital. He was tragically prophetic. In 1973, Inge killed himself by running the motor of his car in a closed garage. 'Hemingway, Fitzgerald, Inge . . . oh, the debris,' cried Williams. 'The wreckage . . . once they become known everyone wants a piece of them.'

For Warren Beatty, however, Bill Inge remained for the time being an important link in his rise to stardom and mixing with that whole group of writers added some experiences which would never be available to other young actors running through the mill.

4

Natalie, Susan and Vivien

Life imitating art and vice versa was the Hollywood story of
the sixties. On screen, the plays of Bill Inge and Tennessee
Williams were intensive explorations of human relationships,
with elements of Freud to make them deeper, allowing the
critics to delve into reasons and roots. Off screen, Hollywood
real life was no less filled with its passions and torments,
grandiose egos built up and knocked down. It was a continual
soap opera in itself as the intensity of the movie plots spilled
out from under the arclights of a movie set into private lives.
There were plenty of players, exploited by the studio publicists and the media but still, for the moment, controlled and
checked by a last remaining clutch of the old-style moguls.

The death rattle of the studios was at its loudest as the
new decade dawned and many would say 1960 was the year
that old Hollywood finally expired. There were still some
dramas being played out as the studios scoured around for
what to do next in the war against television and the declining
cinema audiences. A survey that year showed there were
forty-four million television sets in America, compared with
exactly four million a decade earlier. And where once 200
million people worldwide paid each week to see their favourite
stars on the silver screen, numbers had fallen to a third of
that figure.

The moguls had tried every trick in the book, and filmed
every book. Slowly control had shifted from the autocratic
studio dictators to an assortment of deal-makers, conglomerates, soft-drink purveyors, lawyers, bankers and a handful of

powerful agents. Hollywood was a mirage, made up of a couple of handfuls of precious and pressurised stars marshalled by a smaller number of 'hot' directors. Their lives were under great scrutiny and the gossip giants like Louella Parsons and Hedda Hopper were having their final fling, with a number of upcoming young rivals following on behind. Movie scandal sheets and even the fan magazines still tracked their lives and their loves, and it has to be said that the stars themselves kept them plentifully supplied.

Warren Beatty, in that year of 1960, began to make his own headlines, caught in the soapsuds of off-screen emotions and ambitions, finding fame before he had even been signed for his first picture. He was on the brink of having his name in lights in the picture for which he was desperately attempting to secure a part. He and Collins, that frosty winter, made the most of their stay in New York after the play folded, doing the rounds of the festive parties and catching up with other more successful Broadway productions. That Beatty and Collins were now an item had reached the gossip columns where they were vying for space with the machinations of Elizabeth Taylor and her new husband Eddie Fisher, who were also in New York filming *Butterfield 8*.

It was snowing and bitterly cold as the new year was ushered in and even the fiery language of Elizabeth, who was being forced, almost kicking and screaming, into the daily routine on location in the city, failed to melt the temperatures. Elizabeth and Eddie were also doing the social round to stay sane while she battled with the scriptwriters, attempting to scale down some of the dialogue that *Time* magazine later described as having been copied from a lavatory wall, although the star herself managed to rise above it and eventually won an Oscar for her performance. Elizabeth was reportedly ill with a severe cold, and producer Pandro Berman sent doctors at regular intervals to prescribe a variety of medications.

Joan Collins, not unaware of the trials and tribulations of Miss Taylor, had still not ruled out the possibility that she might eventually star in *Cleopatra*, now being talked of in the trade papers as the most grandiose production ever to hit

Hollywood, although it would be filmed in England for tax reasons. Taylor had thus far tantalisingly refused to sign for the picture, even though Fox was already recreating the city of Alexandria on eight acres of Pinewood Studios in England and eighteen major actors for supporting roles were being tested and signed. Collins remained on standby.

Later that month, Joan and Warren left the cold and flew back to the warmer climes of Los Angeles, where they installed themselves discreetly in an apartment in the Chateau Marmont where they kept a fairly low profile. Living together in the pre-permissive age of the early sixties was still regarded as living in sin, and her studio bosses, already angry over her refusal to do *Sons and Lovers*, would not have approved of such behaviour by one of their young stars.

Meanwhile, Beatty's daily telephone calls to Bill Inge continued and finally brought good news on the work front. Filming on *Splendor in the Grass* was to begin in May, with most of the shooting on location back in New York. Even with Inge's influence it had not been a foregone conclusion that Beatty would get the lead and Jack Warner, who was financing the picture, wanted Warners' top young heartthrob of the day, Troy Donahue, to star alongside Lee Remick.

Inge put in a good sales pitch for Beatty. The reviews of *A Loss of Roses* were presented to Warner, Inge insisting that he was going to be bigger than James Dean and Marlon Brando. Then Lee Remick backed out. She discovered she was pregnant and the search was on for an immediate replacement. The name of Natalie Wood, under contract to Warner, was being mentioned.

Beatty became involved with Natalie Wood when she had reached what she considered to be a turning point in her career, do or die. It would prove to be a major turning point in her life, too. She was vulnerable and nervous about the future. At the time, Natalie and Robert Wagner were considered by their friends and neighbours who surrounded them in their recently acquired $150,000 mansion on the exclusive Beverly Drive, Beverly Hills, as the perfect Hollywood couple. They were young and glamorous and known by everyone in Tinsel Town. Natalie had been in pictures for seventeen of her twenty-two years and by 1960 had appeared in thirty-one films. Wagner had come through the studio system as a contract player for 20th Century-Fox and had made twenty-two films, but neither he nor Natalie had quite matured to 'big star' status.

Before they married, they had been running into each other for years at parties and had many mutual friends, including Elizabeth Taylor. Natalie's teenage life and her involvements with James Dean, Elvis Presley and other young Hollywood men had been well documented. She and Wagner were on the verge of engagement in the spring of 1957 when he was sent overseas for three months with his Fox co-star, Joan Collins, to make *Stopover Tokyo*. Natalie, lonely and confused, found solace in the arms of Joan's current boyfriend, Nicky Hilton, who was Elizabeth Taylor's ex-husband. The word around was that she was about to marry him until Elizabeth telephoned and warned her: 'Don't – he's a very unstable man. You'd be much better off with R.J.'

Natalie and Wagner were lovingly reunited when he returned that summer and were married at Christmas 1957. Outwardly, everything appeared to be going their way. In truth, they lived on a permanent knife-edge of financial and professional insecurity, with Natalie especially torn by the possibility of failure. She had found the transfer from child star to young adulthood especially traumatic, and her studio superiors were never certain how to cast her. Since her role in *Rebel Without a Cause*, she had starred in a number of films, but none was good enough to bring her the big breakthrough. There were many arguments as Natalie rejected one bad script after another. She was placed on a fourteen-month suspension by Jack Warner when she refused to go on loan to Fox to star alongside Kirk Douglas, Burt Lancaster and Laurence Olivier in *The Devil's Disciple* because it would have entailed a three-month stay in England so soon after her marriage.

It took Ronald Reagan, then president of the Screen Actors Guild, to negotiate her return. Reagan, a former Warner contract player himself, used her case to argue that the vast majority of actors were underpaid, overworked and treated like sweatshop slaves. More importantly, they were unable to seek work outside the studio. Natalie's plight led to the begin-

The new star:
Warren Beatty in
the style of the era,
looking mean and
moody, a stance
which did not
altogether suit him
(*Yardley
Collection*)

His first major romance: Joan Collins saw him playing the piano at a Hollywood party and asked, 'Who is that boy?' She was soon to find out. They were inseparable for almost two years, until he fell in love with Natalie Wood (*Syndication International/Hulton Deutsch*)

Vivien Leigh, going through the trauma of her own divorce from Laurence Olivier, was flattered by his attentions, on and offscreen when they made *The Roman Spring of Mrs Stone* (1961) (*Syndication International*)

Surrounded: Natalie Wood's separation from her husband Robert Wagner and affair with Warren Beatty caused headlines around the world. Wherever they went, they were beseiged by the media, as here in London in May 1962 (*Syndication International/Hulton Deutsch*)

Mentor: Elia Kazan, the director of some classic American social dramas and who first brought Marlon Brando and James Dean to public acclaim, also picked Warren Beatty and made him a star in his first picture, *Splendor in the Grass* (1961), co-starring Natalie Wood (*Yardley Collection*)

Enter Leslie: After Natalie Wood, it was Leslie Caron who was on the receiving end of Beatty's affection; they also made one film together, *Promise Her Anything* (1966) (*Daily Mirror*)

A rare picture: Warren Beatty with Leslie Caron meet the Queen at the London royal premiere of *Born Free* in March 1966. Next in line to Leslie was Julie Christie, which was a rather prophetic positioning as things turned out (*Hulton Deutsch*)

The looks, the eyes, the smile were obvious attributes (*Daily Mirror*)

Early co-stars: Above, Warren Beatty in his first appearance with Goldie Hawn in *Dollars* (1971). Below, with British actress Susannah York in *Kaleidoscope* (1966) (*Yardley Collection*)

Expressions which typified the clashing temperaments during the making of a difficult film with Jean Seberg, entitled *Lilith* (1964) (*Yardley Collection*)

He wanted Natalie Wood to co-star in his biggest personal project to date, *Bonnie and Clyde*, but she turned him down. He ended up, instead, with Faye Dunaway which many considered just as well, considering the strength of the role (*Yardley Collection*)

Stars in the making: *Bonnie and Clyde* was Beatty's first film as a producer. He chose unknown actors as his co-stars and had to battle to get it made. It was a watershed picture, controversial in its violence. Gene Hackman (above) and Faye Dunaway (below) became overnight stars, and both won Academy nominations (*Yardley Collection*)

nings of the reforms that benefited many Hollywood actors but the pressure had been so great for her that she had resorted to sleeping pills, uppers and the services of an analyst. Her husband, meanwhile, was also in a state of apprehension, and was coming to the end of his five-year contract with Fox, where he was being overshadowed by new male leads like Paul Newman.

Their position had not been improved when they made their first, and only, picture together, called *All the Fine Young Cannibals* which, if the pre-publicity was to be believed, was the most important film either had made. It was a disaster, savagely mauled by the critics. They knew it when filming was completed, and returned miserable and edgy to their heavily mortgaged mansion. Suddenly, their world was brightened by a call from Warner about a new film prospect for Natalie. Elia Kazan was looking for a late replacement for Lee Remick. Jack Warner told him he could have Natalie 'cheap' because they were looking for someone to take her over and return her as an asset to the studio.

Kazan admitted his first reaction was that Natalie was 'a washed-up child star.' But he agreed to see her. He recalled their first meeting: 'I detected behind the well-mannered "young wife" front a desperate twinkle in her eyes. I knew there was unsatisfied hunger there; I could see that the crisis in her career was preparing her for a crisis in her personal life. Then she told me she was being psychoanalysed. That did it. Poor R.J., I said to myself.'

There now remained the resolution of the male lead and Kazan was still undecided. He had tested other young actors and when Beatty telephoned for the umpteenth time, Kazan told him, 'I've got to be honest with you, I don't know if I want you.' He suggested that he should do another screen test, this time with Natalie. They met at the studio, and Beatty was hyped up and anxious. He complained about a couple of lines he was speaking, and thought they might be improved.

'Really,' said Kazan, but made no move to aquiesce.

Beatty complained about where he was meant to stand, and suggested movement. 'Why don't I go over and play the piano? I can play the piano.'

'Really,' said Kazan with sublime lack of interest.

After about twenty minutes, Karl Malden walked in and Kazan said, 'Hi Karl. Take over for me, will you?' He walked away and Beatty thought he had blown it.

When the test was done, they agreed to meet later that night at Natalie's house. Kazan appeared distant and moody and Beatty wanted to know if this meant he was not required. Kazan grabbed him by the lapels and shoved him up against the wall. He said, 'Look kid, you got the part. OK? Now shaddap!'

Beatty felt the hairs on his spine stand on end, and knew he had finally got a shot at something that could be good. All they had to do now was convince Jack Warner. This time, Kazan went in to bat: 'This boy is as bright as they come, with all that thing women secretly respect: complete confidence in his sexual powers, confidence so great that he never has to advertise himself, even by hints.'

So Beatty got the part.

They prepared to go to New York, where the film would be filmed entirely on location on Staten Island. Kazan asked actress Norma Crane, a graduate of the Actors Studio and another exponent of the Method, to take Natalie through the script. He told her to strip off the Hollywood star trinkets, the make-up, the diamond bracelets, the six-inch heels and the false eyelashes. The part called for a plain and virginal girl. 'I used paint remover on her,' said Kazan, 'and I told her that if she worked hard and listened we could free her from all those bad habits she had picked up in years of lousy films.' Natalie said she would follow his every dictate.

Warren Beatty's moment had also arrived. His first film was ready to be made and his billing would read '. . . and introducing Warren Beatty.' But suddenly his dreams about all that the future might hold were shattered by an unexpected drama – or, as Joan Collins put it, 'the inevitable happened, just like a bad novel.'

Having not long before complained to a friend that Warren's sexual appetite was such that she felt like a sex object, she now discovered she was pregnant. When she told Beatty, he slumped down on a sofa, puzzled and shocked, inquiring how such a thing had happened. Collins replied with all the sarcasm that such a comment merited that perhaps the butler had done it, or maybe it was an immaculate conception. Beatty reached for his vitamin E tablets, gulped several down and wondered what they were going to do about it.

Several days and many anguished hours of discussion later, they had both agreed that a termination of the pregnancy was the only answer. He had a friend in New York who would arrange it. At one point, Joan demurred and said she would have the child. Then they talked again, and she recalled what had happened to Ingrid Bergman, who had been hounded out of Hollywood when she became pregnant out of wedlock.

Beatty said having a baby would wreck their careers, and Joan agreed. He had his picture to do, and she had been given a new script, for *Esther and the King*, a tedious biblical drama with a muddled plot which she had no alternative but to accept after her recent suspension. Furthermore, it was being filmed in Italy, and she was expected to report there for work at the beginning of June.

They travelled to New York where the operation was performed in a high-rise apartment building 'on the wrong side of the tracks in Newark, New Jersey.' It was all over in a day, and they moved into a tiny apartment off Fifth Avenue they had rented for the duration of Warren's filming.

Meanwhile, back in Los Angeles, the Wagners were preparing to move east. Wagner had no filming commitments until the autumn and had decided to accompany Natalie to New York, to give her moral support. Elizabeth and Eddie, by then back home, gave them a farewell party and bought them a portable hi-fi as a going away present. When they arrived in New York, they rented an apartment on the Upper East Side of Manhattan and settled down for what they both knew was going to be a difficult time, both professionally and personally.

Natalie was at the edge of her nerves, worrying about the film and whether she could match Kazan's expectations. R.J. was supportive, but surely harboured his own fears about the scenes his wife faced with that new actor Warren Beatty, whom he knew only by reputation.

Bill Inge's screenplay, which would throw the two together in steamy clinches, was based upon an incident in the writer's own youth. It was set in the puritanical mid-west of the 1920s but the story easily slotted into the modern age. Natalie and

Warren were teenage sweethearts whose romance ends because she will not go all the way. Frustrated, he leaves her for the school tart, who does, and ends up married to second-best, with a baby. Natalie turns to another schoolfriend for comfort and ends up being raped. She slides slowly into madness and the county mental asylum, where she is brought back to health by a doctor whom she eventually marries.

The story was so real and the actors so involved, that they got carried away. Kazan pushed them harder and harder, closer and closer, to get the emotions he wanted. Beatty looked down at Natalie's adoring face, and had to say, 'You know you're nuts about me' and the melodrama built, moment by moment, around the two young lovers.

While all of this passion was being acted out, Joan Collins and Robert Wagner shifted uncomfortably upon their specially provided director's chairs, watching their respective lovers go through their supposedly make-believe clinches. Barely a day passed without their presence on set, and Wagner especially was demonstratively and publicly affectionate to his wife when work was done, as if to repel amorous invaders.

When did Natalie and Warren fall in love? 'When we weren't looking,' said Elia Kazan. 'All of a sudden they became lovers, and I wasn't sorry. It helped their love scenes. My only regret was the pain it was causing R.J. His sexual humiliation was public.'

Joan Collins had flown to Italy before the tell-tale signs that a closer relationship was developing between Warren and Natalie began to appear. R.J., who had barely let Natalie out of his sight, returned to the set one day after a trip into Manhattan and found Beatty standing with his arm around Natalie's waist while they were waiting for their next scene. 'Keeping tabs on me, Bob?' Beatty said in a loud voice, and before they knew it, Dorothy Kilgallen suggested in her show-biz gossip column, syndicated nationwide, that Warren and Natalie 'are staying up nights rehearsing their next day's love scenes.' The Wagners' lawyer, Woodrow N. Irwin, fired a warning shot across the columnist's bows with a telegram demanding a retraction. He said the story was defamatory and untrue. Kilgallen refused, and instead printed a collection of gossip, crediting various sources, about Bob and Natalie and Warren and Joan. Mr Irwin did not pursue the matter.

Joan Collins, fuming with boredom on the set of *Esther and the King*, could not bear to be apart from Beatty a moment longer and flew to New York for the weekend, arriving on Saturday and returning on Monday, a breathtaking journey at a time when transatlantic travel was no mere seven-hour hop. They rowed and fought, and then reaffirmed their love for each other and decided they would marry in January. Joan said she would look for a wedding dress when she went back to Europe.

The Wagners, meanwhile, tried to patch up a marriage that according to Natalie's sister Lana was already in deep difficulties because of the emotional pressures of Natalie's career. They returned to the close-knit village atmosphere of the film community of Los Angeles when *Splendor in the Grass* was wrapped up and resumed their role, temporarily, as Hollywood's perfect couple, against an undercurrent of whispers that Natalie was in love with Warren.

That, in the event, proved to be true, but for the time being their love was left simmering on the back burner, waiting to be brought back to the boil. In the meantime, Joan and Warren were having long-distance rows after the tabloids had splashed it about that she was dating an Italian actor named Gabriele Tinti. Such were the conflicting passions, in front of and behind the cameras.

Elia Kazan had heaped personal praise on his two young stars. They had both exceeded his hopes, and when the film went on general release, reviewers gave it a warm reception. The influential *New York Times* critic Bosley Crowther described it as a frank and ferocious social drama of two late adolescents yearning but not daring to love, played against the harsh backdrop of obtuseness and hypocrisy in a Kansas town.

Crowther's praise for Natalie and Warren was plentiful. They played their roles with amazing definition, he said, and Beatty, who talked like Marlon Brando and had the mannerisms of James Dean, was a 'striking individual'. Of the few who demurred, the unsigned assessment in *Films in Review* struck a nerve, complaining that the movie was merely pandering to 'Hollywood's present conception of how to make money, i.e. tell teenagers that fathers are either dominating or henpecked nitwits, that mothers are neurotics and the adult world isn't worth the powder to blow it to hell.' Natalie Wood gave a good performance, said the reviewer, but Warren Beatty 'is too inexperienced to be able to project anything.'

That he was a star from his first picture was already beyond doubt. It was too early for the rest of the world to agree. As the film was wrapped up, it would be months before those glowing reviews appeared. The no-man's-land between the completion of filming and the appearance of a movie in the cinemas and public reaction is the time that drags the longest and Beatty was already intent on securing his position. As Kazan had already observed, he wanted it all, and he wanted it his way.

Word was out that Kazan had found a bright new star. The reviews from *A Loss of Roses* and the publicity surrounding the making of *Splendor in the Grass* brought a flurry of offers and scripts for him to consider, most of which he returned to sender without so much as a second thought. Beatty had already set his heart on the next movie *he* wanted to make. There would be no lightweight, glitzy crap; no youth movies. He wanted strong meat. Intellectual stuff. Fired by his ambition and ego, he began to pursue his next part with the vigour and determination few actors in his relatively lowly station in the profession would have dreamed possible.

He had learned from Bill Inge, and from preliminary announcements in *Variety*, that Tennessee Williams's novel *The Roman Spring of Mrs Stone* – the only one he ever wrote – was soon to go into production, starring Vivien Leigh as a lonely expatriate American actress in Rome whose life is taken over by a young Italian gigolo. The story behind the story bears repetition. Williams started the novel while living in Rome with his companion Frank Merlo in 1950 and had just written the last page when he was invited to London by Laurence Olivier and his wife Vivien Leigh, who were interested in staging a West End production of his play *A Streetcar Named Desire*.

Williams went to stay with the Oliviers at their Sussex home and was enchanted by them, and especially by Vivien

Leigh, whom he felt was the perfect Blanche Dubois for *Streetcar*. Williams contacted Elia Kazan, who was about to go into
production with a screen version of *Streetcar*, and Miss Leigh
was offered the starring role. Marlon Brando, then virtually
unknown outside of New York, was to co-star, and make his
explosive entrance in the role of Stanley Kowalski. Now, a
decade later, when a film was being made of the novel he had
written prior to his meeting with the Oliviers, Williams
wanted Vivien for the role of Mrs Stone, and as yet the part
of the Italian gigolo remained open.

Whether or not Beatty deliberately mapped out his own
career to follow as closely as possible the rise to fame of
Brando or Dean can only be speculated upon. The parallels
were there to see. Both Brando and Dean had studied Stanislavski, as he had done. Both were brought to stardom by Elia
Kazan, as he had been. Dean had co-starred in *Rebel Without
a Cause* with Natalie Wood. Brando had burst into public
acclaim alongside Vivien Leigh, and now, here was Beatty
making a play to do exactly the same.

Coincidence? Perhaps, but a good deal of groundwork went
into making it happen. He made his bid for the gigolo role
and heard back that Williams, who had casting approval written into his contracts, had turned him down flat. Warren was
not easily put off. In his memoir of Tennessee Williams,
Dotson Rader, the author's friend for many years, relates an
intriguing story, which Williams told him, of how Beatty came
to be cast in *The Roman Spring of Mrs Stone*:

'I was in a gambling casino in Puerto Rico,' said Williams,
'when all of a sudden a waiter came up to me with a little
glass of milk on a silver platter and said, "A gentleman has
sent this to you." [There had been stories in the newspapers
about his ulcer.] I said I did not appreciate that kind of
sarcasm and went on playing roulette.

'After I had lost the amount of money I allow myself to lose,
I started to leave. And there standing grinning at the door
was Warren Beatty. "Tennessee, I've come to read for you," he
said. He was very young then, and a handsome boy. He
wanted the part in *The Roman Spring of Mrs Stone* and had
somehow discovered where I was and had flown to Puerto
Rico. I didn't know Warren's work and I thought that the role

should be played by a Latin type, since he's a Roman gigolo.

'I said, "But why, Warren? You're not the type to play a Roman gigolo."

'He said, "I'm going to read it with an accent, and without. I've come all the way from Hollywood to read for you."

' "Well, that's very lovely of you," I said. And I went to his room, and he read fabulously. With an accent and without. And I said, "Warren, you have the part."

Back in Los Angeles, the domestic non-bliss of Collins and Beatty resumed in a house they had rented on Sunset Plaza Drive. They were officially engaged now, but they acted and rowed like an old married couple. The beige chiffon wedding dress she had bought in London still hung untouched in its protective wrappings in her wardrobe. They fought and squabbled and then made up.

There was a brief and fretful separation. Before going to London to begin work on his second film, Beatty had to attend to the pressing matter of doing his duty for President and country. Military call-up beckoned under the Selective Service which had classified him as A1, in 1958, although at his physical in February 1960 he had been graded 1D, which placed him in the category of a reservist, and this required that he completed three weeks' training at George Air Force Base in Victorville. Once he was there, Joan was plagued by his usual flood of cables and telephone calls professing his miserable plight, that he was lonely and missing her madly. She flew down to spend a weekend with him, and they ended up arguing again.

Beatty returned to Los Angeles to prepare for England. Joan planned to go with him since she had no film in view. Fox was on the verge of releasing her from her contract, but kept her hanging on until the position of Elizabeth Taylor in *Cleopatra* had been clarified.

Elizabeth had finally accepted the role and had gone to London with Eddie and her entourage, whom she had checked into the Dorchester. She had barely begun filming when she was taken ill, and rushed to the London Clinic suffering from pneumonia. Naturally, fearful for his star's well-being, Spyros Skouras, head of 20th Century-Fox, called a hasty production meeting to discuss their plight. The whole future of the studio virtually rested upon this one film; millions had already been committed and so far not a single foot of usable film had been shot.

The telephone rang around nine in the morning, and Joan's agent blurted out the news: Elizabeth was dying and Fox wanted Collins to be packed and ready to fly to London that night. If Taylor didn't pull through, Collins would take her place. It would make her a big star. Joan said that was shitty, making such a call when Liz lay dying. Beatty replied that he thought it was shitty, too, but 'that's showbiz, babe' and went back to sleep.

Twenty-four hours later, the news came through that E.T. was making a remarkable recovery. They had put the whole production on hold until the situation clarified. Joan was off the hook. A little while later, she was off the hook completely: Fox released her from her contract and she was out of work and drawing no salary.

They were making ready to go to London anyway. Filming for *The Roman Spring* was about to start and they rented a house in Kensington for the duration. Joan said it would give her the chance to see her mother, who had recently had an operation, and to catch up with other family duties. There would be little time for Beatty to socialise so she made plans to go off on her own, leaving life and art to continue merging its fact with fiction, and Beatty with Vivien Leigh.

It was an unlikely encounter between Beatty and the forty-eight-year-old star of *Gone with the Wind* and other great works, but he came into her life at a particularly traumatic time. The boy, as Noel Coward described him, then barely twenty-four, was playing on screen a scenario that was matched in real life, opposite an older woman, an actress who had just lost her husband.

The plot of the movie was more complicated, bound up in typical Tennessee Williams subterranean movements and general nastiness. Beatty plays Paolo, a cunning opportunist and male whore who uses Mrs Stone to get publicity for himself, so that he is talked about by the film people he seeks to use him in the movies. There is the Contessa, strong and forceful in the hands of the German actress Lotte Lenya, who plays the pimp providing gigolos for lonely women, and there is Jill St John as the younger woman who offers better sex than the ageing Mrs Stone. Vivien finds herself troubled by some classic Williams lines, such as 'The beautiful make their own rules.'

It was only a movie, of course, although there were some rather stark similarities to real life which did not go unnoticed. Indeed, Beatty had walked right into the heart of another heated and emotional scene in which his leading lady was vulnerable and unsure of herself. At the time, Miss Leigh had just lost her husband to a much younger woman.

Laurence Olivier had recently requested a divorce to finally end their traumatic marriage so that he could marry Joan Plowright. Noel Coward best summed up the situation in a diary entry: 'The Larry and Vivien situation has now bust wide open and they are going to divorce . . . Poor Vivien is, I am afraid, on her way round the bend again. I am deeply sorry for her.' And later he added that Vivien had appeared in London 'making a cracking ass of herself . . . she looks ghastly. What has driven her round the bend is the demon alcohol; this is what it has always been. She arrived . . . almost inarticulate with drink and spitting vitriol about everyone and everything. But however upset she may be about Larry she should control herself and behave better.'

Vivien, making her penultimate film before she died in 1967, had leading-man approval written into her contract. She was charmed by Beatty, who looked the picture of health and virility. His hair had been darkened to look the part of a Latin lover and he was bronze from the California sun. As Joan Collins noted often in her account of her eighteen months with him, he could charm any woman within moments of meeting her.

Vivien Leigh was in the frame of mind to be flattered by the seemingly flirtatious attentions of her young co-star, looking sexier than ever in his tight Italian pants. On the set, where all good rumours begin, it was being suggested that Warren and Vivien were becoming 'involved'. She was smitten by his eyes and his mouth. The thought occurred to Joan Collins as she watched them working at Elstree Studios, London. She knew Vivien enjoyed his company and there were to be plenty of opportunities when the crew moved to Rome for location work while Joan went back to stay with her sick mother. But she never did discover whether this intriguing relationship was ever consummated. There were other matters about which Joan was also blissfully ignorant at the time. Sarah Miles, also in the cast, had attracted his attentions.

And during his sojourn in Rome, Beatty met Susan Strasberg, daughter of the mentor of Method, Lee, while taking coffee with actress Inger Stevens. Susan was fascinated to discover how he managed to sit down in the tight trousers he wore for the gigolo role. Such a topic of conversation led to a deeper interest, and that night she and he met for dinner. Before long, he moved into her apartment for a brief but exciting stay, and in off-duty moments they raced to each other's company. It was a mad fling, taken and enjoyed on the spur of the moment and with incidents of high passion. One day they visited the studio of film director Luchino Visconti. He was discoursing on the subject of communism to a small gathering when Beatty suddenly excused himself and, heading towards the bathroom, whispered low in Strasberg's left ear. She waited a minute or so and followed him to the smallest room, where they remained ensconced for fifteen minutes or so, of which a mere second or two was passed admiring the exquisite marble flooring. They emerged having regained their composure and normal pulse rate to rejoin the group, he beaming his enchanting, toothy grin and she pinkish around the gills.

Yet it ended as quickly as it began, and Warren returned to Collins and onwards back to Los Angeles. Their romance was as good as over, and Joan knew it. The wedding dress still hung in the closet where it was to remain, unused. He did love her madly, he would say later, and she was the greatest fiancée anyone could wish for. Joan heaped praise on his ardour, but criticised his selfishness, especially when she brought her mother back to Los Angeles for a holiday in the home she shared with Warren on Sunset Plaza Drive. There were career differences too. He was on the up, being talked about all the time, being featured in the fan magazines and the glossies, while Joan was currently static. This was in part due to the advice Warren had given her, discarding script after script which he said was not right for her. Finally, against his advice, she accepted *Road to Hong Kong*, a comeback vehicle for Crosby and Hope. He said it was crap. She rejoined that she was going to do it if for no other reason than to get away from him.

As for the film which was at the centre of this frenzy of activity, there has been wondrous speculation ever since as to why Beatty was so desperate to do it in the first place. It was not a youth-sex film, like *Splendor in the Grass*, and there was a whiff of mouldering decadence about the whole project that did not seem to fit the image he was apparently trying to project, and certainly not the image the media had written for him.

There was general praise for himself, and thankfully, in her present fractious state, a good deal for Vivien Leigh. She was not as strong as her Blanche Dubois, but she was Mrs Stone, uncertain and jealous of rivals. She stood up well against the blatant competitiveness of the cast. Sadly, a *Time* magazine prediction that a new screen career lay before her could not come true, although the writer correctly forecast good things ahead for 'Shirley MacLaine's little brother'. Other comments were less pleasing for him. *Films in Review*, which had castigated him in *Splendor*, apparently enjoyed this one no better: 'Warren Beatty plays the male whore. Because I am unfamiliar with such lowlife, I suppose, he seemed well-cast to me, although his Italian accent kept slipping. At least his deadpan face suited this degraded role...'

Beatty is sensitive to such indirect sideswipes and especially those which used his private life as a viewfinder for his professional activities. He now discovered the downside of being a star, and the expectations of studios to help talk up a film. But at the time that duty came around, his personal life had become the subject of microscopic examination, caused in the main by Natalie Wood's imminent decision which was to come as a bombshell in Hollywood.

5

Whirlwind

Even if Warren Beatty had never consciously modelled himself on anyone, and he always denied that he did, the media likes to make comparisons. His name was everywhere, long before his films had been released and his work assessed by the critics. Neither *Splendor in the Grass* nor *The Roman Spring of Mrs Stone* appeared in the cinemas before the winter of 1961, but with his liaison with Joan Collins and the advance hype of both movies, he was already a major celebrity. Publicity men would have given a valuable part of their anatomy to secure the kind of press attention he was receiving for any one of their major star clients. As Dustin Hoffman, then struggling towards his own discovery,' would say later, 'Warren was famous before he was alive.'

Beatty was getting hotter, more attractive and mysterious, and all the glossies wanted to talk to him. Well-known writers of magazine portraitures sought him out for interviews and an avalanche of words on the discovery of Warren Beatty was about to hit the streets even though no one had yet seen him on the silver screen. As the *New York World Telegram* pointed out under the headline 'Mystery Surrounds Mr Beatty', '... the young actor had been a provocative mystery to the public for almost two years.' Everyone knew he was the brother of Shirley MacLaine, everyone knew he was the lover of Joan Collins, a lesser number knew he had appeared for twenty-five nights on Broadway, and every so often news trickled out of Hollywood that he had signed for a new picture at an escalating salary. The movie-going public, however, were still waiting for a glimpse of his movies and most could not even pronounce his name, which he pointed out rhymed with 'weighty' and *not* 'wheaty'. Even then, an early interviewer came away thinking to himself, 'I've spent an hour with Mr Weighty and I still know virtually nothing about him.'

When eventually that bastion of American establishment media, *Time* magazine, chose to feature him, he could truly be said to have arrived. Not unlike the rest, *Time* chose to run through the comparisons to the most recent crop of male icons: 'With a facial and vocal suggestion of Montgomery Clift and the mannerisms of James Dean, he is the latest incumbent in the line of arrogant, attractive, hostile, moody, sensitive, self-conscious, bright, defensive, stuttering, self-seeking and extremely talented actors who became myths before they are thirty.' Beatty did not much care for that description, but where *Time* went, others followed.

Developments in the Wagner household merely served to fuel this aura of celebrity status which he was gathering around him. Whatever else Natalie Wood could thank Beatty for, the knock-on effect on her own career from the hype surrounding *Splendor in the Grass* had done her jaded confidence a power of good. She had resumed the role of big star, with the furs and diamonds and six-inch heels that Kazan had stripped from her body for her virginal role in his film. Now she desperately wanted a role in which she could consolidate her position.

The first new film she was offered would not do that, and she knew it. *Parrish*, the project that had first brought Beatty to Hollywood two years earlier for a screen test, had resurfaced. Troy Donahue was to play the role originally intended for Beatty and Jack Warner was insisting that Natalie was his co-star. She read the script and tore it into shreds. The crap word entered the stream of descriptive adjectives which she applied to it.

There was another one, better and far more enticing. Kazan had recommended her to Jerome Robbins, who was casting the screen version of the stage hit musical *West Side Story*. Natalie wanted it more than she'd wanted any other. A convenient bout of tonsillitis ensued. Years later, Natalie laughed about it and said she had been saving her tonsils for 'the day they offered me something really awful, like *Bride of Godzilla.*' *Parrish* presented such an occasion, but if the tonsillectomy was her excuse to duck out of Jack Warner's pet project, and he would surely suspend her again if she refused it, the scheme backfired. A routine operation went wrong. She caught an infection, contracted pneumonia and almost died. She was on the critical list for three days and her health remained delicate for weeks afterwards.

The role in *Parrish* went to Connie Stevens, leaving Natalie free to do *West Side Story* if Robbins agreed. Actually, he was not bowled over by the idea, and director Robert Wise certainly had doubts. Natalie was the girl of the moment in terms of publicity, but she could neither sing nor dance. There were other background arguments. Robbins wanted to run a troupe of unknowns and make them famous. Executive producer Walter Mirsch countered that without stars the film would surely fail. He wanted to stack the cast list with well-known faces, such as Elvis Presley in the role of Tony Romeo, and others like Frankie Avalon, Paul Anka and Fabian in the support cast. Robbins threatened to quit, but agreed to compromise. Natalie came into the negotiations for a star name, and was called for an audition.

She was offered the part at a flat fee of $250,000, the largest single payment she had ever received in the movies, or an alternative of $50,000 and a percentage of the net profits. Since she and R.J. were strapped for cash, she took the bundle up front.

Wagner himself had now left 20th Century-Fox after his old friend Spencer Tracy advised him against signing a new contract which called for a million dollars over five years, but without script approval. That meant, as Tracy pointed out, they could put him into any kind of rubbish they wanted and it could be the death of his career. Wagner chose to go elsewhere and signed a three-year non-exclusive deal with Columbia, whose first project for him, *Sail a Crooked Ship*, was a low-budget crime story that was hardly what he had hoped for. But he accepted anyway, and he and Natalie prepared for their respective new roles. All of this background would have a bearing on forthcoming developments. Wagner had little time to see Natalie ensconced on the set of *West Side Story* before going off to make his own film,

However, he was there to accompany her on her arrival, which she performed in big-time Hollywood style. It was, by any standards, to be a spectacular entrance. She was wearing sunglasses specially selected from her collection of 200 pairs, with a Cossack hat, a fur draped around her shoulders over a skin-hugging dress and carrying a long, diamond-studded cigarette holder bearing a Chesterfield king-size held aloft and sparkling with her diamond rings. Her newly acquired entourage followed on behind: a hairdresser, her male secretary, her dresser, with poor R.J. bringing up the rear, dragging a reluctant miniature poodle named Gigi.

Beatty, meanwhile, was back from Europe and remained for the time being with Joan Collins. The point at which he resumed his contact with Natalie is a secret known only to himself, but one day on the set, Natalie was called to the telephone to hear a voice say, 'What's new pussycat?', the familiar opening line Beatty used for many such conversations and which became so famous that his friend Charlie Feldman, the producer, got Woody Allen to write a film script with that title. The film starred Allen, Peter Sellers and Ursula Andress, and Tom Jones sang the title song.

Beatty discovered Natalie at her wits' end. She badly needed a shoulder to cry on. All was not well on the set of *West Side Story*. She had known it would be demanding, but never in her life had she imagined the pressures she now faced. Jerry Robbins, the ultimate dance perfectionist, was giving her a hard time. Director Robert Wise recalled, 'She really tried hard but she had great difficulty making the routines. Her singing voice was weak, too. She did all her tracks and then sang back to them. They were good, but not good enough.'

Natalie was rehearsing with Robbins, almost step by step, sixteen hours a day. She was shattered when they told her they intended to dub her singing voice and the relentless struggle to conquer the intricate dance routines finally drove her back to her analyst, whom she would dash off to visit during her lunch break.

'Warren, oh Warren!' she was heard to cry into the telephone when he called soon after a screaming match with Robert Wise. Beatty listened sympathetically, and tried to calm her. When and where they met was their secret, but not for long. George Chakiris remembered that Beatty was to be spotted around the set by the end of April 1961. By early June, Natalie finally finished *West Side Story* and was exhausted. Wagner, too, was wrapping up his film and had thrown a party on the lot at Columbia. Natalie had promised to act as hostess but half an hour after the appointed time she had not arrived, and they began without her. Some time later, she arrived with Warren Beatty at her side. She went straight over to her husband and kissed him. He coolly asked her what had caused the delay and she said that she had been posing for stills, and had run into Warren. The atmosphere, as a Columbia producer recalled, could have been cut with a knife.

Natalie circled the party, embraced her friends and congratulated everyone on the film. Then she and Beatty disappeared. They were gone for an hour, and when they returned Beatty had Joan Collins on one arm and Natalie on the other. Natalie said that they would all go out to dinner when the party had ended, and Warren and Joan and Natalie and Robert went off to the Villa Capri. The occasion brought more problems than it solved. In fact, it spelled the end of the Wagner marriage. R.J. and Joan looked on uncomfortably at their giggling lovers until finally Wagner stood up and announced they were going home.

At the mansion on Beverly Drive, where the refurbishment was still unfinished, the Wagners argued their way around the house until finally R.J. slammed the front door and went to their boat at Newport Beach. Natalie was so angry that she squeezed an exquisite Venetian goblet containing her drink so tightly that it shattered and cut her hand. She arrived at dawn on the doorstep of her parents' home in Van Nuys, with a scarf wrapped around the hand.

The following day, the Wagners' press agents, Rogers and Cowan, sent out a short note to the media announcing that it was with regret that Mr and Mrs Robert Wagner were embarking on a trial separation, although there were no immediate plans for a divorce. Shockwaves reverberated around Hollywood at a time when marital problems among the stars were big, big news. This one was especially so – the perfect couple had split up. Louella Parsons said it was the worst news Tinsel Town had received since Mary Pickford and Douglas Fairbanks called it a day. Elizabeth Taylor, herself on the very brink of meeting Richard Burton in *Cleopatra*, said that when she heard the news she took two tranquillisers and went to bed. Joan Collins, meanwhile, showed Beatty to the door of the apartment they shared in Sunset Plaza Drive and slammed it shut behind him.

Events moved on quickly. The trial separation began a bitter parting. A 'For Sale' sign was hung on the Wagners' beloved mansion in Beverly Hills and the builders cleared away the Italian marble and South American mahogany that was still to be fitted in the refurbishment. It now stood as a forlorn monument to what was being described as a Hollywood tragedy. It was the house of dreams: they had redesigned it at enormous construction cost in the style of a Roman palazzo, described by one visitor as early Liberace, with its marble and glass basilica of a living-room; its his-and-hers everything; the designer library that R.J. had lined with books he never read; the music equipment that blared their favourite discs; the glorious swimming pool around which they had entertained the rest of Hollywood. It remained empty for many months until it was finally sold for a bargain price of $155,000, far less than they had put into it.

Natalie rented a house in Bel Air and Beatty, not being a man of property nor possessed by any wish to own his own home, moved in. Rumours abounded that Natalie was on the verge of dashing down to Mexico for a divorce so that she would be free to marry Beatty. Joan flew off to London to begin filming *Road to Hong Kong* with Crosby, Hope and Lamour while Wagner himself headed to Europe to make his appearance in Darryl F. Zanuck's *The Longest Day*.

In London, he telephoned Collins and they met for dinner to discuss their woes. The Fleet Street gossips soon had them headlined as changing partners, but of that notion they were soon to be disabused. R.J. had bought tickets to a new show, *Stop the World I Want to Get Off*. The star was Anthony

Newley, and he and Joan were so enthralled by his performance that they went backstage after the show to congratulate
him. Miss Collins was smitten, and Newley with her. They
married a couple of years later.

Stuck in the middle of these events, and partly the cause of
them, Beatty had little time to think of his career, but somehow private life and screen persona rolled into one. Steamy,
soapy passions were the stuff of the current genre and of
Beatty's life even as a new film came on the immediate horizon. Bill Inge had written the screenplay and there were
cruel rumours that Warren's mentor was pushing his career
along at an incredible rate. It was true, and not true. Beatty
was doing the pushing, going so fast that there was a trail of
blue smoke in his wake, and all of this before his first two
films had been released.

Inge had been hired to write the screenplay of Leo Herlihy's
novel *All Fall Down*, which producer John Houseman had
persuaded MGM to purchase and finance. Houseman would
attest that 'almost against my will' Beatty's suitability for the
starring role in this film was being pushed behind the scenes
by Bill Inge, and then by Beatty himself in what was 'an
astonishing campaign of self-promotion, using his charm and
unmitigated gall.'

He was signed in July, and in August of 1961, as the split
in the Wagner household took on its air of permanency, Beatty
flew down to Florida to prepare for work on the film which
was to put him alongside more excellent actors, with Karl
Malden and Angela Lansbury now cast as his parents and
Eva Marie Saint as his love interest. Would she too be smitten? Few could resist the speculation, so Natalie Wood braved
the prospect of being branded a scarlet woman and flew down
to join him, a fact which the gossips immediately blasted
across their news pages.

But what of Beatty's role? In this instance, let us put the
cart before the horse, and read the review of the film by
Bosley Crowther, that doyen of critics who, when the film
opened in New York the following April, seemed overcome by
an attack of acidity. 'Everybody in this story is madly in love
with a disgusting young man who is virtually a cretin. At

least, Warren Beatty plays him like one. The persistent assumption that everybody should be blindly devoted to this obnoxious young brute provokes a reasonable spectator to give up, finally in disgust. Surly, sloppy, slow-witted picking his nose, being rude beyond reason to women and muttering how much he hates the world, this creature that Mr Beatty gives us is a sad approximation of modern youth.'

That, of course, was not meant in any way as a reflection upon Beatty himself. He was certainly never rude to women. But, truthfully, *All Fall Down* gave him one of his best roles and he matched it with his most excellent performance to date, and one of the best in his career. It provided the intensity that he enjoyed in a story scripted and performed by a writer and actors well-versed in portraying a gallery of middle American failures. It was a tantalising but ultimately unanswered question whether Inge had written the screenplay of James Leo Herlihy's novel with Beatty in mind. Though by no means on screen throughout, he was central to some of the most powerful scenes. He plays a ne'er-do-well son of a middle-class family which has some occasional flashbacks to Beatty's own. The story takes us through his adventures in Florida, and his life of womanising, driven by his endless reservoir of sexuality. He comes home to rejoin the family, and the younger brother who idolises him, and discovers the character played by Eva Marie Saint, an older woman whom he gets pregnant and rejects, and she commits suicide. And so on through the disturbing, coil-snake tension that Inge so proficiently builds . . .

When the film was done Warren and Natalie spent an idyllic weekend in the Bahamas and flew back to New York to begin the publicity round for *Splendor in the Grass*. It was the beginning of an horrendous six months for Beatty and a period which would affect the way he mapped out his future, and especially how he dealt with the media.

His affair with Natalie was punctuated by the release of *Splendor in the Grass* on 10 October, his second film, *The Roman Spring of Mrs Stone*, on 28 December and *All Fall Down* on 11 April 1962. In between time, Natalie Wood was nominated for an Oscar for *Splendor*; *West Side Story* opened to massive acclaim, there was initial hype for the start of her new film, *Gypsy*, in which she was to star as the sensational stripper, and she filed for divorce from Wagner in the spring of 1962. The upshot was that the Beatty profile was at its highest. His arrival was billed in the *New York Sunday News* as 'Hollywood's best-known unknown'. *Life* magazine ran a cover story on him and pronounced he was 'the biggest new name in American entertainment, whose fame is so fresh that he is likely to burst out in sudden blushes.'

Never had there been such a media furore over a new star. With all the publicity that he had received in the preceding months during the making of the movies and over his liaisons with Collins and Wood, the critics were literally straining at the leash to get a look at him on film, to see what all the fuss was about. When his films finally made their appearance, the denizens of the New York critics were on the edge of their seats.

During those winter months of 1961–2 it was barely possible to pick up any magazine or newspaper without finding a mention of Beatty, Wood or both. He was the newcomer, she was a child star who had finally crossed the great divide that few others of her ilk had managed, and had suddenly rocketed in the eyes of Hollywood to status and notoriety normally afforded to no less a personality than Elizabeth Taylor, to whom she was being compared.

It was a mad, exciting, tiring, ego-boosting, ego-deflating, godawful time in which their private lives became totally and utterly intertwined with film fiction. Both were in such demand for interviews that big-time writers and editors were queuing up for appointments. Initially, Beatty was cooperative, but soon he became morose, unapproachable, elusive and downright difficult. On the one hand, he faced the pressure of the studio publicists, who were trying to maximise on the Beatty-Wood situation to boost their respective films, and on the other, he faced the rampant evils of the gossip columnists, who were not the slightest bit interested in his work, but merely wanted the lowdown on his love life.

When Warner booked them into the Plaza Hotel for the first round of publicity interviews, they made sure that their star couple were in suites separated by several floors. The gossips had their spies on all levels. Their every move was monitored. Housemaids and room service boys were interviewed and tipped fresh dollar bills for information. They reported that Warren spent half the time tripping up and down the back stairs to Natalie's room, hoping not to be spotted. Dorothy Kilgallen, who regarded this story as her own, kept up a running commentary for her readers and suggested that the way the two lovers were carrying on it was a wonder they had time to eat.

Sandwiched between the exploitative vagaries of the studio publicists and the gossip columnists were the more serious writers who wanted to get inside the head of this new star, find out what made him tick, compare him to other big stars, rifle around in his past and discover the motivations of his alleged blossoming greatness. They, too, soon began to find it a difficult assignment. John Springer, a former newspaper man and movie publicist, ran the New York office of Arthur P. Jacobs and Company, which handled Beatty's press contacts. Springer, whom Beatty liked and respected, had the dual role of seeking favourable publicity and keeping his client from offending the media. He had lined up a series of major interviews, even before Beatty's films were released, with such eminent publications as *Life, Cosmopolitan* and the *Saturday Evening Post*, mentions in which other more famous stars would die for.

However, Springer found it necessary to write to his client to lecture him on his dealings with the press. He said several interviewers had been infuriated and upset because he had not taken them seriously and pointed out several occasions when he had been just plain uncooperative. Springer concluded by saying that he would not be writing at all if Warren was just a kook who didn't know any better, and pointed to several intelligent, articulate interviews he had given to intelligent and serious writers. Springer would soothe the complaints by stating that Warren was prone to becoming self-conscious about questions he was being asked, or nervous about the approach to certain topics. He also wanted to retain some areas of privacy. But Beatty did not improve. Just as he had thrust himself into the face of the world, so the world was coming back at him and the experience gleaned so far was fermenting. He weighed the realities and the risks and dealt with them in his own taut and frustrating way, and never really altered in the next three decades.

These early interviews will console present-day seekers of a journalistic audience with Beatty, for he was seldom an easy subject. Jon Whitcomb, who came with tape recorder for *Cosmopolitan*, recalled that he found Beatty grudging and suspicious while the tape was running, but as soon as it was switched off, he grinned and relaxed. For example, Whitcomb questioned him about his first meeting with Bill Inge. Beatty was typically monosyllabic in his replies, and said that the meeting was entirely conventional, arranged through his agent. Later, Whitcomb talked to Inge himself, who explained: 'This young man is still high, still exhilarated at the turn his life has taken. His birthday comes in early summer; he's just turned twenty-four. I think he may start closing doors on the press pretty soon. I doubt if he will give interviews at all much longer. When I first met him, he seemed marked for success ... the kind of boy everyone looked at, knowing he was going to make it big ... he has a basic confidence that's made of iron.'

Another of the famous painters of media portraits, Joe Hyams, upset Beatty with the report of his encounter with him which appeared in *Showbusiness Illustrated*. Hyams described him as opulently handsome and astonishingly foul-mouthed. He said Beatty's constant vulgarity and frequent use of the fuck verb – not in such common usage in 1961 – was not necessarily the product of a dirty-minded young man but more of a camouflage to stop the interviewer spotting anything significant in his replies. It also enabled him occasionally to be startlingly candid without fear of being quoted. Hyams likened his interview with Beatty to a child's therapy session, with the subject rambling on in virtual gibberish without giving an answer to the question, while happily picking his nose, scratching his head and fiddling with any object that came to hand.

There was a mask of resolute anguish permanently on his face, yet he agreed that if people weren't interested in talking about him, or reading about him, then he would be dead. But on the other hand he didn't want readers of articles to decide that he was an ass. Such protestations were to become commonplace and even to lead to the occasional point-blank refusal to give interviews to certain magazines. He would not see a *Time* reporter because he considered that the interviewer would only write like a comic who entered a room and had to say something funny, even if it was cruel.

There was a distinct pattern to the emergence of the myth and legend which would surround Beatty for the rest of his life, and which was being created during this whirlwind of astonishing media coverage. First, he put himself about, seeing everyone who called, and then when everyone began calling, he made himself scarce, aloof, morose and all those other adjectives applied to him by interviewers who either did not get to see him, or to whom he gave a hard time. Later reticence to giving interviews is perhaps explained by these experiences, but also of equal use was his learning of the craft of manipulation, which he could and would use with considerable skill in the future. There would be enough writers around, even experienced journalists, who would still fall for it.

The moment of Beatty's final arrival in terms of being visible on screen has as much to do with his notoriety as with his pictures. Throughout Hollywood, the major studios were in financial crisis. Dwindling audiences and spiralling production costs were hitting them hard, and more and more movies were being made in foreign locations for lower costs and tax breaks. Major stars of the old school were being put out to grass and left to fend for themselves as the studios battled with one theme after another to try to generate better business at the box office.

Probably the best example was the state of 20th Century-Fox, which had just sold 250 acres of its massive studio complex in Beverly Hills to a property development company, in part to finance the burden of the cost of *Cleopatra*, which was being shot in Italy. The result of all this background activity in the smoke-filled rooms of the money men and deal-makers was that hot stars suddenly escalated in their importance. Nothing was sacrosanct in this heady, swirling world of movie-making, least of all the private lives of the stars themselves, which seemed to be outplaying anything that was on at the local Roxy.

As Natalie and Warren returned briefly to Hollywood for the new year of 1962, Natalie telephoned her goodbyes to Elizabeth Taylor who, having recovered from her illness, was heading back to Europe with husband Eddie to embark on the filming of the most costly film in Hollywood history. On 22 January 1962 she came face to face with Richard Burton, who had earlier confided to director Joe Mankiewicz: 'I do not relish the thought of meeting your Miss Tits.' The reality was rather different. Within a month, the beginnings of what Burton later termed *Le Scandale* was hitting the headlines, and vying for space with the Beatty-Wood romance back in Hollywood.

In the third week in March, the Taylor-Fisher camp announced the formal ending of their marriage, and the media, which had been driven to a frenzy by the antics of Taylor and Burton in Rome, where planeloads of gossip columnists had been arriving daily, then pounced upon the news from the Wood-Wagner-Beatty scenario.

First, it was breathlessly reported that Beatty and Natalie had become engaged, even before the formalities of a divorce had been dealt with. He had given her a Chihuahua puppy instead of an engagement ring. True or false, it did not matter. They were the intermittent focus of attention between the Taylor-Burton saga. Then, as the year's Academy awards neared, Natalie was nominated for best actress for *Splendor in the Grass*, and Beatty was disappointed that he did not get a nomination too. They quarrelled and he walked out but returned the following day. They turned up hand-in-hand for the award ceremony on 9 April, and caused a near riot among the paparazzi, with Natalie determined to out-stun her rivals by wearing a sensational multi-thousand-dollar evening gown and white mink stole. Natalie did not get the Oscar – it went to Sophia Loren for *Two Women* – but she had the distinction of being in the cast of *West Side Story*, which won ten Oscars. *Splendor in the Grass* scored only one – Bill Inge for best original screenplay.

The headiness became headier. Beatty and Wood were dubbed by Sheilah Graham the poor man's Taylor and Burton.

They were all being mentioned in the same breath, the same conversations, the same stories. Money was talked about. Beatty had put his fee up to $200,000 a picture. Natalie was asking $250,000 – although this was still no match for Taylor's $1 million. Hedda Hopper said Natalie was 'robbed' because she did not get the Oscar, but had a nice consolation prize in Warren Beatty, whom she suggested she should marry without more ado because living together was not a good example to be set by two role models of American youth.

To remove the only apparent hurdle to this prospect, Natalie filed for divorce a week later, claiming mental cruelty by Wagner, who had gallantly volunteered to be the guilty party. In her statement, filed in the Santa Monica Superior Court on 17 April, she claimed her husband had become 'cold and indifferent and was very critical of my friends. He criticised my management of the household and would go off by himself. He preferred to play golf than stay at home with me.'

The divorce was granted in double quick time, ten days later, after Natalie pleaded she had to leave for Europe, although she failed to state that the only reason she was going was to accompany Beatty, whose film *All Fall Down* was an American entry at the Cannes Film Festival. She received an interlocutory decree, which meant she would be free to remarry one year hence. The following day, she and Warren flew off to Europe to begin a new publicity round, heading for Paris, Cannes and Rome, and always checking into two separate suites.

The scene switched to Rome a couple of weeks and a thousand headlines later. Taylor and Burton were at the height of *Le Scandale*, and Wagner had recently completed his scenes in *The Longest Day*, in which Burton had also appeared. Wagner had remained in Europe to begin a new film, coincidentally moving on to Rome, where he had looked up his old pal, actress Marion Marshall. She had in turn recently fled to Italy during a bitter split and custody battle for her two children with her husband, the director Stanley Donen. Marion had been a contract player at Fox at the same time as Wagner and they had much to reminisce upon, and much to comfort each other about, both having recent broken marriages.

Out of the blue, Natalie and Beatty arrived, and purely by chance walked into the same restaurant where diners had just witnessed an almighty bust-up between Taylor and Burton, and where this evening Wagner was entertaining Marion Marshall to dinner. R.J.'s face was a picture of enlightened joy when he saw her, giving way to sadness when he espied Beatty coming in behind. Ever the gentleman, he beckoned them over and ordered a drink, a bottle of Natalie's favourite champagne. The evening passed uncomfortably; conversation was difficult, and when R.J. and Natalie danced, they barely touched.

Later that night, R.J. telephoned Natalie at her hotel. He could not get her out of his mind and he decided to propose an attempt at reconciliation, but the telephone line was permanently busy, apparently with Beatty making many calls to Hollywood. When she learned of this years later, Natalie confessed that at that moment, she would have run back to him like a shot. She was already tiring of Beatty's virility and fast-lane life. But the moment passed and she jetted away with him again, leaving Wagner and Marshall consoling each other. They married in July 1963. Natalie was less lucky with her new man.

6
Wanted

If Warren Beatty was truly a self-created illusion, a man whose mystique and not his talent had made him a star, as some of his critics were saying, then he had pulled off one of the greatest coups of self-projection in the extravagant history of Hollywood. Every major studio and every major director began to seek his services. He had moved into the celestial high ground where fame was a doubled-edged sword. It was one thing being famous, and quite another sustaining himself as an actor.

Bill Inge, in the wake of all the publicity and gossip headlines that surrounded Beatty during that early part of 1962, suggested that his friend might even quit acting altogether, a possibility which he had presumably gleaned from conversations during Beatty's moments of despair about the pressure of being in the constant glare of the arclights. Inge said: 'I don't think he really knows how he acts. He's got a healthy ego, a good ego, but has a negative side too. There's an awful lot of negativism in Warren but he has real intelligence. He's been so intent on his career that he's devoted his entire self to it. He's just sitting around now, waiting for the rest of his life to come back to him.'

It was true that Beatty had concentrated hugely on his career, although not to the exclusion of all else, such as his affairs, although even these, in a curious way, had been turned to his general advancement. He had probably been in love with Joan Collins once but the publicity of the relationship opened more doors for him than it did for her. Close friends of Natalie Wood were now wondering about the extent of Beatty's devotion to her, and whether she was merely infatuated by him. Neither, it appeared, had the strength and depth of feeling to sustain a long and healthy romance.

Quite apart from the continuing round of headlines which followed them wherever they went, Beatty was astounding his media observers and colleagues alike by what Bill Inge had called 'waiting for the rest of his life to come back to him'. He was simply refusing all offers of work. There was a necessary period of deliberation on his future after the quick-fire arrival of his first three films, premiered within a space of six months of each other. The box office would give a good pointer to the future, and perhaps it was time to sit back and take stock. In those roaring few months, he had to ascertain if he was a success in *Splendor in the Grass*. If so, then he hoped there would be a rush to see him in *The Roman Spring of Mrs Stone*, and then a dash to see him in *All Fall Down*.

That was what happened with Dean's trio of films, *East of Eden*, *Rebel Without a Cause* and *Giant*. But they were all popular films, with a definite appeal at a certain edge of the cinema market. It was difficult to put Beatty in the same category, although comparisons with others seemed a necessary ingredient to any writer on the topic of Beatty.

The comparisons ended on screen. *Splendor in the Grass*, which had taken Kazan so long to bring to the cinemas, did reasonable business but was certainly not a smash hit. *The Roman Spring* did not do as well as expected commercially, and with such strong rivals around for the Oscars, it picked up only one nomination, Lotte Lenya for best supporting actress. Beatty's third film, *All Fall Down*, fared badly. But in spite of his mixed fortunes at the box office, Beatty was singled out for three good performances. He was also, by his own choice of material which verged on the realism genre, caught up in the questions-marks being raised over the American cinema's preoccupation with social dramas. Critics used these portraits of life and relationships, which had been the focus of so many plays by writers like Inge, Williams and Arthur Miller, as a good excuse for some high-blown discussion. They provided ample material for debate but the critics themselves were as much in the doldrums at the time as were the studios. It was all very well producing meaningful pictures and arty reviews, but the fact of the matter was that the audiences gave them a very, very patchy response in the cinema.

Exactly the same trend had been noted in England when the new wave of writers like John Osborne were producing what the popular newspapers disparagingly called 'kitchen-sink dramas'. Plays like *Look Back in Anger* and *The Entertainer* fared well in the theatre but did not enjoy the same success in the cinema. In America, the giants of the literary scene were delving into all kinds of topics that the public at large was embarrassed to discuss, and found uncomfortable to watch. That was the stark reality of realism. It was *too* real. It was tolerable and experimental in the theatre. But somehow, that great big screen brought the drama a touch too close. After little more than five years of this genre of movie-making, cinema audiences were already signalling their displeasure by not attending. There was enough grimness, oppression and misery being experienced by the masses, be it in the heart of England or middle America, without having to sit and watch it exaggerated and re-enacted as entertainment.

Was it even entertaining? Often it was not, and the novelty of the realism, the swear words and the pregnancies out of wedlock and all those taboo topics like homosexuality, incest and even cannibalism tackled by the literary élite was insufficient to hold the customers' attention. It was no good calling the public names, either, as Bosley Crowther had done when he described Warren Beatty's performance in *All Fall Down* as an 'approximation of modern youth' – i.e. surly, sloppy, nose-picking, slow-witted, given to scratching himself and muttering to himself about how much he hates the world.

Upon modern youth rested the future of the cinema, or had he forgotten that? The older generation was firmly stuck in the sitting-room, eyes fixed to the smaller screen. Perhaps in the scheme of things, when all the murky waters surrounding Warren Beatty began to clear, it did not really matter what the critics were saying, at least not as far as he personally was concerned. They may have been an important influence on the box office, but it made no difference whatsoever to his immediate future.

Beatty had just stopped work. Charlie Feldman, his agent,

recalled that he simply could not understand what was going on. Script after script arrived in the post, and script after script was rejected, some of them returned unread. 'No other actor I have ever known could do this,' said Feldman, 'if for no other reason than egotism and the need to continue working and keeping his face before the public and prospective employers. That's what acting is all about. You become famous, you become a star and you'd like it to stay that way.'

It was inexplicable. They were not *all* bad scripts he was turning down. There was Neil Simon's *Barefoot in the Park*, which he and Natalie considered doing and eventually rejected. It was made five years later with Robert Redford and Jane Fonda. There was *The War Lover*, which had two ideal roles from which he could pick. No again, and they went to Steve McQueen and Robert Wagner. Luchino Visconti telephoned and said: 'Warren, I need you; I need you badly for my film *The Leopard*. I have Burt Lancaster and Claudia Cardinale and I want you . . . it is your part.' Visconti knew why he wanted Beatty, and the film suffered because he did not get him. Warren read it and said he did not do costume dramas. Alain Delon took the role instead. There was *Act One*, a film based on the autobiography of director and dramatist Moss Hart, director of the stage versions of *My Fair Lady* and *Camelot*. Beatty was emphatically wooed for the role, but turned it down. Producer Dore Schary signed George Hamilton instead, and it was not a success.

The next offer had some topical prestige. He was wanted to play John F. Kennedy in a story of the current US President's wartime exploits as the commander of a PT boat. Now, there were rumours about this film having been promoted by those who wished to find grace and favour with the President, and to assist in his re-election with a propaganda message of a wartime hero, to be released strategically as close as possible to the next election, without getting into trouble with the opposition. Warren Beatty, a known Kennedy supporter, was earmarked for the starring role in the film, entitled *PT 109*. Elia Kazan, coincidentally, had decided that if ever he wanted to portray Kennedy on screen, he would choose Beatty. This assessment came from observing both men at close hand, Kazan having been twice invited to the White House. 'Warren had everything Jack had,' said Kazan. 'Looks, intelligence, cunning and a commanding eye with the girls. Not many escaped either man. Warren also suffered from lower back trouble. I once asked him if this hampered his sex life and he said, "It doesn't hurt then." '

But although Kazan wasn't making this film, Kennedy knew of his belief that Beatty was the man for the job. He may have been impressed by the thought of himself being played by Beatty. When Warner Bros contacted the White House to enlist Kennedy's cooperation, the President agreed, and even suggested Warren Beatty to play him.

Producer Bryan Foy was apparently not too happy about having his lead actor selected for him, but Warner agreed to the President's wishes. Kennedy went so far as to instruct his press secretary, Pierre Salinger, to act as liaison man between himself, the studio and Beatty. So here was another seemingly high-profile opportunity to play the most famous and powerful man in the world at that moment in time. Who would turn down such a chance without running the risk of being castigated for snubbing the President or displaying a considerable lack of national spirit?

Warren Beatty would. He had already been criticised for supreme arrogance when a trade paper related the tale that Jack Warner had specifically asked him to fly to Washington to see the President and talk over the film with him, and to 'soak up the atmosphere.' Beatty was alleged to have replied, 'Let the President come here to California and soak up my atmosphere.' He later explained he said it as a joke, not seriously. The fact was that he did not think *PT 109* would make a good picture, and he could hardly turn it down if he had already been to Washington to meet Kennedy.

Anyway, the whys and wherefores were all academic. He was adamant about not doing it. Although he was a left-wing Democrat, destined for future back-room involvement in politics, he weighed up the risks and the possible advantages, as he always did. He decided the risks were too great. The script was weak, there was a surprising lack of action and he could see that opponents of the President, of whom there were many, would become his own opponents when the film was reviewed; he would be on a hiding to nothing.

Beatty, controversial and on the move, could have given the kind of star profile that the film needed. In the event, his assessment was right. Cliff Robertson played Kennedy in a low-key and ordinary movie. The whole project seemed to be in awe of the subject matter and fearful of speaking out of place; consequently Cliff Robertson and Ty Hardin, who eventually starred, looked leaden and dull. The film flopped. Months later, when the dust had settled, Beatty and Kennedy met. 'You were right,' said Kennedy, and Beatty grinned.

He studied and analysed with a greater degree of sensibility than most in his position. He jumped at nothing, and mystified the pundits as one project after another came and went. Why had he turned down so many offers? Was it because he would not have been the centre of attention? Did he look at any script with the eye of a solo player to whom other actors were merely performing a supporting role? These questions were not unnaturally posed.

Louella Parsons was keeping count. Between the time he finished his last film, *All Fall Down*, and the start of 1964, she recorded that he had turned down seventy-five scripts and $2 million in fees to her personal knowledge. What was he afraid of? The crap word continued to figure in his replies, and certainly there was an abundance of it on offer. Warren was not interested; he told everyone he was holding out for a quality picture and was not even lured by the low-money-but-interestingly-arty films being touted by Continental directors. He may have admired their work, and talked seriously and meaningfully in endless transatlantic telephone calls, or in quiet conversations in the booths of the trendy restaurants. But still nothing. He said that unless he could put his heart into a project, then he did not believe there was any point in doing it. He was also adamant about big money and star billing. And yet that in itself was one of the reasons he gave for turning down these multitudinous offers.

He moaned that the pressure of his fame had hit him hard. 'I was not prepared for it,' he said, 'I was not ready for the agony, the coarseness, the vulgarity, having to do things here, being pressured there until finally they rub out your talents. I was insecure. I'd lost the spark and I felt like I was being sold like a can of tomatoes.' It was the bleeding-heart cry of many like him, only he was doing something about it. The trouble was that as the publicity surrounding the three films subsided and his career languished, the headlines reverted to his social and domestic life.

Occasional interviews in major magazines continued to give readers an account of his reluctance to show his hand, and no one was quite sure what he was up to; didn't he like acting or something? Louella Parsons called him and demanded to know why he had turned down so many films. He moaned about the media's predilection for getting into his trousers. Parsons replied that he had chosen the wrong career if he resented questions about his love life. That was no reason for giving up work, she rebuked. He replied that he was going through a barren period, when the mere thought of work revolted him. In actuality, he was setting a pattern which would become familiar throughout his working life.

Beatty's workshyness continued to intrigue, and without the available addition of film talk, there was nothing left in his current calendar for writers to discuss other than his social arrangements. They continued to focus on the problem of getting him to say anything of substance, while he countered that all the questioners ever wanted was to talk about trivia. He said to the esteemed Rex Reed of *Esquire* on this topic: 'There is as far as I can see no reason to do a story on me. Most of what I have to say is unprintable, anyway. Most movie stars are not interesting, so to sell papers and magazines in the fading publications field, a writer has to end up writing his ass off to make somebody more interesting than he is, right? What do I need with publicity?'

So the magazines were now writing stories about how he didn't want to be interviewed. He would even call up a writer for whom such an interview had been rejected and explain at length why he did not wish to talk to him, thus giving the writer enough for a whimsical piece, anyway. Was he acting at being not interviewed? Was his reputation as the *enfant terrible* of Hollywood based upon an act? Was it satire or truth? Only Warren Beatty knows, and thus there were more questions to add to the growing list of imponderables that helped build the portrait of mystique.

Meanwhile, Warren's romance with Natalie had progressed to the point where the debating societies of La Scala and elsewhere were wondering who would marry first, R.J. and Marion Marshall or Natalie and Warren.

Beatty was a roaming, untethered lover. He had no home of his own, only borrowed apartments and hotel rooms, and for the time being he was staying at Natalie's new place in Benedict Canyon. It was a large house, befitting her new major star status. There was a waterfall in the garden, levelling out into a stream which ran through the middle of the house; swimming pools, a jacuzzi, monogrammed linens and bedroom silks. Natalie had it all, and she had Warren, for the time being.

'They were something to behold,' said her sister Lana, then sixteen and living occasionally in Natalie's home. 'Their love affair became very intense. They were beautiful, exciting and sophisticated.' Especially, Natalie wanted sophistication. No tackiness. They had important friends to dinner, entertained without embarrassment as if they were husband and wife (early sixties, remember!) and they maintained a high profile among the glitterati. They were guests at the party at Peter Lawford's house in Malibu, that fateful party which last saw Marilyn Monroe alive. The passion of their romance overshadowed the reality, that which many stars have faced after the heat of co-starring movie scenes. It was an infatuation and not true love, and the cracks were already appearing by the beginning of 1963. They began to fight, just as he had done with Joan Collins.

Natalie gradually became aware of the sandy foundations of their affair, especially when R.J. and Marion Marshall married. She even had a brief affair with Tommy Thompson, a writer who came to interview her for *Life* magazine and who, in the end, became her lifelong friend and confidant. They were sharing a suite in a New York hotel where she had flown for a publicity round for her new film, *Gypsy*, when Beatty turned up. He invited everyone out to dinner, apparently unaware that Natalie and Thompson were special friends, and the evening was fraught and quiet.

They rowed and drifted, and Lana reported a distance growing between them. There was sufficient space in the Benedict Canyon house for them to spend hours in different rooms. Their differences were not merely those of disenchantment.

Natalie had moved to the very brink of the higher echelons of Hollywood greatness, signalled when Jack Warner gave her Joan Crawford's huge dressing-room on the Warner lot, from which the older star had won her Oscar as Mildred Pierce. Although Natalie would never quite assume the mantle of superstardom, she was as it turned out at the zenith of her career. While she was deeply involved in her relationship with Beatty, he had little or no influence over her work, except in helping her prepare. Her manager was a bare-knuckle fighter in the kick and rush of Hollywood, and secured the very best deals for his client, which put Beatty's own career and present inactivity in the shade – and Beatty was not a man to be overshadowed by a woman.

The wrench came one night during dinner at Chasen's, another of their haunts, best known for serving the best chilli in Hollywood. There was a fair smattering of local dignitaries, including James Stewart and party, Gregory Peck with his wife and Mr and Mrs Alfred Hitchcock. Halfway through the meal, Warren disappeared and Natalie hung around drinking coffee, expecting him to return at any moment. Before long, proprietor Dave Chasen was seen walking to the table where Natalie sat and whispering something in her ear. Natalie was left to pay the bill, which she signed, forcing a smile, and nodding to her friends as she left. Beatty surfaced a week later at Benedict Canyon. Natalie refused to see him. She told her maid to tell him that she had burned his clothes. There was nothing left for him to collect and goodbye!

Tommy Thompson, on the receiving end of many calls from Natalie in her times of personal stress which verged on the suicidal, said the break-up had a tumultuous effect on her, and sent her racing back to her analyst. 'I think it went deeper than most people realised,' he said, 'because the hurt was so public and it was humiliating. As far as Warren was concerned, I think he had reached a crisis point, knowing that he either had to marry her or get out, and marriage was never part of his plans, ever. He ended it in the only way he knew how, by forcing it through his own guilt, and allowed Natalie to call him all the rotten bastards under the sun.'

She was hurt and shattered just at the very time her career demanded at least a public showing of glamorous confidence.

In 1963 she completed *Love with a Proper Stranger*, in which she co-starred with Steve McQueen, another migrant from New York who had made it big. She had also just signed to make *Sex and the Single Girl* for $750,000, the highest fee she had ever received and which put her within an ace of the £1 million a picture being charged by Elizabeth Taylor.

Her importance to Warner, who made the film, can be seen by comparing her salary with those of her co-stars in that movie. Tony Curtis, also a big name of the day, commanded just $400,000; Henry Fonda received $100,000 and Lauren Bacall $50,000. It was also more than three times the figure Beatty was demanding for a picture. Some even suggested that Warren, in the midst of his own crisis about what to do next, had become jealous and bored by watching Natalie wallowing in acclaim and acting out the big star syndrome, and evacuated himself before he went down the same road feared by Wagner, that of becoming Mr Natalie Wood.

Her friend and colleague, the actress Hope Lange, who was going through similar trauma with the end of her own marriage, recalled that she and Natalie would sit around for hours discussing their problems. Natalie clung to those friends for support; she was fragile and shaking in spite of her success, and told Hope that she knew she was a step away from 'going over the edge.'

Fortunately, the gallant white knight Arthur Loew Jr, who had given shelter and support in the past to Elizabeth Taylor, Joan Collins and Debbie Power, rode forward to pluck her from the doldrums. A few months before Natalie's break-up with Beatty, he and Debbie Power had divorced. A kindly, caring man, he offered Natalie some stability when she needed it most; cool, calming words from a softly spoken man who was a gourmet and connoisseur of the arts. He and Beatty were total opposites. Very soon, he bought her a diamond boulder and announced they were engaged. But the unlucky Mr Loew himself suffered rejection when Natalie called it off a few weeks before they were to marry.

The whole scenario offered the gossip columnists a huge new ballpark of speculation and one suggested that, given the plethora of romances recently in the headlines, it was not beyond the realms of possibility that Warren would now steal

Marion Marshall away from Wagner, Natalie could fall in love with Tony Newley and steal him from Collins, who would then seek consolation with Richard Burton after Wagner had eloped with Elizabeth Taylor, while Arthur Loew waited patiently in the wings to assist any temporarily displaced females. Anything was possible, as indeed was proved the following April, when the Academy awards for 1963 rolled around.

Natalie was nominated for the second time in three years, this time as best actress for her strong and captivating performance in *Love with a Proper Stranger*. The irony of the situation was not lost on anyone as Natalie swept into the foyer of the theatre on the arm of Arthur Loew, looking the absolute star in another shimmering, stunning blue gown and white mink. Among her competitors for the title was Warren Beatty's sister, Shirley MacLaine, for *Irma La Douce*, and the French actress Leslie Caron, for her highly acclaimed performance in the British film *The L-Shaped Room*.

As Natalie and Arthur lingered for the photographers and film crews and she did her interviews in front of the live television cameras, in walked Miss Caron, nervous and shy, competing in style and elegance as well as professionally.

And on this great night of nights, her escort was none other than ... Warren Beatty.

7

In Swinging London

Young careers were made and lost in the mêlée of the emerging sixties when the Beatles and the Rolling Stones burst on to the music scene and brought with them all the bandwagons and influences of swinging London and magnificent Merseyside. A clutch of supposed new romantic idols to replace the Hollywood image of the old-style romantic idols came and went. The conventional Rock Hudson school of beefcake actors, handsome, tanned and all-American, which had run parallel to the Method-ists throughout the fifties and early sixties, populating some pretty awful movies aimed at displaying their virility and physique and little else, was already in decline. There were strident moves towards a more liberal view of censorship of sex and violence in films and the constraints which forced studios to churn out those endless twee boy-meets-girl plots were at an end.

Oddly enough, the emotive styles of graduates of the Actors Studio and other allied groups like Stella Adler's were also going out of fashion. The tutorials were still strict and intense, but the studio was racked with conflict and Kazan's disaffection with Lee Strasberg led him to resign as a director of the studio in 1962. Only then did the basic disagreements over actor training that existed between Kazan and Strasberg come to light, with the former focusing on actions and movement while the latter concentrated on emotions.

In an article for *The New York Times* magazine, Kazan pointed out: 'The Actors Studio has made an historic contribution to the American theatre. It is now no longer a young

97

group of insurgents. It is itself an orthodoxy ... regrettably too much talk of the "Method" among actors today is a defence against new artistic challenges, rationalisations for their own ineptitude. We have a swarm of actors who are ideologues and theorists. There have been days when I felt I would swap them all for a gang of wandering players who could dance and sing and who were, above all, entertainers.'

A new breed of film actors, as opposed to those steeped in the quite different demands of the theatre, had come through some hard schooling, often – as Charlton Heston identified – via the medium of live drama on television. Now the cinema was veering towards the promotion of its dashing, extrovert anti-heroes, of whom the ultimate would be Jack Nicholson, in his arrival in *Easy Rider* at the end of the decade. They had to be tough, rugged and stylistic, like Steve McQueen (in *The Magnificent Seven, Hell is For Heroes* and *The Great Escape*) and Paul Newman (*The Hustler* and *Hud*), who were setting audiences alight.

Newman was still a great supporter of the Actors Studio and its theories for the theatre, but the cinema was demanding excitement, escapism and veering strongly away from the mumbling, stuttering, laid-back vogue of the fifties. They had all moved on from their origins in the New York Method scene to meet the changing demands. The anti-heroes, beyond Brando, were becoming the driving force of American cinema in the sixties. Brando was Brando and would remain unique and unassailable, though disenchanted and reclusive because of the films he was being offered and the press he was receiving. Monty Clift was in the last painful throes of his career and life, torn by his emotional problems and addictions.

Beatty was positioned uncomfortably in the middle of these schools and, though not a product of the Actors Studio itself, was still wallowing in the kind of material it favoured because some of his closest allies – like Kazan, Inge, Clifford Odets and soon, the director Arthur Penn – were working in those areas where the frailties of human relationships were examined and dissected. Virtually everyone who had so far played any significant part in his career was actor-orientated, as opposed to script-led.

Because of his attachment and fondness for fifties Americana, some wondered whether Beatty would make it through the maze and be able to cope with the changing scene bearing down upon Hollywood with fierce intensity. He had the handsome features that pass for beefcake, he had the actor training that brought all those early comparisons to Brando and Dean, but above all he still seemed to be driven by artistic desires which were almost genteel. They harped back to the origins of his early devotion to the American playwright, and even that genre of social melodramas was fading.

The two and a half years between the time Beatty finished filming *All Fall Down* and his next project, which was to be *Lilith*, were wasteful and barren. He did nothing except reject scripts, travel and have fun, and more fun, sex and more sex. The combination of self-indulgent idleness and the search for the right script for whatever ambitions remained for self-fulfilment kept him off the screen and out of critical observation. The only headlines were those, as we have seen, which were concerned with his social life, and not without reason, the pundits were already beginning to label him as a spent force, a playboy.

The script for *Lilith* arrived at the time when he was reaching a crisis in his life, and was perhaps accepted with a degree of desperation in his search for a movie. It was near enough to his ideal, but not quite. It was an art movie that would require exceptional skills to become the commercial success he badly needed.

Beatty was approached by the writer-director Robert Rossen – to whom he had been recommended by Clifford Odets – with an outline from J.R. Salamanca's novel, published in 1961. Rossen, one of the outlawed directors of the McCarthy era after his powerful drama *All the King's Men*, which won Broderick Crawford an Oscar in 1949, had recently come back to the fore with his direction of Paul Newman and Jack Gleason in *The Hustler*. The 1961 movie won eight Oscar nominations, including Newman's for best actor, Gleason and George C. Scott for best supporting actor and Piper Laurie for best actress. It was Beatty's good fortune, once again, to work with a man of depth and, some would say, genius.

With that kind of pedigree and a story which appealed,

Beatty believed he had finally found his next success. The appeal of the story was difficult to define; it could have been the sexual content, which would have him back in the midst of the activity for which he had become most famous, or perhaps it was the intensity of the drama, which he believed would allow him to show off his own talents. Later, when *Lilith* flopped, he would say it was none of those things. He had taken the role because he so admired the work of Rossen that he had hung around waiting for him to come up with the right script. When Rossen finally offered him *Lilith* he was so broke after two years of doing nothing that he had to accept.

Lilith was the tale of a young war veteran who returns to his home in Maryland to contribute something to humanity. He lands a job at a private mental hospital as an occupational therapist and there encounters a young woman who is overcome by sexual desire. She is a nymphomaniac who ruthlessly selects her partners for sex, male or female, and causes havoc among them, drives one fellow-inmate (to be played by Peter Fonda) to suicide, and then slides into total madness. Rossen saw the story as one which examined the way society considered those outside the norm as sick. He seemed to be approaching his task with the idea of producing something that would shock his audience with explicitness. But it was still only 1963, almost a decade before *Last Tango in Paris*, and even the hint of a semi-nude scene in *Lilith* enraged a few puritanical hypocrites in the media.

Whatever the underlying reasons for Beatty taking on the film, it must have been obvious from the start that in extending the boundaries of movie eroticism at that time, it would hardly be classed as a subject for mass entertainment.

However, Beatty was involved from the outset with casting and in script revisions, which was in itself a privilege rarely bestowed upon an actor of such relative inexperience. The title role was still open, and they discussed a number of names including Sean Connery's wife, Diane Cilento, who had just become a smash hit in the British-made *Tom Jones*, which won great acclaim and nine Oscar nominations, including one for Cilento as best supporting actress.

Beatty was also captivated by Jean Seberg, who had faded

quietly into the Parisian landscape after the role which made
her an international star in Otto Preminger's *Saint Joan*.
More recently she had appeared in two French movies for
Jean-Luc Godard, in which she had acquitted herself rather
more favourably than in her first movie. Seberg, selected by
Preminger from an alleged 80,000 applicants for Joan and
then driven almost to distraction by his directorial demands,
had been living in Paris virtually as a recluse until Rossen
and Beatty flew there to meet her. She was impressed by
their arrival, and would later say that the two men had
developed a very fraternal, intimate relationship, bouncing
conversation off each other.

The three of them talked and discussed the role and Beatty
implored her that it was exactly the right one to bring her
back into the mainstream. They agreed terms, hers being a
quarter of what Beatty was being paid, and then began weeks
of further discussions and work on the script. They visited
mental hospitals and they discussed the intricate nuances of
the script. The rest of the cast names were filled in, including
Peter Fonda as the mental patient who commits suicide. Well
down the credits is a young Gene Hackman, making his very
first movie.

Filming began after several false starts in the late summer
of 1963, by which time the fraternal relationship between
Beatty and Rossen had already become strained. Somewhere
along the line, the great hopes that director and star had
for this film disintegrated into a mess of rows and general
discomfort. For one thing, the director became ill, and brown
liver spots appeared on his skin. No one could have imagined
then that it would be his last film. Beatty was allowed his
head, but not sufficiently, he would say, to command a great
influence on the outcome.

As his friend, the writer Robert Towne, was to observe later,
'If a director was indecisive, Warren could destroy him. He
would ask so many questions – and he can ask more questions
than a three-year-old – the director would not know whether
he was coming or going.'

Those around the set believed Beatty saw this as his film
and a promising screen partnership with Seberg gave way to
disagreement and anguish, with many stops for discussion

and retake. Peter Fonda was so angry he voiced his disapproval to Beatty in no uncertain terms.

Later, when the film was universally panned by the critics at its premiere at the New York Film Festival in September 1964, Beatty would excuse himself by laying some of the blame on Rossen. He said he told the director he was making a bad film, but he would not listen to Beatty's own ideas. Rossen, mortally sick, though the seriousness of his illness was then not known (he died in 1966), was defended by his supporters, who were vitriolic in their dismissal of the opinions of a 'snot-nosed, wet-behind-the-ears actor' who had made three pictures against the genius of Rossen.

Reviewers were once again anxious to see how Beatty had fared. The high profile of the actor, placed alongside the combination of Rossen and Seberg, attracted much consideration and attention. *Variety* put *Lilith* in the mould of an art-house film not suited to general audiences, and commented that Beatty tackled his role with a hesitation that was jarring to the watcher, not helped by the staccato dialogue of single, and no more than double, sentences. Beatty was roundly attacked with uncomplimentary adjectives for his performance and Seberg was given the most, if restrained, praise. In actuality, it wasn't that bad. Seen today, out of the context of sixties pre-liberal Americana, it ranks far higher than a good deal of the movies being pumped out by Hollywood, certainly not as bad as it was portrayed by the critics and the disastrous box-office returns. For Beatty at the time, it was not a good comeback after his long lay-off. In fact, with two box-office duds out of four, lesser men might have been permanently floored.

By the time *Lilith* opened in New York, he was already engaged on his next project, another deep and mysterious story entitled *Mickey One*. Behind the scenes there was another affair, too, equally deep and mysterious. A real-life scenario of the kind which had helped carry him forth to international notoriety over the past four years was bubbling towards the surface. Until then, it was known to only a few.

By Leslie Caron's own admission, after she met Beatty at the party given to promote her Oscar-winning chances in *The*

L-Shaped Room, 'We practically did not leave each other for the next two years.' Apart from Caron's arrival on Beatty's arm for the presentation of Oscars at the Santa Monica Civic Auditorium on 13 April 1964, their liaison had been low-key. She was a controversial young woman with a career record that was spectacularly more successful than Beatty's, and it was during the making of these earlier hits that she had accumulated some foes.

Until the early part of 1964, Leslie Caron appeared to be happily married to Peter Hall, director of the Royal Shakespeare Company, by whom she had two adorable children, Christopher, then aged six and Jennifer, four. It was her second marriage. She was barely out of her teens when she married handsome American meat tycoon George Hormel, although they were divorced after three years. She and Peter Hall had been married for almost eight years, and had two superb family homes, one within a stone's throw of Peter's theatre at Stratford-on-Avon and another in London.

She had been famous far longer than Beatty and was six years his senior, although elfin-faced, with almond eyes and a largish mouth, and schoolgirl features, even at thirty-two. She had been plucked from nowhere in 1950 to become an overnight sensation alongside Gene Kelly in his Oscar-winning *American in Paris*, and later to co-star with Fred Astaire in his 1955 remake of the 1931 hit *Daddy Longlegs*. In the meantime, her films included the superb *Lili*, for which she won an Oscar nomination. In 1958, her star ascended to even greater heights in the multi-Oscar-winning *Gigi*, with Maurice Chevalier and Louis Jourdan. Cecil Beaton, who was hired to do the décor and costumes for the Lerner-Loewe musical, recalled in his diaries his first impressions. He said Caron showed signs of being difficult and pernickety, and he feared trouble.

Beaton observed that Caron was 'generally unpopular' among her colleagues on *Gigi*, although he eventually formed something of a rapport with her himself and decided that she was a basically charming young woman whose shyness was often wrongly taken as snobbery. 'Through sheer intelligence,' he wrote, 'she has become a very good actress. She [can be] ... argumentative and stubborn, but there is nothing glib or slipshod about her. She has to have everything clear in her brain before she proceeds.'

In the theatre, she had been directed by Jean Renoir in his play, *Orvet*, and by Peter Hall in his stage version of *Gigi*. She had acquired a considerable versatility as an actress, sufficient for Richard Attenborough and Bryan Forbes to cast her, somewhat surprisingly, alongside Tom Bell in *The L-Shaped Room*. This was a powerful drama, important at the time and mildly sensational in its content, about a young girl seeking an abortion in a seedy London suburban house. And so Leslie Caron had blossomed again, and the years following instant acclaim and her marriage to one of the supreme figures of the British theatre establishment had provided her with a degree of confidence, perhaps masking insecurity. Her career, boosted by the attention attracted by her performance in *The L-Shaped Room*, brought her back to the attention of Hollywood.

In February 1964, Hall and Caron were parted seemingly by the pressures of work. Peter was working on a huge Shakespearean festival to mark the 400th anniversary of the Bard's birth, and Leslie was preparing to fly to Hollywood, announcing that she could not find suitable work in England and intended to spend the next six months in America. 'It's very tough on my husband, I know,' she said at the time, 'but I am an actress and I cannot change. I have never intended to stop work; I have been working since I was fourteen years old. Peter knows that. For the sake of my marriage and family, I never wanted to make another picture outside of England. But now I realise I must, if I am to continue working.'

Leslie admitted then that the conflicting working arrangements would put pressure on their marriage, but she and her husband had talked it over and agreed that it was the only solution. It was intended that the two children would fly to Hollywood to join their mother during school holidays when she was working.

On 4 April, they ended the speculation among friends by announcing in a joint statement that they were separating: 'We have found that the demands made upon us by our very different careers, often in different parts of the world, make it no longer possible for us to remain together. We are both deeply sad . . .' Later that month, on 13 April 1964, Caron was seen on Beatty's arm at the Oscar presentations and a couple of months later, she flew off to Jamaica to begin work on her new film, *Father Goose*, with Cary Grant and Trevor Howard. Beatty's arrival on a distant corner of the island went relatively unnoticed. Beatty moved into her house, and remained at home and out of sight during the hours of daylight, waiting for her to finish work.

A difficult situation was building, and one which Leslie Caron must have known then would lead to an explosion of tempers and disarray in her domestic life. Beatty knew that, too, but as Caron has said, once he had zoomed in on a woman, he would never let go. He also seemed equally concerned with his own plight. Caron would recall that during those hours of after-work conversations she had with him, fears over his career and his future were never far from his mind. He talked endlessly about how he wanted to be recognised as an actor to be taken seriously. He complained that the media had branded him a playboy, and seemed incapable of recognising the cause, which was himself.

The discussions continued in Chicago the following month when he began filming *Mickey One*, and her flights into the Windy City also went apparently without the gossip columnists getting wind of their affair. Back in London, Peter Hall was so aggravated by his wife's liaisons with this young scallywag that he confronted her about it at the end of May. Leslie was in love with him, she had to confess. She had not wanted it to happen, but it had and there was nothing she could do about it. Hall responded angrily and pointed out that she risked a scandal, and might drag the children into a public dispute.

Leslie Caron knew then she was risking everything for the love of Warren Beatty. In June, Peter Hall filed for divorce in London and named Warren Beatty as the co-respondent. On 17 June 1964, as the headlines blazed, Hall obtained an interim order banning his wife from taking their two children out of the country. Hall's counsel told the London Divorce Court that he was 'fearful' that the children might not be returned if they were allowed to leave England.

In those days, of course, there was no such thing as a quick and quiet divorce in Britain. There was no possibility of an out-of-court settlement in some far-off place away from the public eye. Everything had to be done according to the book, which meant lawyers in wigs and gowns, detectives and evidence to prove adultery. The divorce court judge would also need to hear proof of the submissions by Hall's counsel over his claim for custody of the children, which could only be achieved by showing that Caron was not suitably placed to take charge of them.

A messy matrimonial dispute was in prospect. Peter Hall, in his sworn statement read to the court, said his wife had said she wanted the children to be brought up in America, and that she planned to set up home in Hollywood. Extracts from an interview with Leslie Caron by Roderick Mann of the *Sunday Express* were read in court, in which she said: 'When I first went to Hollywood years ago, I hated it. But it's different now. I have some marvellous friends there . . . After Peter and I broke up, I felt as though I had been left alone on the sea to drown. But not for long. Soon I began to feel my own life flowing again and it's wonderful. I need respect, you see. I need to be admired. And Peter and his friends were solely concerned with the theatre, and they didn't really care about films.'

Hall's counsel said it appeared that Miss Caron felt she had an absolute right to take the children out of the country without her husband's consent. The judge granted an interim order giving Hall custody of the children pending a divorce hearing.

In the months before it came to court, Caron relied even more heavily on Beatty. In between times, he planned to take a house in Beverly Hills to provide Leslie and her children with a home if ever they were in Los Angeles, although that prospect had been temporarily halted. It was the first time in his life that he had taken a step of some permanency in his living arrangements, having always in the past preferred the convenience of hotel living. The house would be carefully selected, to provide a swimming pool and play area for Leslie and the children, although whether she would ever be able to have them around her when matters were settled remained in some doubt.

The heat and ferment of the split in the Hall-Caron household focused upon Beatty with a much greater intensity than any of his previous romances. The sheer weight of formality surrounding proceedings in a British divorce court, the fact that he had wooed the wife of a leading establishment figure and all the subsequent publicity of the hearing would lie heavily upon their situation, like a black cloud positioned above them waiting to rain heavily upon their future together. It was then the case that there had to be a 'guilty' party in any British divorce. Caron, through her association with Beatty, would be branded the guilty one.

For once, even Beatty looked vulnerable, and the ring of steel-like confidence was at last being penetrated. His closest friends – and there were actually very few in the strictest sense of friendship – had visions of him being forced, finally, into taking the ultimate step of marriage, if only to save the honour of Miss Caron after she had been put on the rack by the media. There seemed little alternative, inasmuch that if Caron was eventually to supply evidence that she could provide a stable background for her two children in the eyes of the strict British courts, there would have to be a visible matrimonial home and a stepfather if she were to fight a case for custody.

Beatty had found no easy match in Peter Hall; much more was at stake than in the Collins affair, or the break-up of the shaky marriage of Wagner and Wood, and Hall's lawyers would undoubtedly pursue the worst elements of Beatty's recent romantic wanderlust to secure the result they required for their British client.

While preparations for this legal onslaught were being made in London, Beatty remained in Chicago filming *Mickey One* and, as he arrived with Arthur Penn, that superb off-beat and occasionally off-beam director, there was an immediate challenge. His career was central to his concerns; his love life was a matter which could be pushed to the back of his thoughts when he was working. Primarily, all he was interested in there and then in Chicago was restoring himself, getting his name back into the realms of professional recognition.

Once again, he had made a strange choice of film, almost as if he did not want to appear in any kind of popular movie, and was saving himself for more artistic, serious stories. And *Mickey One* was to be art with a capital A; a surreal, contemporary drama which was to be described by one reviewer as modern, garish and hectic as neon.

There was a huge risk involved. His career must surely have been on the line now with all that was going on, but he trusted Penn like he trusted Kazan. The two directors were old friends. Penn had, like Kazan, a long-standing affiliation with the Actors Studio and the New York theatre. In the late fifties, he and Bill Inge had run a Playwrights Unit within the studio with Kazan's wife Molly, and in the early sixties he had been a regular lecturer to actors and directors, although his work there was gradually curtailed by his own success as a film director, which began when he directed Paul Newman in *The Left-Handed Gun* in 1958.

Beatty's search for his own perfection within his selected arena of investigating human relationships led him back into the realms of experimentation and controversy. It was one of those films no one could fathom a reason for, or how any studio had been persuaded to stump up the cash in the first place. Actually, it was a low-budget movie, made for less than $2 million and Columbia, who backed it, did so in the belief that the package of Penn and Beatty, along with Franchot Tone in the co-starring role, would at least get their money back. There was a chance that they might even make a profit.

Penn knew the movie was going to be difficult, and he was apprehensive about Beatty, but wanted him nonetheless. 'I saw him in *The Roman Spring of Mrs Stone*,' he recalled, 'and took the script of *Mickey One* to him at Delmonico's. I found him a deeply confused young man, but attractive. He had a reputation for being uncooperative and difficult, but overall, I never found him lacking in his willingness to engage and I think that is an admirable trait. He was strong in native intelligence and possessed a richly inventive mind. Oddly, his literary taste is exquisite, not from a broadly educated base but from a visceral appreciation of good writing. Also, I don't think anyone could question his integrity. I would take his word on anything.'

Mickey One is on two levels, a fable and a nightmare. Beatty plays a Detroit comedian who flees to Chicago to escape gangsters, and then works himself into a schizophrenic state working in cheap dives and seedy surroundings, convinced he is being persecuted. His paranoid retreat to escape the gangsters and reality form the two levels of the action. The movie, filmed in moody black and white, with lots of camera tricks and lighting effects, is filled with complications, self-indulgent messages broadcast by Mickey in his deluded state, and populated by a small but weird cast which includes dwarfs and giants. It was being sold as a screenplay in the mould of Franz Kafka, but perhaps more truthfully displayed the work of a leading actor who was bent on rebelling against Hollywood conventions and a director who, now and again, wanted to bring his motivations from the theatre into the cinema. It attracted Beatty's interest and energy as much as any project he had tackled in the past.

In the end, it disintegrated into its own complications. Done another way, more commercially, it had the definite possibility of being made into a film with popular appeal. That was never the intention. During filming, Penn allowed the production to set its own pace. Beatty, troubled occasionally by private thoughts, was sullen and reclusive on set.

Franchot Tone, another expatriate from the Actors Studio, was used to such behaviour. She found Beatty alternately quiet and studious, and then angry and disruptive. She believed that Beatty, at his best, could conjure up far more anger than Dean. Some of his colleagues voiced another complaint, one which was reminiscent of Maureen Stapleton's story of rehearsals with Brando, Joanne Woodward and Anna Magnani, when she protested that she couldn't hear a word Brando was saying. Actors on this set, in Chicago, apparently faced the same problem with Beatty, although, sadly, there was not a strong voice like Stapleton's present to shake him up, and consequently there were many moments when it was difficult to hear exactly what he was saying.

Mickey One was one of those movies which immediately polarised its audience. They either loved it or hated it, and that was obvious from the reviews when the film opened for its first screening at the New York Film Festival in September

1965. Judith Crist, of the *New York Herald-Tribune*, praised it as a 'brilliant original screen work, visually exciting, intellectually satisfying and a credit to everyone involved.' Bosley Crowther, however, complained that it was difficult to know whether this 'lurid demonstration' was intended to represent what goes on in the psyche of the hero, or was meant as a symbolical allegory of the agony of life for those who can't face it. So you paid your money, and took your stance. Commercially, the film was a failure, but as a contribution to a body of work amassed by an actor, it was a worthwhile addition to Beatty's portfolio.

If, on the other hand, *Mickey One* was ever intended to display Beatty in a role that would have mass-market appeal, and increase his bankability in Hollywood, then it failed. This was the enigma of the man at that moment of his life, and thereafter for that matter. He seemed to have no inclination towards becoming involved in movies aimed determinedly at the popular end of the market, preferring instead to immerse his talents in the sometimes leaden, occasionally pretentious melodramas and the behaviour of society at large. Since this route had been selected by personal choice, rather than being imposed upon him, he was giving the distinct impression that he was becoming an actor who neither wanted nor needed popular acclaim in the way it was being attached to some of his more swashbuckling contemporaries.

Yet, as Leslie Caron would say, he was profoundly ambitious. Even so, Beatty possessed a contumacious inner probity that would not be moved by opting for easy routes to either money or professional status. This was easily misinterpreted as confounded arrogance and reckless irresponsibility. He had managed to alienate the media and the Hollywood money men with a reputation as a self-seeking smart-ass which was not wholly deserved. It did mean, however, that the word fame as applied to pedlars of dreams would have been more difficult to sustain through his most recent work had it not been for the ongoing and very public saga of his private affairs.

8

Promise Her . . .

The title, the timing and the presumed intent was rather blatant. *Promise Her Anything* was a screenplay produced out of the hat in the aftermath of the torrent of publicity and press abuse that surrounded Beatty following Leslie Caron's divorce from Peter Hall. He had decided they should do a film together, and according to Caron had selected the script. Compared with his recent material, heavily laden with melodrama, it was a flimsy piece which took him well away from the moody material that had failed to give him status at the box office.

So would this movie. It was an American comedy interwoven with an undercurrent of sexual content that may well have been considered near the knuckle in 1965, when it was made, but which quickly dated during the rapid movement of the advancing permissive age.

At the beginning of 1965, the scenario of an on-screen romance appealed to Beatty despite the hostility surrounding him in the British press. The new movie was being filmed in London, and he and Leslie walked straight into the lions' den. Such a divorce in Hollywood would have been a routine affair, but in Britain it was still viewed as a far more serious matter, despite the emerging era of 'Swinging London'. Beatty perhaps did not quite appreciate the way in which it would be treated as he arrived in almost cavalier style into this new stamping ground, largely unexplored.

The social scene had moved on apace since his earlier visit during the making of *The Roman Spring of Mrs Stone*. Even

111

so, friends of Leslie Caron wondered why she allowed herself to be exploited in such a way, in such a movie. Today, she still defends it as a delightful comedy which she enjoyed making. She could not escape the murmuring, though, which suggested that Beatty was cashing in on their situation to help pay for the costs.

Their notoriety over the affair was at its peak and the last place Beatty-watchers would have expected him to turn up was at the epicentre of the action. Peter Hall's reputation and standing was also at its highest so far in his career. He had just completed the Royal Shakespeare Company's year of huge 400th anniversary celebrations. The most outstanding event was Hall's acclaimed direction of Peggy Ashcroft as Queen Margaret in *Richard III*, while the National Theatre had mounted a showcase of incomparable talent, which included Laurence Olivier playing Othello for the first time in his career. England was being heralded as the outstanding leader of world theatre and Peter Hall was among those who received much of the appreciation. Had Warren Beatty not intervened in her life, Leslie Caron would have been at Peter Hall's side, sharing the accolades.

London was the scene of change, in everything from attitudes to clothes. In the world of popular culture, the people that were to shape a generation were gathering. The Beatles and the Rolling Stones were leading the music revolution while in their wake came the artists, models, writers, photographers, fashion designers and film-makers who were all in place by the time *Life* magazine pronounced that London was the 'city of the decade' in which the key words were 'uninhibited' 'now' and 'young'.

New boundaries of style, expression and phoney exhibitionism were being forged daily as the Age of Aquarius gained its momentum. Quite coincidentally, Hollywood was engaged in a massive movement of activity in Europe to take advantage of various tax benefits, and London was experiencing a welcome revival as a movie-making centre, apart from its own upsurge of activity, which had centred around a string of superb international successes and with Sean Connery as the first and best James Bond.

Fresh from his appearance in the media pages of cultural review, interest in Peter Hall was moved with ease and, in some quarters, carping glee to the news and gossip columns when the divorce came to court in February 1965. The public hearing before the officious Sir Jocelyn Simon, president of the Divorce Court, gave formal acknowledgement of Caron's adultery with Beatty, and exercised that commonly known phrase of 'discretion' over Mr Hall's own admitted adultery with another woman. Beatty was cast as the villain of the piece and was ordered to contribute to the costs of the divorce. The question of custody of the children was left to a private hearing in the judge's chambers, and later, when passions and tempers had been quelled, amicable arrangements were concluded.

Neither Caron nor Beatty joined Peter Hall for the divorce hearing. That afternoon, they were to be found together at Shepperton Studios, in Middlesex, making preliminary pre-production tests for their movie together. In the aftermath of this bitter domestic parting, indeed on the very day of its finale, they had begun work on *Promise Her Anything*, a title which certain writers found both amusing and distasteful in the circumstances. Sheilah Graham, for example, managed to extract a quote from Beatty which fitted exactly – he was ready to marry Caron whenever she wanted. When she said 'Now!' he would be quite happy to go to the altar.

This, his friends believed, was Beatty being serious, and they speculated upon him being forced into a corner at last by the intensity of what had happened in London. 'He just could not walk away from this one,' said a close associate of both. 'We were really expecting him to marry. He gave the impression of being more definite about Leslie than any other person in his whole life. He seemed to be ready to set up home and become stepfather to her two children when they came to visit; he had even rented a home for that specific purpose. Always, in the background, there was the feeling that, with Warren, nothing was permanent. Nothing in his whole lifestyle signified a man ready or able to settle. He was constantly on the move, constantly talking on the telephone, travelling like a panther on the prowl, living out of a suitcase in borrowed homes and hotel suites. There was no base, no roots. And we were all asking ourselves if Leslie would alter all that and pin him down, although in retrospect I'm not at all sure she knew what she wanted in that very difficult period of her life.'

The togetherness, in part forced by the pressure of the divorce and then by their co-starring commitments on *Promise Her Anything*, moved to London, where Beatty took up residence with Caron for the duration. Acceptance of the project came before the reviews of his last film, *Mickey One*, had made their point about his choice of script, and he seemed to have been taken with the notion that his career should move into the area of romantic comedy, in the mould of Cary Grant, perhaps.

Beatty's career was certainly ready for a change of direction. The fashionable genre of films which had held his attention so far had run its course, and yet with his determination to pick his own script, this film was hardly one which would aid his wish to become a major force in Hollywood. Quite the reverse. The natural awkwardness was derived from his background in what someone once described as the 'scratch and mumble' school of acting. Only Leslie Caron lifted the whole film from failure.

Beatty was reminded of an off-hand prediction by Elia Kazan who, interviewed soon after the release of *Splendor in the Grass*, said he thought Beatty was good in that role and showed every promise of becoming a very good actor, but 'we should wait five years, and see if he is as good then.' Asked if the bloom comes off with fame, Kazan replied. 'It isn't the bloom that comes off, it's the humanity. The bloom comes on – the wax fruit look!'

The comment puzzled and troubled Beatty. 'Why do you suppose Kazan said that about wax fruit?' he mused at the time. 'I don't think someone really interested in working is going to come out like wax fruit.' He could not understand why Kazan had made such a remark. If he was good then, would he not get even better? Now he knew what Kazan knew – that getting better with experience was not a foregone conclusion, and in the here and now of sixties frivolity and escapism, the five years was almost up and, on current evidence, he had lost some of the early power of his youth, otherwise he would have not been there, in Shepperton, doing what he was doing.

Promise Her Anything was little more than a good-natured romp, set in Greenwich Village but filmed in London where the surroundings were anything but authentic. That basic flaw was the least of the film's troubles. He was cast as a young film-maker who wants to make important, artistic movies but has to settle for pornography. Into his life comes a young French widow (Leslie Caron) who moves into his apartment building with her infant son.

Caron, meanwhile, is in love with her boss, who doesn't like children, and she has to hide hers from him. Beatty, the film-maker, uses the child in one of his sex movies, then redeems himself and wins the widow's love by saving the child's life. Attempts at humour, rolled up in satirical discussions of child psychology and mild pornography, largely miss the mark, and Beatty is left with the least auspicious picture he has made to date, prompting the critic Judith Crist to observe acerbically that they succeeded in proving one thing, that 'neither gifted professionals nor eighteen-month-old babies can rise above some material.'

Leslie Caron was more jarred by the divorce than she had shown publicly, but was not ready to rush back into marriage – merely films. By July, there appeared to be no haste on her part to dash to the altar, although Beatty proposed several times. 'I want to live while I am alive,' she said often, as if indicating that life with Beatty was a whirl, compared to less hectic refinement with Peter Hall. 'I'm having tremendous fun. I'm enjoying my work, and making money. It is terribly satisfying. I'd like things to stay exactly as they are. Life is great and I love Warren. Marriage? Not yet . . .'

Beatty, meanwhile, had already signed to make a third film in London, *Kaleidoscope*. It was to be another romantic comedy, co-starring a largely all-British cast, headed by Susannah York who, not long before, had come from the galling experience of watching Montgomery Clift disintegrate under the harsh, occasionally cruel, directorship of John Huston in the making of *Freud*.

Susannah was among the best of Britain's young and glamorous actresses of the day, and was much sought after along with other Brits, who included Eric Porter, George Sewell, John Junkin and Yootha Joyce, when Warners sent over a production team from Hollywood, headed by director Jack Smight, who had just directed Paul Newman in *Harper*. In fact, the two stars struggled with lifeless dialogue that raised the eyebrows of the theatrically experienced cast who surrounded the two stars.

The movie, as fans of those fashionable crime 'capers' in which the villains were the heroes will recall, revolved around a playboy card-sharp who plans the ultimate gambling coup by breaking into a factory which makes the playing cards for a casino, and marking them with an ink visible only through his special spectacles.

In 1992, Susannah York recalled for the author: 'My agent sent me the script, and I thought it was funny and said yes, I'd like to do it. I hadn't met Warren then, but as he was playing a charming card-sharp I thought it seemed rather good casting. It was a very frivolous, frothy script, and if I knew him at all by reputation, it seemed an appropriate part for him. I played Angel Maguire, a dress designer who was what was known as "kooky", a young eccentric who was the daughter of a police inspector. I was Warren's love interest.

'The dialogue was bright and fun but the film didn't really work because it fell between the two stools of the comedy and the thriller elements.'

For those seeking a film which is pleasurable without taxing the brain, this one would suffice. Beatty, however, was even more lacklustre than in *Promise Her Anything*. His co-actors felt the same. Susannah York did not find the experience particularly exhilarating, especially when compared with her work with Monty Clift. With Warren Beatty's reputation travelling well in advance of him, she had been expecting a Clift-like actor, deep and sensitive. 'I fell in love with Monty,' she said. 'I found him a generous, excessive, totally truthful and very courageous actor, though maddening for the wrong sort of director.' Monty gave of himself to help his colleagues. She was unsure about Beatty from their first meeting. Acting with him provided some taut and tense moments, but she was captivated by his absolute charm off screen.

In fact, part of the trouble was that this kind of light comedy provided him with no inspiration whatsoever, and very little challenge, either. As a previous co-star had once observed, Beatty needed to draw down into his well of anger to fire himself up for a good performance. In comedy, there was no anger, no well to draw upon. He was not a natural comic, and it showed. As far as Beatty's professional reputation was concerned, *Kaleidoscope* did nothing to rescue him from the plateau of the mundane, which threatened to do for him exactly what Kazan had predicted – to present him as an also-ran, blown out of ideas and tricks by the end of his five-year apprenticeship, success and failure before he reached thirty. For the time being, he had only the love and constant companionship of Leslie Caron to keep him warm.

There was one thing above all else that he could eventually thank her for, however, and with it she probably saved his career and a decline into depressive oblivion. Indeed, it was her introduction that jerked him out of the downward spiral and secured his future once and for all.

They had flown to Paris to meet the famed director François Truffaut for lunch. Leslie Caron had arranged it especially, at Beatty's bidding, in the hope that he could secure a role in Truffaut's new film, *Fahrenheit 451*. As Truffaut spoke English intermittently and not very well, Beatty said he would not join them for the meal because it would be too much of a strain to communicate, but would instead come in for coffee and a discussion.

Truffaut said he had already cast the German actor Oskar Werner for the lead, but that if Warren was looking for a script that might suit himself and Leslie, he had recently read something that would interest them. It was *Bonnie and Clyde*. Leslie translated the sentences that Warren could not pick up. It turned out that Truffaut had been sent the script by a couple of American writers named David Newman and Robert Benton. 'Heard of them?' asked Truffaut.

'No . . . I don't think I have,' replied Warren. In fact, he had barely heard of Bonnie and Clyde, either, and there was no reason why he should have remembered a cheaply made 1958 B movie version of the story entitled *The Bonnie Parker Story*, starring Dorothy Provine and Jack Hogan.

Truffaut said: 'You should read their script; it might interest you.'

Beatty showed a mild flicker of interest: 'We are casting our net,' he said to Truffaut, gesturing that he meant himself and Leslie. 'We are looking for something special.'

'This, maybe is right . . .' said Truffaut. 'I think it is right for you. It needs to be made by an American.'

He explained that he had first received the script in 1964 and had been so intrigued that he had commissioned a French translation. This was a curious demonstration of faith, because it was based on the story of a couple of outlaws, a man named Clyde Barrow and his girlfriend Bonnie Parker, whose activities in the early thirties gave them brief notoriety before they were shot to death in an ambush by the Texas Rangers in 1934. They robbed banks and killed people and were themselves dead before their twenty-fifth birthdays. In the story, Clyde Barrow was said to have been impotent or homosexual while his girlfriend Bonnie Parker led him to casual adventure and thrill-seeking crimes.

'How come,' said Beatty, 'two unknown American writers send you a script about American gangsters?'

There was more to their story than gangsters, said Truffaut. There was an undercurrent of relationships going on, and the reason Newman and Benton had posted their script to him was because they had been inspired by his film *Jules et Jim*, with the *ménage à trois* of two men and a woman. They had projected the same movement of characters in their own script but they believed that only a Continental director like Truffaut would understand their meanings and intent. It was also a fact that they had been unable to raise a flicker of interest in their project in America. Eventually Truffaut had been sufficiently interested to suggest small improvements to Newman and Benton, but by the time the script had resurfaced, he was already committed to make *Fahrenheit*.

The whole project appealed from the start. For Caron and Beatty read Bonnie and Clyde. As far as the gossip columnists were concerned they were already outlaws, and they became more and more caught up in the story as the discussion progressed. There was a problem, instantly visible, however.

118

Caron spoke, and still does, with an undisguisable French accent. How would she fit into a story about a couple of all-American gangsters? In all honesty, she realised it would not be for her, but that did not stop her goading Beatty into going for the script. After his initial interest, he began to have doubts. He wondered whether *Bonnie and Clyde* would be perceived as a Western, since it was set in Texas, and Westerns were not doing very well. He wondered, too, if the recently announced film version of Truman Capote's *In Cold Blood* might detract from it.

Leslie Caron swept his doubts away. There was no way *Bonnie and Clyde* could be seen as a Western, and *In Cold Blood* would be long forgotten by then. What was more, she said, he ought to consider making this film not just as an actor – he should steer the project from the beginning, as its producer.

Caron was right. It certainly possessed all the ingredients to float him out of the backwater into which he had drifted: popular appeal, with sex, violence and anger. It had depth of story and seemed to be populated with characters who were by no means one-dimensional. It also had a pair of authors who were as desperate to develop the original concept, a story hinged equally upon sexual relationships, as they were the story of Bonnie and Clyde itself, so that it wasn't just a wild gangster movie about two relatively obscure characters resurrected from the depths of American criminal history. What they sought was more an experimental, uninhibited production.

Something more than just acting ambition was stirring. Beatty had been discussing with Caron during these past months the future, their future, and their careers. They were both exceedingly ambitious, competitive people. Beatty was already talking of quitting acting and going for directing or even producing, just as soon as he had secured himself financially. Caron encouraged him. Her years with Peter Hall had brought her as close as anyone could come to observing the tough negotiating skills required for an impresario. She impressed this upon Beatty, and insisted that with careful thought and tight controls on his own ambitions, making sure that he did not overreach himself, he could become the master of his own destiny – at least on this picture. She said that the story of Bonnie and Clyde presented him with the ideal opportunity of creating his own movie.

Beatty dashed to New York alone. He was anxious and eager, toying with the idea of doing something *really* special. Immediately he arrived, he telephoned Robert Benton to inform him of his interest, and that he would like to read the latest version of the script of *Bonnie and Clyde*. Benton was surprised by the call. The normal route for such contact was through agents and managers.

Benton said he would be happy for Beatty to read it, and less than an hour later, Beatty appeared on the threshold of his apartment in Lexington Avenue. Benton invited him in, and they talked. Benton expressed his reservations, however, about whether Beatty – or any of the mainstream studios who might back the picture – would be prepared to accept the important homosexual undercurrents going on between two of the leading characters, Clyde Barrow and his partner C.W. Moss. Beatty said Truffaut had already mentioned them, and considered them to be an integral part of the script. Would Warren really play a homosexual? Benton wanted to know.

'Well, for the time being I would really love to read the script. Then I can tell you what I think.'

Benton, hardly the master of salesmanship, cautioned Beatty that he may not like it.

'Let me read it . . . I just want to read it, please.'

Benton handed over the script, and Beatty said he would be in touch just as soon as he had read it. Three hours later, he called Benton and said he just had to say how much he was enjoying it, and wanted to do it. Benton said he was pleased to receive this news, but remained cautious. He said he would prefer to hear Beatty's views when he had finished. How far had he got? Beatty said he had read thirty-five pages or so. Benton said that he should wait until he had read another thirty pages before he made any rash statements: 'Page sixty-four will make your hair curl.'

'Don't worry,' said Beatty. 'I'm sure I want to do it.'

Benton muttered to himself that he would believe that

when he saw the signature on the bottom of the contract. The following day, his hopes went up a further notch. Beatty had finished. He enjoyed the script very much and wanted to put together a package to try to rouse the interest of a backer for at least some development money. It might never get made, of course. Only one in a hundred good ideas ever made it onto celluloid. It would be difficult; the script was very lumpy and he wanted to let another, more experienced Hollywood writer take a look and make some suggestions. Nothing substantial, just general advice.

In the circumstances, the best offer he could make for the script was $10,000, and yes, he knew that was peanuts in Hollywood terms, but even so he was taking one hell of a risk and for them it was better than nothing. Since nothing was the only other alternative on the table, Benton and Newman agreed.

Having been virtually talked into the role of impresario by Leslie Caron, Beatty gained more confidence in his negotiating abilities as he followed through and became a deal-maker. It was an unusual stance for an actor; few had tried and with limited success in the past. And frankly, anyone who knew Beatty closely at the time would not have given him many marks out of ten for his organisational abilities. His life was haphazard and impromptu. He was just as likely to dash to the airport and catch a plane to some distant place as he was to drive down Sunset Boulevard. Business matters especially were an aspect of his life to which he afforded little attention. He was as cavalier with money as he was with his women.

Accounts rendered lay unopened in his briefcase or littered the floor of his fairly ordinary saloon car. Like royalty, he seldom carried much money and displayed little propensity towards paying bills, referring creditors to his manager. He also often omitted to put his salary cheques in the bank. Once, when his briefcase accidentally fell open, a clutch of uncashed cheques worth thousands of dollars fluttered on to the floor.

So, at that moment in his life, he had little to recommend him as businessman, which is what a movie producer is supposed to be. However, he steeled himself for a battle, half expecting that at the end of the day all he might achieve was disappointment in the volatile world of Hollywood which, to put it mildly, was less than enamoured by his reputation of the moment.

Yet, there was a new determination emerging. The list of requirements needed to satisfy any prospective backers was formed and ticked off. The well of friendships and past acquaintances would be drawn upon. He first considered directing the movie himself; it was his ambition to get to the other side of the camera. But there was much to be done, too much at risk and he was unsure he could produce, direct and star. He had the good sense to realise that this might not be a wise move. Success was more important than his own ego. He put the job out to a proved and hot exponent, going straight for Arthur Penn, who had directed him in *Mickey One* and was one of the few directors on the American scene in the mid-sixties who were bold enough to experiment like their European counterparts.

Penn agreed to read the script, but did not rush to sign up. He was worried about certain aspects, and surprisingly did not like the suggestion of a homosexual relationship between the two leading men. He thought it got in the way of an otherwise fast-moving tale.

In the meantime, Robert Towne was consulted. He was a friend of Beatty's and an up-and-coming young writer who had cut his teeth turning out plots for Roger Corman quickie drive-in movies for Jack Nicholson to star in; later he would become renowned for more famous work, like *Chinatown* and *Tequila Sunrise*. He, too, did not like the implications of homosexuality and suggested they were downplayed to the extent of being barely visible. Towne was brought in officially as script consultant and the Benton-Newman partnership found his advice helpful and easy to accept. Slowly, some of the less commercial elements were drained away and the script began to take on a far more viable appearance. Penn came back for a second look and finally agreed to take it on, provided the casting was right.

This element was, of course, vital if Beatty was to raise the finance. He would star but he needed an attractive co-star as Bonnie Parker. Beatty had long ago ruled Caron out, and had said from the start it needed an American. Caron agreed. He had already telephoned his former lover Natalie Wood, whom he believed would make an ideal Bonnie. Now it was decision time. Agreement on a co-star was vital in presenting the package to a studio. One afternoon, he turned up unexpectedly at Natalie's house, hoping to persuade her to join his movie. Natalie was in a dark and deeply depressed state. After some promising films at the beginning of the sixties, she had just completed three in a row that were absolute disappointments.

In two of them she starred with Robert Redford, *Inside Daisy Clover* and *This Property is Condemned*. The third was produced by her former fiancé Arthur Loew Jnr, who had paid her an enormous salary of $750,000 to star in *Penelope*, a comedy which had great potential but which she knew even as she was making it was going to be a dud. When she finished filming, she went home, took to her bed and would see no one except her analyst, Dr John Lindon. Her only other company was her long-time live-in companion and former secretary Mart Crowley, who resided in a guest cottage in the grounds of Natalie's mansion and where – at the time – he was writing what eventually became his first success, a play and a film about homosexuals entitled *The Boys in the Band*.

Crowley was in constant touch with Lindon over his concern for Natalie, who spoke constantly about the disasters in recent months which she believed would wreck her career. She saw herself as a failure in her work and in her life. Although Loew had paid her a huge fee for *Penelope*, she knew the film would be a flop, and wrongly blamed herself. Crowley said she was also worried about her disastrous love life; she had no permanent man, and no prospect of one. Above all, she wanted a family of her own and life was passing her by at an alarming rate. She was vulnerable again, her confidence was shattered and she was fearful of the future. The reason she gave for turning down the role of Bonnie Parker was that filming would demand her presence in Texas for three months, and she could not bear the thought of being away from her analyst for that long. At the time, she was seeing him almost daily.

Beatty's uninvited arrival came as no relief. He pleaded with her to reconsider appearing in *Bonnie and Clyde*. What happened thereafter is known now only to Beatty, but it is likely that Natalie told him that she would never work again; she was a failure. Beatty would have pleaded, of course, that she was not finished, and that he would show her this if she agreed to do his movie. But Natalie refused to accept his assurances and later that day she attempted suicide. She swallowed barbiturates and staggered out of her room.

Crowley heard her cry out and found her slumped at the top of the stairs. He telephoned Dr Lindon, who advised Crowley to drive her immediately to Cedars of Lebanon Hospital in Hollywood. Lindon warned the hospital to stand by and he was ready and waiting with a stomach pump when Natalie was brought in.

Natalie was kept in hospital overnight and when she came round, she and Lindon had a shouting match that could be heard through the hospital corridors. The psychiatrist berated her over the foolishness and futility of her actions. She said that she did not want to live any more; she said she would never work in movies again. Lindon, who had gone through the sympathetic stage of treatment and now had to force his views on her with ramrod brutality, talked her into living again, but not into making movies. She did not appear in front of the cameras again for almost three years.

Beatty, though shocked and despairing over Natalie's actions, pressed on. He went back to tackle the task of casting his picture and surprisingly took a different tack. He sought no star to join him. The only near-famous contender was Tuesday Weld, who ruled herself out by revealing she was pregnant. No one in his final list of players was well-known. This move was one of expediency, to keep the budget tight.

He advertised the co-starring role widely, and eventually selected Faye Dunaway, then a virtually unknown fashion model turned actress. She had made one off-Broadway appearance and two movies to date, appearing well down the cast list in the heavily panned Otto Preminger film *Hurry Sundown*, starring Michael Caine and Jane Fonda, and lately had just finished filming *The Happening*, a curious comedy starring Anthony Quinn.

Gene Hackman, hired to play Clyde's brother Buck, had a similarly limited CV. Since appearing with Beatty in a minor role in *Lilith* in 1964, he had been seen in only one other credited screen role, in the heavy-going *Hawaii*, which starred Julie Andrews and Richard Harris. Estelle Parsons, the character actress, was signed as Buck's wife, and Michael J. Pollard as C.W. Gene Wilder in a one-scene role completed the cast list. With some veteran names among the list of technicians, Beatty was ready to take his package to town and attempt to get financing. It was an audacious plan, and few would have given him the slightest chance of succeeding . . .

9

Achieving the Impossible

Nobody wanted to know. The famous young actor who had appeared in a few films, of which only a couple could be classed as successful in terms of money – and that is the only consideration Hollywood backers look at – was touting around this picture that had no stars apart from himself, was filled with violence and anti-heroism and was about two obscure figures of American criminal history that only the Texas Rangers remembered. Warren's star had waned greatly as the issues of talent and bankability became clouded by the rampant publicity in his private life. And anyway, Hollywood was full of people with good ideas.

Beatty wasn't fighting only for the recognition of what he believed could be a rewarding project. He was up against the whole desolate, nerve-jangling system that pervaded the film-making capital of the universe. Hollywood, in the mid-sixties, was reaching a watershed in its financial turmoil. Studio after studio fell into new hands where artistic merit, or what remained of it, was seldom a consideration. The trade press was full of gloomy stories of rolling heads, cutbacks and unemployment in every single department. The years of featherbedding, nepotism and over-manning was being hit by the recession and middle-aged men who had spent their lives in film were being unceremoniously dumped on the labour market.

Production after production was going abroad, to Europe, South America and even Canada, for tax avoidance schemes and less costly production bills. Another factor was the impact of the influential New York contingent of producers and directors, who shunned the make-believe of the Californian hothouse and those massive, specially-built sets on the backlots and stages and preferred instead to find the real thing with location shooting. Huge backlots where every memorable scene in movie history had been played out were being dismantled and sold off. MGM was preparing for the first major auction of props and costumes, such as Rhett Butler's top hat and Tarzan's loincloth; memorabilia gathered over almost half a century of film-making was to be sold off just to raise money. Others followed, leaving only the ghosts of movies past to wander the mythological dream factories of the century. Some studios resorted to renting out their facilities for made-for-television productions; others began making films and series for television themselves. The unthinkable had become reality.

The retrenchment brought greater power for a handful of people. Creative artists, whether they were directors, actors or writers, began to acquire enormous sway and influence so long as their films were successful. The 'few' demanded higher fees and profit-sharing deals. 'Power,' Elizabeth Taylor observed as she increased her up-front fee by another quarter of a million to $1.25 million per picture plus a percentage, 'is being able to do what you want.' Every project was looked at in terms of being a financial winner; no studio could afford to make films for artistic posterity as they once did, knowing that their routine productions would carry the day. The 'bottom line' became the be-all-and-end-all of pretty well every production.

That was the scenario as Beatty went back west with his script honed and hopes high. But Beatty did not yet have the power of Taylor or Burton or Brando or anyone else. He had no power at all, because he had no track record to speak of, and it was touch and go whether he would ever get his picture made.

'Right from the beginning of trying to get a deal on *Bonnie and Clyde*, no one took Warren seriously, and especially not as a producer,' said co-writer Bob Benton. 'They don't take actors seriously in Hollywood, and he was one of the first actors to make the move out into producing. So they just laughed in his face.' There were two or three straight 'nos' from studios he contacted, but Beatty had got the bit between his teeth and he wasn't going to let go. As Leslie Caron later recalled, he had decided that this was a crucial moment in his career. He was fed up with the thought of becoming just another actor, walking the treadmill and hoping against hope that the next picture would be the greatest ever made.

To any casual observer, *Bonnie and Clyde* hardly seemed to offer that vision of success he was promoting. There was even some confusion as to the writers' intent – serious violence or dark comedy? – and it was a fact that between Beatty saying he wanted to do it and actually beginning the task of filming seventy per cent of the screenplay had been rewritten. This was nothing unusual with Beatty, who became well-known in Hollywood for his desire to 'tinker' – except that tinkering quite often meant locking himself in a room with a writer and arguing and pleading and restructuring until it was to his liking. He would blow hot then cold, work up a head of steam and then inexplicably pull back. 'Most of the people who don't like me in Hollywood,' he admitted to Tommy Thompson, 'are guys whose pictures I wouldn't do.'

Eventually, Beatty got in to see Jack Warner, who'd had a kind of love-hate relationship with the actor since he first met him with Kazan and had introduced him to the press as Warner Beaker. Warner, then seventy-five, did not much care for some of the brash New Yorkers whom Kazan and others brought to him; for one thing they never did as they were told.

Beatty was prepared to beg.

He admitted years later that he did some crazy things with Jack Warner, just to keep up the charade and confirm, every now and again, Warner's belief that he was a little crazy. Jack used to like to put his desk between them. He did not enjoy eyeball-to-eyeball conversations with Beatty, and appeared sometimes even intimidated by him. 'These young punks,' Warner once said, 'show no respect. They think they're God's gift to the movie business and nothing will shift them.'

Jack Warner was the last of the great Hollywood moguls still in position, although controlling interest in his studios had long ago passed elsewhere. He was the epitome of the image of the mogul; loud, flashy and fervently addicted to a

personal lifestyle of garish extravagance. He was a bully, and
renowned for his long-running battles with some of his contract stars. In the old days, anyone who challenged his authority got it straight between the eyes: 'I pay 'em and they do
what I tell 'em.'

Humphrey Bogart, who had an epic contractual fight with
Warner, called him the Governor of San Quentin. Those who
questioned his judgement would be pushed towards the
window of his office overlooking the great Warner acreage,
and with a wave of his hand, he would say: 'Would all that
be there if I didn't know what I was doing?'

That kind of boast was seldom heard in 1966 because 'all
that out there' was shrinking rapidly. He was still the great
autocratic figure, trying to live up to his reputation while the
industry disintegrated around him. Thus it is easy to picture
the scene in that vast expanse of plush-carpeted office space,
where Warner sat behind his great antique mahogany desk
with inlaid leather top, bearing nothing but a bank of telephones and the paperwork that Beatty had laid before him.

'Give me one good reason, kid,' said the great man, 'why I
should back you?'

'Because this is a very good story, Jack, and I am going to
make a very good film.'

'But will it make money?'

'Sure. It will be very successful. I guarantee it.'

'How many times have I heard that before! So what's so
special about Warren Beatty? Look at your record. You haven't
made a film yet that has made money. Some people are saying
you're washed up, kid.'

'*Splendor* made money.'

'Not a lot.'

'Anyway, I was not in control. I can't be blamed.'

'So who do you blame? You chose the pictures, didn't you?'

'Yes, but this time it will be different. I am in control and
I will make it work. I'll lay my life on it.'

The story of his meeting with Beatty ends with Beatty
laying on the floor ready to kiss the old man's feet until
Warner says: 'OK, OK, Warren. You're embarrassing me. I'll
do your little picture but I warn you, don't go a cent over
budget.'

In the event, he nailed Beatty down to an exceedingly tight $2 million, which meant that the actor also had to put up some of his own money. For this he was granted thirty per cent of the profits, which rather displayed Warner's lack of confidence about the eventual outcome. If he had believed for one single moment that *Bonnie and Clyde* might make a little money, Beatty's percentage would have been far lower. Warner must have believed that he had granted Warren a thirty per cent share of nothing.

Jubilant, Beatty called his team together. He gave a little speech about working to a very tight schedule, but he did not intend to allow this to damage the quality; this was paramount. He wanted a top-class movie that would knock their eyes out. Then they proceeded to Texas for location shooting.

They checked into a modest hotel. They worked from dawn to dusk. Beatty was calm and cool and the actors were slightly in awe of him. They would see him pass through a gamut of characters and emotions; bully, coach, colleague, impatient then patient, the good guy and the bad guy rolled into one, and they would all end up respecting him without reservation. Faye Dunaway did not display, at this stage of her career, some of the traits of formidable resolve as an actress that she acquired later on and which put the fear of God into a few directors who shall be nameless.

Arthur Penn was the linchpin of the whole business. A fine director, he was also a patient man who had an uncanny knack of being able to get what he wanted without pain. He had to contend with a producer who was also the star, and who also would have liked to have been directing himself.

Robert Towne was also a key figure in many respects. He helped in the rewrites, some of which became necessary when old relatives of Bonnie and Clyde heard about the film and came out of the woodwork to view the action with curiosity. Clyde's nephew, who was eleven when he died, provided some excellent recollections that enabled Towne and the writers to inject added realism into their scripts. Towne can be credited for the creation of some of the undercurrents in the relationships between the fivesome of Beatty and Dunaway, Hackman and Parsons, with side-kick Michael J. Pollard, who make up the Barrow gang. *Bonnie and Clyde* provided Towne with an arena for developing a style which would emerge more demonstrably later in his career, in such moody pieces as *Chinatown* and *Tequila Sunrise*.

The landscape around Dallas had barely changed since the period, and provided authentic settings that could never have been recreated on a Hollywood backlot. It was all vital to the mood and pace of the film itself, which was a movie about rebels, above love, sex and death at its most violent.

On the set, it appeared that Beatty never slept. He was up late and around again before dawn. As the star, he was giving the best performance of his career; those who worked for him would willingly testify that off screen he was also performing some superhuman feats of organisation. Did Penn and Beatty really imagine they were creating something special? When did they know they had crossed that line? When a film is a failure, there is often no way of telling that it is a failure until it is too late, when the film is in the can and the actors have gone home. Does the same apply when there is a success? Did they imagine they were creating a movie that would be hailed as a trendsetter of its age, one that would polarise the critics and capture the imagination of the movie-goers like no other film that decade?

What they were creating here was an orgy that expresses itself through a hail of bullets, beginning from the moment when Bonnie strokes the barrel of Clyde's revolver in a kind of phallic caress. Thereafter the violence becomes their aphrodisiac for sex, because Clyde is having trouble getting it up. The sex is ever-present. The violence is greater, more bloodthirsty, more realistic and more casual than anything that will have been seen in non-Western movies. The comedy is there to ease the crescendo of bloodletting.

'This is a stick-up,' says Beatty politely and quietly, repeating it louder so that the victim can hear him. *Bonnie and Clyde* is a movie in which you can see the objectives clearly laid out by the producer and the director and they are met with an eerie ease and considerable skill. Beatty, Penn and Towne were a powerful trio. They studied the rushes every day, going back over scenes to get them right, with Beatty meticulous in his eye for detail. 'He was a great producer,' said Robert Towne. 'And that's not bullshit.'

As the production moved along at a pace to keep ahead of the budgets, Beatty found himself paring back and occasionally chipping in extra finance from his own resources. Jack Warner let him get on with it, although he was continually riled by Beatty's refusal to let him see the rushes. When they returned from Texas with much of the picture completed, Warner demanded to be allowed to view the work so far. Much of it had been tight and was shot with minimal retakes, but one scene in Dallas, where Hackman and Beatty are together for the first time, was shot about fifteen times. Then there were some technical shots, over the shoulder and close up. When Warner saw the number of shots for this one scene, he came out of the screening room and called Beatty. 'Hey, kid. Bogart wouldn't do that. Errol Flynn wouldn't put up with it. For Chrissakes, kid, how many takes do you have to make?'

When he finally received a viewing of the full film, he growled uncomfortably. He showed no enthusiasm for it at all and was ready to take it out of Beatty's hands for the final edit, the titling and the music. Beatty had to fight off intervention, and had to plead on bended knee to be allowed to retain control until the completed picture was delivered. By now, Warner was calling it Warren's picture, and Warren's share of the proceeds had been elevated to forty per cent on account of the extra funds he had injected during the filming. If *Bonnie and Clyde* was a failure, as it surely must be if all predictions were correct, then Warner could distance himself with ease and grace and say, 'I told you so.'

Just to ram the point home, he yawned as he came out of the viewing room after watching the final two-hour ten-minute version and said it was the longest two hours and ten minutes he had ever spent in his life. But he always made such comments about films of dubious future, and the finished print was slimmed down by nineteen minutes.

There was a round-table discussion at Warner to which Beatty was not party. There was general agreement that not a lot of money would be spent on the marketing and distribution. It would go out on limited general release, vanishing quite quickly unless there was widespread acclaim from the critics. No one considered this likely, and so the opening was limited to just two New York cinemas, the Murray Hill and the Forum, against the normal clutch of prime locations given to any new movie which had half a chance of success. Worse, Warner decided to launch the film in August, known as the graveyard month for film release. 'Warren spent about three days in a black funk when he heard,' said a producer friend. 'I think if anybody had gone near him, he would have strangled them. Then he got up and started fighting...'

In the normal course of events, Warren Beatty's film would have been already doomed to be cast into the great wastebucket of B movie oblivion, probably never to be heard of again, except to crop up in some pre-dawn television slot in years to come. That was undoubtedly the fate of this movie, but for one thing that the studio had not accounted for: Warren Beatty himself. Although he was about to be shot to pieces by an antagonistic and hostile review body, he was not prepared to let it go; not by any means.

Beatty's relationship with the critics had been patchy but their reaction this time was potentially devastating to his career as both actor and producer. Almost all of the most influential magazines threw up their hands in hypocritical horror. Not in recent times had a film or a Hollywood personality been the subject of such vitriolic abuse, and their comments are worth more than a passing mention, if only to demonstrate that having forced the film into production, Beatty now had to take on the might of the opinion-formers.

First, however, it is interesting to note one particular glowing opinion, which provided Beatty with some consolation amid an otherwise heavy-handed caning. The influential film observer Judith Crist had often given Beatty the benefit of the doubt in the past, and had gone along with his attitude-provoking performances. She maintained that with *Bonnie and Clyde*, Beatty and Penn had established themselves as one of the most excitingly creative teams in American moviemaking. She added: 'Beatty, so often merely a promising performer, fulfils himself as Clyde ... Saturated in time and place we are left with the universality of the theme and its particular contemporary relevance. And this is the triumph of *Bonnie and Clyde*.'

But Crist was pretty much a lone voice among most major

reviewers. The rest were lukewarm; some were destructively opposed to the film and all it stood for, even attacking the poster advertising which, reflecting the best-selling title song and the moods of the film itself, read:

> Bonnie and Clyde,
> They're young . . .
> They're in love
> And they kill people.

Bosley Crowther, of *The New York Times*, had never been a particular Beatty fan, and it showed. His assessment of *Bonnie and Clyde* displayed his outrage at such a film even having been made in the first place. He branded it a cheap piece of bald-faced slapstick that treated the 'hideous depredations of that sleazy moronic pair as full of fun and frolic as the jazz-age cut-ups in *Thoroughly Modern Millie*.'

Crowther said Arthur Penn's combination of farce and brutality was pointless and lacking in taste, and made no valid commentary on the already travestied truth. Not content with one searing review, Crowther kept up a campaign against the film which was to last for weeks. The quiet-talking Arthur Penn bristled. 'We weren't making a documentary any more than Shakespeare was writing a documentary in his Chronicle plays,' he said in defence. 'True, we made conjectures about the intimate life of Bonnie and Clyde. There was much talk that he was homosexual in prison and that she was pregnant by him at the time of the ambush. We just did not know the truth. I suppose we could be charged with romanticism in having beautiful people play Bonnie and Clyde, but I think we were justified in that we were dealing with the mythical aspects of their lives. They were folk heroes of their time. To dismiss them as just killers or pariahs would have been equally wrong.'

The critical onslaught continued. *Films in Review* said the movie displayed incompetence at every level – in its acting, its direction, its producing. It wallowed in sado-masochism and set out to arouse sympathy for this appalling pair of two-bit gangsters with its ending (a slow-motion orgy of blood and bullets in the final scene, when police ambush Bonnie and

Clyde and shoot them to pieces). 'Who is the producer of so adolescently ignorant a film? Warren Beatty [who] adds his own ignorances. Who directed? Arthur Penn, whose artistic integrity is about on the level of Beatty's acting ability – i.e. close to zero.'

Newsweek's Joseph Morgenstern attacked 'the most gruesome carnage since Verdun, and for those who find killing less than hilarious, the effect is stomach-turning.' He described *Bonnie and Clyde* as a squalid production for the moron trade while *Time* magazine said Beatty and Penn had elected to tell their tale of bullets and blood in a 'strange and purposeless mingling of fact and claptrap that teeters uncannily on the brink of burlesque.'

All of the above displays of derogation and disparagement more or less fell into line with the view of the distributing council of Warner Bros executives who, by and large, had fallen into line with the first thoughts of their boss, that the film was 'a piece of shit' that was worthy of no more than a limited run as a B movie and which might, with any luck, cover the cost of the prints.

Two things happened that would quickly reverse that opinion. First Beatty himself, angered by the critical reaction and the doom-filled attitude of Warner, began a personal fightback with a tenacity for which there are few precedents. Secondly, audience reaction was at complete variance with the critics. As the controversy about the violent content raged, the film grossed $59,000 in the first week in the two New York cinemas, and in the second week the take went up to $70,000.

The reason for this phenomenon was to be identified by one other favourable reviewer, Penelope Gilliatt, writing in the *New Yorker*, who saw it more as a contemporary statement. The film was about violence, but she maintained that *Bonnie and Clyde* looked like a celebration of gangster glamour only to a man with a head full of wood shavings. Their motive was not gain but an urge to be theatrically remembered. Finally, she said, the film made its audience think of Kennedy and Lee Harvey Oswald. And herein lay the key to its success.

The newsreels of the days were filled with violent scenes from around the world, Vietnam, Biafra, the Six-Day War and race riots in American cities. Nothing in phoney gun battles and bloodthirsty killings in *Bonnie and Clyde* could match the true horror of reality that was also being portrayed in living colour by the same magazines that had ripped into Beatty's movie.

Beatty began his campaign by attacking the reviews and virtually forced a retraction out of two of the most influential writers. First, Joseph Morgenstern came out with an unheard-of reversal of his first review, apologising for the fact that his first attempt had been grossly unfair and regrettably inaccurate. He had seen the film again, and had observed the audience reaction, which he described as 'enjoyment to the point of rapture.'

Meanwhile, the success in New York was being repeated throughout the US, with Beatty zooming in and out of each major city laying on interviews like he had never done before. Within eight weeks of its original opening in New York, it had become the third most popular film on the circuit, behind *To Sir, With Love* and *Thoroughly Modern Millie*. In October, the *New Yorker* published a 9,000 word appraisal of Beatty by Pauline Kael, who said that for the first time in his life, Beatty seemed less burdened by his limits as an actor and had at last got away from portraying self-preoccupied characters in a lifelike but boring, self-conscious way.

The bandwagon of favourable opinion finally reached a climax when the December issue of *Time* magazine ran a cover story on 'The New Cinema: Violence, Sex and Art', in which Beatty was now to be characterised as the leader of the new wave. *Time* said it had been an irrelevant exercise by earlier critics to compare the film's fictitious portrayal with the real Clyde Barrow and Bonnie Parker. It proved that the American audience was ready and able to discern the complexities of such movies, and view them as art. Even this new assessment was a touch high-blown.

The truth of the matter can now be seen to have had very little to do with audiences appreciating art. *Bonnie and Clyde* was an enormously appealing orgy of escapism, with a glamorisation of violence that could be compared with the runaway success of the James Bond films. Sean Connery had created the opening, brilliantly playing the violence for laughs with

137

his classic one-liners as he emptied his Smith and Wesson into the villain's heart while using his leering sexuality for total entertainment. Beatty had gone further, challenging his audiences with his mixture of comedy and violence, sexuality and rebellion. That *Bonnie and Clyde* was also now being seen as some carefully planned artistic pointer of the sixties may well have been entirely accidental, although Beatty and Penn must be given the benefit of the doubt.

Beatty, meanwhile, was tear-arsing around the countryside and using this reversal of fortune to attack the distribution policy of Warner. He collected box-office returns almost daily, and went anonymously into cinemas to gauge audience reaction, which he would then use in his pleadings to Jack Warner for more support and a better distribution and promotional effort, which to date had been abysmal.

Actress Judy Carne, who was dating him intermittently around this time, Leslie Caron having ended her relationship with Beatty because she could no longer stand the pace, recalled one particular evening out. He had driven her to a theatre where *Bonnie and Clyde* was showing and spent most of the time watching people going into the theatre. Actually, she thought it was 'marvellously exciting' to have a picture you'd produced becoming such a hit. He got out of the car and looked up at the marquee. He watched everyone who walked into the theatre as though he was trying to figure out what kind of people wanted to see it, or as if he was counting the number who came. 'I was fascinated. I could have said, "Is this your idea of a date – making a survey of how your picture is doing?" But I didn't. I knew he was waiting for that reaction and when I did not make a fuss, it threw him completely,' said Carne.

To use a cliché, he left no stone unturned; minutiae took on gargantuan proportions. In Chicago, for instance, where *Bonnie and Clyde* was to open in a downtown theatre, he tried to arrange for a young projectionist because he thought a younger man might show more care.

By the end of 1967, Beatty was exhausted but still fighting. In Hollywood, his film was being talked of in terms of a contender for an abundance of Oscar nominations, even though there was some outstanding competition from such movies as *Guess Who's Coming to Dinner, The Graduate* and *In the Heat of the Night*. He went back to Warner Bros and literally demanded that *Bonnie and Clyde* be re-released with a properly developed campaign, new posters and publicity in prestige sites around the world.

According to one source, Beatty stormed in clutching box-office figures and a sheaf of the latest glowing reviews. 'Here's the evidence. What more do you assholes want?' he insisted. 'You never gave this film a fucking chance and it has made it in spite of you. Now, will you re-release it, and do it right this time?'

'Impossible. It's unheard of. You can't re-release a film that has been out on the circuit for four months.'

'There's an exception to every rule – and this is it!'

Warner refused point blank. Beatty threatened to sue unless they re-released the picture. This, Warner continued to point out, was not only unprecedented, but the movie had by now played out most of its American dates and was already in the smaller neighbourhood movie houses. Then word of the potential hype from the forthcoming Oscar nominations became a reality. In January 1968 it was announced that *Bonnie and Clyde* had picked up ten Oscar nominations.

Every one of *Bonnie and Clyde*'s five stars had been nominated – Beatty for best actor (along with Dustin Hoffman for *The Graduate*, Paul Newman for *Cool Hand Luke*, Rod Steiger for *In the Heat of the Night* and Spencer Tracy for *Guess Who's Coming to Dinner*). Faye Dunaway was nominated for best actress in this her first starring role, with Anne Bancroft (*The Graduate*) Edith Evans (*The Whisperers*) Audrey Hepburn (*Wait Until Dark*) and Katharine Hepburn (*Guess Who's Coming to Dinner*). Gene Hackman and Michael J. Pollard were both nominated for best supporting actor and Estelle Parsons for best supporting actress. Arthur Penn was nominated for best director, David Newman and Robert Benton for best screenplay and Burnett Guffey for Best Cinematography, while the film itself collected nominations for best picture and best costume design. Although only two of the nominations were converted to actual awards (Estelle Parsons and Burnett Guffey), the volume of nominations was sufficient justification for *Bonnie and Clyde* to be acclaimed as one of the pictures of the decade. The nomination of three virtual unknowns, Hackman, Michael J. Pollard and Faye Dunaway, was in itself a remarkable achievement.

Now Warner had to concede to Beatty's demands to re-release *Bonnie and Clyde*, which it proceeded to do in a manner that matched its success. Even so, Beatty had to agree to give back a portion of his percentage as an act of good faith, so that if the grosses did not match his expectations, Warner would be covered. It also meant that if his expectations were met they would grab a larger slice of the rewards. It was a decision that cost him dear either way, but he was happy at last.

The film went back into first-run theatres, again an unprecedented move, and everywhere the business was between five and eight times higher than it had been first time around. In the first year, it became one of the most financially successful films of the decade in terms of profit against cost.

The swarming new audiences proved that *Bonnie and Clyde* was as much a film of its day as the music of the Beatles and the Rolling Stones and the new mood of revolution amongst youth, which had emanated from London and was reverberating in the college campuses around the world. But regardless of the view of the intelligentsia, it was a film that also took off in the small towns and country cinemas where the movie showing at the local Odeon was the main source of excitement.

In that sense, as a precursor for reflection and future development in art and society itself during that exciting period of change, *Bonnie and Clyde* was the first of a series of films that exploded with audience reaction. Interestingly, the next would be *Easy Rider*, then already in the planning stage, which would finally bring Jack Nicholson to the public eye the following year.

For Beatty observers, an interesting topic of discussion at the dinner tables and the trendy restaurants was how this reluctant actor, a man of no fixed abode, no roots, whose lifestyle had been carefree and cavalier, who showed an alarming lack of responsibility or acknowledgement of convention, had been able to nail himself to the floor to deal with the problems that present themselves to the producer of any

140

movie, and particularly one which had been virtually written off before it had begun.

He had been transformed into businessman, director's assistant, writer, acting coach, financial wizard and technical rookie. He did not do it alone, but all those around him on the production of *Bonnie and Clyde* applauded his courage. He had learned things he had never even contemplated in his life as an actor. He had been at the centre of every decision, be it how Gene Hackman or Faye Dunaway should play a particular scene, or how it should be shot, or the mixing of the sound, preparing the soundtrack, the editing, the presentation of the titles. Everything.

When the movie was delivered, he became its chief press officer, publicist and promoter. After succeeding in getting it re-released by Warners, he renewed his campaign, first touring the US and then moving on to London, where he could be found in discussion with the projectionist in the Leicester Square cinema over sound quality, then to Paris, Rome and the remaining European centres, and further still to Scandinavia.

At the end of its first year of release, *Bonnie and Clyde* had grossed $30 million in domestic box-office rentals, from which Beatty himself collected a figure in excess of $6 million, to which would be added later returns worldwide. The number of actors in Hollywood whose fee for a single picture could be counted in millions at that point in history was negligible. Even Taylor and Burton, as a double act, could not match him for his return on a single picture.

In one move, in one picture, Beatty had done more to prove himself than in any of his previous films since *Splendor in the Grass*. But it was a far more important development than just inspiring a bout of one-off accolades for his acting in a particular picture. He had created a new and far more powerful image for himself. Virtually overnight, he had been able to thumb his nose at the doubting Thomases who dismissed him and his project as wild and wilful with no hope of long-term survival. In this one move, he had won the grudging admiration of his fellows as the wily actor-producer-businessman perhaps more comparable to the old-style theatrical actor-impresarios, and in this way he had become unrivalled among his peers for a broad-based display of talent, and certainly had presented a far more crucial, vital and vibrant persona than he could ever have managed in his earlier self-conscious roles as an actor-only.

This was the prevailing truth, then, in 1968, when there was suddenly something new and smart about Beatty which bore no comparison. He actually did not need to be compared to Brando or Clift any longer. He had succeeded in demonstrating that he had moved on from the scratch and stutter era, first in creating an image and a character with which sixties rebellious youth could identify and secondly in carrying off a daring movieland coup that demanded hair-raising tenacity and left his peers wondering what he could do for an encore.

Leslie Caron, who had helped put him on this road, had hardly seen him since he began. She could not go on with it and ended the relationship, in spite of his wish to marry her. The pressure and pace required by his ambitions were too much and she would be left, ultimately, regretting she had ever left Peter Hall. Beatty, the charmer, the great seducer, the passionate lover, was above all else pursuing his career, and nothing could stand in his way.

10
Just Julie

Beatty was in ebullient mood, which he demonstrated one lunchtime when he arrived in the dining-room of Delmonico's in New York, where he stayed when in the city – they provided him with the suite that was large enough to double as his home from home, the other one being his suite at the Beverly Wilshire in Los Angeles. He kept books and personal belongings there and the management was also quite happy to move a piano into his room. He strode in wearing a crumpled brown suit and grimy sneakers. He didn't care about his looks.

He knew the room was watching as he walked across the red-carpeted floor in a confident swagger with his entourage of publicity man John Springer and the two writers he had made famous, Benton and Newman. He stood for a moment surveying the scene. Heads turned and a few unidentified people waved, but he made no response and sat down. He remained there for the next three hours, hunched over the table, in deep conversation between bites of his eggs benedict and coffee. The publicity campaign for Europe and beyond was under discussion.

There were other matters, too.

In between the completion of filming and achieving a proper launch for *Bonnie and Clyde*, Beatty's itinerary had included several trips to Europe. On the work front, his new friend Roman Polanski, the Polish director, was involved in discussions for two new movies for which Beatty had been earmarked by studio executives.

At that point Polanski was really known only in Europe, notably for his arty, moody and often perplexing movies such as *Knife in the Water*, *Repulsion*, *Cul de Sac* and lately *The Fearless Vampire Killers*, but he had become an integral part of the London scene and was commuting between London and his residence in Paris. He had become a member of the exclusive but wild Ad Lib Club, located high up in a building off Leicester Square. It was said to provide a microcosm of swinging London, and was the habitual haunt of the modern crowd.

There, Polanski first met Beatty and another key figure in the swinging society, Victor Lownes, who had a rented house in Montpelier Square, where Leslie Caron lived. Lownes was Hugh Hefner's right-hand man in Europe and was supervising the building of the Playboy Club in Park Lane, which eventually became a magnet for everyone who was anyone in the élite of showbusiness.

Lownes, like Beatty, was a collector of people, and when the club opened enjoyed surrounding himself with the rich and famous, entertaining them in his private penthouse facilities above the gaming- and dining-rooms. Lownes had taken a particular shine to Polanski, if for no other reason than to have a willing partner to join him in the exceedingly lively London social scene, and especially that part of it which centred upon the Bunny Club establishment.

In fact, it was there that Lownes later arranged several parties for Polanski when he married Sharon Tate, and the guest list sounded like a reunion of Beatty's friends. Joan Collins and Anthony Newley, Leslie Caron, Candice Bergen, Kenneth Tynan, Peter Sellers and Britt Ekland and others like current London swingers Michael Caine, James Fox, Mike Sarne, Brian Jones, Keith Richards and Terence Stamp.

Beatty first met Polanski in 1964 when the Polish-born director was approached by executives from 20th Century-Fox to discuss a remake and Americanisation of his award-winning *Knife in the Water*, produced in 1962. Fox had the idea of casting Elizabeth Taylor, Richard Burton and Beatty. Discussions continued, as they do, over many months but eventually it all came to naught. Polanski could never understand why they wanted to remake the film in the first place.

By then, Polanski and Beatty had become good friends and

when Robert Evans, head of Paramount, sought him out to direct the movie *Rosemary's Baby*, Polanski knew straight away who he wanted as Rosemary's husband. The story was, of course, about the young bride who is impregnated by the devil. Mia Farrow was in line for the role of Rosemary and Polanski wanted Beatty as co-star. 'I needed someone who could play a clean-cut young American ... and persuaded Warren to read the script,' Polanski recalled, 'but as usual he procrastinated and finally rejected the role as not important enough. Warren's parting shot was, "Hey! Can I play Rosemary?" ' Jack Nicholson's name was mentioned, but Polanski rejected him because he was then a complete unknown. He finally settled for John Cassavetes.

The Beatty-Polanski friendship would continue, and indeed became so close that eventually, Beatty was one of those who helped Polanski at the time of Sharon Tate's murder, a year or so later.

Beatty's association with the London social scene had brought him into contact with a number of stars of European society. It becomes as monotonous and inaccurate to catalogue the members of his social circle as it does his lovers.

Many reported dalliances never existed. Some were the inventions of the gossip columnists and some invention of the lover herself. He was said to have had a fling with Brigitte Bardot while she was married to Roger Vadim, when the truth was that they had met only twice – both times in public. Another socialite, Mme Dewi Sukarno, the estranged wife of the Indonesian president, was a more intriguing association. She was determined to meet Warren, and did so at a party in Paris given by Mia and Louis Feraud.

She appeared ready to be courted by him, and according to a guest observing the scene, did everything to attract him. 'She looked gorgeous,' said the witness, 'positively exploding out of her dress, which no man could have ignored. Her exit was spectacular, in a full-length brocaded cape, carrying – of all things – a bamboo pole with a lighted candle on the end, don't ask me why. Warren did not leave with her and I have no knowledge of whether he saw her again. If he did he would not say ... But word was they got together.'

If he needed solace or sexual replenishment, it was always available. Women were ready to lie down at his feet, and if he was seen talking to any of them for more than a few minutes, the natural assumption was that a bedroom scene would follow. Casual dates in far-flung capitals of the world were charted and logged by the gossip columnists. Many others were never known outside of his own hotel bedroom; affairs lasting only an hour or two were not infrequent.

Was it all true? Much was the creative invention of scandal-hungry writers, but let that not detract from the bouts of abundance and plenty. Roman Polanski recalled a week-long adventure in Paris, where they had arrived ostensibly to discuss a new picture deal. The first night, they decided they would have a good time. Parties, discos and girls. The second day, said Polanski, was a repeat of the first. So was the third and the fourth. Polanski was growing uneasy and at the end of the fourth night, said, 'OK, that's it. We've got to do some work.'

Beatty replied, 'You're absolutely right. Let's have dinner and discuss it tomorrow.'

They had dinner tomorrow and ended up giving Paris a further coat of red paint. 'I was so frazzled for lack of sleep, I couldn't take any more,' said Polanski. 'That night Warren did not go to sleep again – he stayed up until he had read the book for which we were due to discuss a script and made sure he let me know it the following day.' In the end, the project came to naught, but they had a good time not doing it.

Life magazine, in a new assessment of the star, flatly contended that the girls he had loved, known or unknown, were legion and that with Warren Beatty, there was no worry over whether seduction was possible, only when, where and who was next.

Curiously, he also seemed to have a fear of women, that they might hurt him and find his weaknesses. When he began to date Judy Carne, the *Rowan and Martin's Laugh-In* girl and a short-term visitor to his life, he was also involved in a marathon courtship of Julie Christie, who was eventually to stay much longer and to fill the void left by Leslie Caron. So Judy was in Los Angeles, Julie was in London and occasionally in California.

Judy Carne stopped to analyse her brief association with Beatty, coming as it did at the moment he reached the very pinnacle of his success so far with the acclaim over *Bonnie and Clyde*. She concluded that he was one of the most fascinating men she had ever met and she did not know of any woman who had met him who had not been attracted to him. Many women had fallen in love with him. Judy decided very quickly that such a thing would be dangerous.

His reputation then, in 1967–8, had been headlined for almost a decade and there was much discussion among the chattering classes, as well as Beatty's closest friends, about why any woman became seriously involved with him. Anyone who became his lover knew that there was little likelihood of a long-term commitment. He might say he loved them, and that he could not live without them. Were those also his promises to his past serious loves? And in those wayward moments of passion, like the fling with Susan Strasberg or the flattery of Vivien Leigh, had he ever promised them anything? Or nothing at all? He could charm the pants off pretty well any woman who came within his sphere. 'Actors can't help themselves,' said Judy Carne, 'and Warren certainly could not, and sometimes I got the feeling that Warren did not care what happened to other people, particularly women. In a way, I think he had lost touch with the world outside Warren Beatty.'

She maintained that theirs might have been a very rewarding relationship. She reaffirmed the view of others that he was charming, and yet underneath, deep down, she felt he had very little compassion towards women. 'Sometimes I felt that there was nothing about women that he liked except their bodies,' she said.

Their meeting was remarkably similar to others past and future. She saw him at a party and they hardly spoke, but once or twice she caught him staring at her and she stared back. She recorded a mental picture of him which she was later able to recall. It sounded exactly like the description that Joan Collins or Natalie Wood had given years before... 'He was one of the most beautiful men I had ever seen. His hair, his hands, everything about him ...' About three weeks after the party, there was a message from her answering service: please get in touch with Warren Beatty. He gave the number of the Beverly Wilshire Hotel where he had a penthouse suite.

She called him back.

'I'd like to see you,' said Warren.

'What brought this on? We've only met once, and that was no more than eye contact.'

'I've been away since that party, and I've had a devil of a job getting your number.'

Judy agreed and he turned up at her house, looking immaculate and clean, in sloppy grey slacks and a white sports shirt. She said she did not realise until that moment that he was a game-player; he played games so much that she found it difficult to distinguish fact from fiction, truth or dare.

'Well,' he said, 'we might as well get this over with right now. What do you demand of me in return for seeing me? What do you expect to get out of it?'

Judy replied starkly, 'I'm not demanding anything of you. You're here now just for one reason – I felt we could spend a pleasant evening together. If I had not, I would not have invited you round.'

She reckoned that, really, everything Warren did was a charade. There had to be an opening gambit and then dinner, in a quiet and secluded Italian restaurant. Judy said she felt that all evening she was on trial, and felt Beatty was testing her and watching her reactions. This continued on several dates. He continued to test her and probe her responses. 'I remember one night,' she said, 'he played me three different records from *Bonnie and Clyde* and asked me which I liked best. I got the feeling he did not really care about my opinion, which was OK – but heaven help me if I picked what he considered the wrong record. It was a curious scenario.'

Eventually, after about seven dates, she concluded that to be with Beatty was a nerve-racking experience. He was fascinating, lovable, charming and all the things that make men attractive to women; he had an oversized ego and was often self-centred, but she could not help feeling that it was a blind for a basketful of insecurities, and when they began to show, he just shut himself off. There was a five-hour conversation in his apartment of the Beverly Wilshire about life and about work. His life and his work. Carne was enthralled but was left drained. She said he seemed to distrust women for their motives. Carne might have thought for a moment that it was just her he didn't trust, but why? She had already told him in their discussion about their relationship that she wasn't interested in marriage, and later she was to witness the same trait occurring with other women.

She couldn't cope with it and that was that. The affair ended when he flew off to London to promote *Bonnie and Clyde*. He said, 'Call me' but she didn't. The relationship had no future, anyway, because he was already smitten by Julie.

There was one other aspect that Judy Carne had not spotted. In addition to having a woman prepared to mother him during the depressed times, he also wanted a woman of independent spirit and fire, which is what had so attracted him to Joan Collins and Leslie Caron. Julie Christie, on the other hand, was in so many ways a mirror image of himself, especially in her professional life, where she was as unorthodox as he, refusing to adhere to the Hollywood code and positively rejecting the prospect of being controlled by anyone, and least of all the moguls whom she hated.

As a man and a woman who had moved through early life in completely different surroundings and circumstances, they came together and typified the beautiful people emerging in the sixties, rebellious and independent, owing nothing to anyone.

Movement and motion were their key words. Julie Christie was alluring and mystical, with a need for liberty and freedom. He was the same in male form. They were both driven to frantic bursts of activity, often running until on the verge of collapse. Once enveloped by 'fame', they were both chased, constantly, by the media and others. They ran and never looked back. Their success would hold a strangely empty feeling and both were capable of rejecting it. It lacked meaning, yet they still lived in fear and dread of failure and criticism. They had other remarkably similar and conflicting traits and ambiguities. They could both be bold and yet incredibly shy; they could be totally modest yet self-promoting, they could be careful and reckless, charming and glamorous, and then lapse instantly into some clumsy, unaccountable behaviour.

One pundit's description of Julie almost exactly matched one made about Beatty a few years earlier: 'She has become quite neurotic about being Julie Christie, to add to her existing neuroses ... she wants to be talented, to be seen to be talented and special. But she does not want to be Julie Christie.' The parallels were extraordinary.

She had a shaky start in the performing arts in British repertory and a couple of minor film roles, but came to the fore in the play of its time, Keith Waterhouse's *Billy Liar*, the brilliant urban comedy in which she starred with Tom Courtenay. It was this and other theatre work that brought her to the attention of the Royal Shakespeare Company, then under the directorship of Peter Hall, and she was signed for a five-month run in *A Comedy of Errors*, which was going on a world tour to commemorate the Bard's 400th anniversary.

The play took her through Europe, Budapest, Bucharest, Warsaw, Leningrad and Moscow, and then on to America for two months. She found new friends and soul-mates in Greenwich Village but remained, for the time being, apparently devoted to her long-time companion, Don Bessant, the artist.

Charlton Heston, then involved in packaging a production of *The War Lord*, arranged a private viewing of *Billy Liar* for his backers at Universal. 'I tried very hard to get her,' Heston recalled, 'and I could have, for $35,000, which her agents were asking. Universal balked at the fee, and wanted someone cheaper. It would have been a bargain. She was on the brink of becoming an international star.'

This she became when John Schlesinger created *Darling* especially for her, and the fact that he wanted a relative unknown in the lead put the project in jeopardy. Approaches to several major studios got the same response: 'Give the role to Shirley MacLaine and put Paul Newman alongside her and you can have your money.' Schlesinger stood his ground. He wanted Christie. Newman turned down the role, as did several other American names, and he ended up, thankfully, with Dirk Bogarde and Laurence Harvey as the important threesome in Frederic Raphael's smart and fashionable mid-sixties screenplay about swinging people and their amoral activities, in which Bogarde says to Christie: 'Your idea of being fulfilled is having more than one man in bed at the same time.'

Thus, like Beatty, Christie arrived in Hollywood with a film which drew a controversial and mixed reaction for its exploration of relationships. Like Beatty, Christie became an international personality overnight, with the press pack in constant attendance. This interest heightened to breathless pursuit when she was nominated for an Oscar, and again when she won the title for best actress at the ceremony in April 1966, beating the favourite, Julie Andrews, nominated for her performance in *The Sound of Music*.

Christie furthered her sensational arrival, and attracted much indignant press comment, by walking on to the stage of that very, very, formal occasion wearing a polka-dot chiffon mini-dress which made her look like a naughty schoolgirl beside the elegantly gowned *grand dames* of Hollywood.

The accolades were doubled by her appearance the same year as Lara in *Doctor Zhivago*, which won six Oscars at the same ceremony and vied with *Darling* for the best picture award (won that year by *The Sound of Music*). There was another coincidence in the intertwining of Beatty and Christie: François Truffaut had given Beatty the script of *Bonnie and Clyde* because he was too busy to contemplate doing it himself; at the time he was writing and directing *Fahrenheit 451*, based on Ray Bradbury's novel, and had chosen Julie Christie as his leading lady. After that, she dashed straight into Schlesinger's screen version of Thomas Hardy's *Far from the Madding Crowd*.

Somewhere among these frantically crossing paths, which had been occurring since Beatty was with Leslie Caron in London, Paris and Los Angeles, Beatty and Christie one day stood face to face and realised their similarities and their desires. It was, said one close to Beatty at the time, like holding the ends of two live electric cables together: the sparks were almost visible.

As with most of his previous romances, other than the brief flings, he had been chasing her since their meeting in Hollywood when she won the Oscar. It had developed to such an intensity by the time the next Oscars came around that on the day he received the news that *Bonnie and Clyde* figured so strongly in the nominations, the first person he called with the news was Christie, then in London.

'It's heady,' he shouted loudly over the transatlantic wire.

'It's more exciting now than when it happens,' she laughed, and said she would see him soon in Los Angeles.

She flew in for the awards and was there to watch the accolades for *Bonnie and Clyde* and to ponder the euphoria of the moment. She checked into the Beverly Wilshire, where Beatty also rested his hat in the Escondido Suite, which had taken on the appearance of his permanent residence. The affair of the two beautiful people began to take the meandering course which would envelop them for the next seven years, although not exclusively.

In the immediate future, the relationship prospered with the usual kind of Beatty intensity. Though torn by her singular devotion to Bessant, Christie found in Beatty all that she admired in a man and their togetherness flourished while she was filming *Petulia* for Richard Lester, with George C. Scott and Joseph Cotten, on location in San Francisco. As the summer wore on, they stole every moment between their commitments to be together.

Don Bessant, the rock of Julie's life for the past few years and with whom she shared her house in Fulham and their Continental home, left her life quietly and Beatty came back in the eye of the hurricane in every respect.

Scripts, manuscripts, books and ideas for movies began to arrive by the sackload. People he had never heard of were leaving messages, but Beatty was in no rush to go back to work, and when he did it would be on his own terms. The irony of this situation was that by turning down so many major films, he provided considerable opportunity for several other male stars of his generation at a crucial time in their careers.

He had already passed on *Butch Cassidy and the Sundance Kid*, which would receive an Oscar nomination as best picture of 1969. Then Robert Evans, the head of Paramount, came up with an offer which they believed he would not refuse – to produce and star in *The Godfather*. The pedigree was good:

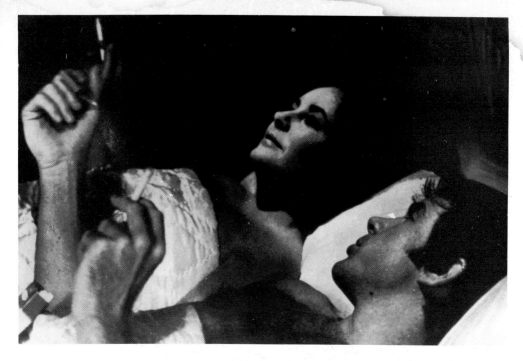

Substitute: It should have been Frank Sinatra in bed with Elizabeth Taylor, but he called off and Beatty came in as a late replacement in *The Only Game in Town* (1970). Richard Burton was watching this scene from behind the cameras, throwing in some taunting remarks between takes. In fact, they weren't naked, but wrapped in towels (*Twentieth Century-Fox*)

New love: Julie Christie, the British actress seen here in her role in *The Go-Between*, met Beatty in London in 1966. After Leslie Caron, she became prominent in Beatty's life for the next four years. Their first film together (opposite) was specially selected for them, *McCabe and Mrs Miller* (1971) (*Yardley Collection*)

Running mates: They met in Canada in 1970 when they were both making movies there . . . and became best of friends. Beatty and Jack Nicholson were introduced by director Mike Nichols, who also brought them together for the first time on screen in *The Fortune* (1975). Offscreen, they became known as the Two Boulevardiers (*Yardley Collection*)

Reunited: Although their relationship had ended, Beatty chose Julie Christie to star in his next major film which he produced, co-wrote and co-starred – *Shampoo* – a controversial mix of sex, comedy and politics (1975). They were together again for *Heaven Can Wait*, which he also produced, directed and co-wrote (*Yardley Collection*)

Classic close-ups: On screen, most of Warren Beatty's best-known portrayals centre around relationships, as indeed they did offscreen, too. Here are some intimate moments: top left, with Leslie Caron in *Promise Her Anything* (*Yardley Collection*); top right, with Vivien Leigh in *The Roman Spring of Mrs Stone*; below, with Julie Christie in *Shampoo* (*Columbia Pictures Industries Inc*)

Above, with the most controversial of all his co-stars, Madonna, as she appeared as Breathless Mahoney in *Dick Tracy* (© *Touchstone Pictures. All rights reserved*)

Left, a major match, and an electrifying partnership in every respect. Beatty as he appeared in *Bugsy*, the life story of gangster Bugsy Siegel, with his co-star Annette Bening who also became his real-life wife and mother of his child

Another early onscreen love interest was Eva Marie Saint with whom Beatty co-starred in *All Fall Down*, rated by many as one of his best pictures. Offscreen, however, Ms Saint apparently did not join the ranks of his conquests (*Yardley Collection*)

James Mason made a cameo appearance in *Heaven Can Wait*, in the role played by Claude Rains in the original 1940s version, *Here Comes Mr Jordan* (*Yardley Collection*)

Mario Puzo's novel had been on *The New York Times* bestsellers list for sixty-seven weeks and had been bought by Paramount on a modest option of $12,500 against a $50,000 fee with escalators if it was produced.

Beatty had been earmarked for the role eventually taken by Al Pacino, but he turned it down. He has never given more than a cursory explanation. Did the scale of the project scare him? Did the violence, which made his own boundary-breaking efforts in *Bonnie and Clyde* look like a Sunday School outing, worry him after all the stinging criticism he had just received? He said not, explaining merely that he did not think the movie was right for him at that time – and the time was around the fresh eruption of violence on the streets of America and elsewhere, and the assassinations of Bobby Kennedy and Dr Martin Luther King.

The violence of movies was not a matter which he dismissed lightly, a factor of current trends that was not unique to him. It challenged all of those in the world of performing arts who showed more than a passing interest in political affairs and who lent their support to political causes. This, in Beatty's case, had become a theme of recurring personal interest and debate. Like a clutch of other Hollywood names, he campaigned for Senator Robert Kennedy's bid for the presidency in 1968. Hollywood had always had an incestuous relationship with politics, which had become more personal when John F. Kennedy moved to the White House. There were many among the political establishment, not to mention the media, who questioned whether it was wise for these young men of influential sway in the movies to take their fame out into the heartlands of American life, knocking on doors on behalf of a particular candidate.

Beatty was the first person to admit that it 'scares up a lot of publicity'. But publicity was not the key as he saw it. He was always willing to debate whether an artist should engage in politics and would argue, as would Paul Newman and Robert Redford, that the mere celluloid portrayal was an insufficient response on the part of the artists to the turmoil of severe national problems like the war in Vietnam or the burning of inner cities. They believed it was possible to detach themselves from their fame and their screen image to go out and campaign, and to come to terms with the problem itself. 'There is no reason why the artist is not a part of his times,' Beatty insisted. 'The artist simply says in an uncompromising way what the truth is. People were dying in Vietnam and the racial problems at home were very immediate things. And you had the sexual revolution of the 1960s. This was a very immediate thing. And all of this ancillary fall-out was immediate . . .' Making films about social issues was not the answer; artists had to become involved in the issues.

Beatty's involvement with Robert Kennedy was more than a mere flirtation with a glamorous politician. He took the trouble to read every speech Kennedy had ever made in the Senate, and according to observers of the Kennedy campaign, he talked to hostile students on the college campuses and won them over as skilfully as Kennedy himself.

When Robert Kennedy was assassinated in June 1968, some considered it ironic that Beatty – then on the crest of a wave from his success in *Bonnie and Clyde* – should speak loudly towards the cause of gun control in America. Critics claimed that he had glamorised the very violence he was speaking against. He countered that the film showed the bloody reality of violence and he agreed to speak at public meetings and other gatherings on behalf of the groups sponsoring gun control.

He also made an instant foray into the controversial area of gun law, for so long a part of the American way of life and the freedom of the individual to defend himself and his property. The second Kennedy assassination added to his own feelings about involvement. He worked with the John Glenn Emergency Gun Controls Committee and went out into the public arena to campaign for it.

On 6 July 1968, exactly a month after Bobby Kennedy's assassination, he and Julie Christie went to Candlestick Park, San Francisco and before the game between the San Francisco Giants and the St Louis Cardinals spoke to the massive, and irritable crowd. It was a mistake! 'A sound and reasonable gun control law will only help curb violence in our society,' he shouted above the hubbub of the impatient multitude. 'Now is the time to act and Americans should wire or write to their congressmen to approve a law that will impose reason and

154

good sense on possession of firearms.'

He was booed loudly from a crowd more interested in seeing their football stars than discussing the implications of gun control. Beatty was not put off. He and Christie moved on to Cow Palace to make a similar impassioned plea before the start of Sonny Liston's heavyweight fight with Henry Clark, and met a similar response. He was pelted with bottles and beer cans but stood his ground.

Soon afterwards, Beatty met one of the contenders to replace Bobby Kennedy as the Democratic candidate for the presidency, Senator George McGovern, for whom he was to become a tireless worker. Beatty launched himself into politics in what would be a long and influential involvement with McGovern. His approach was to be far different from the support on the hustings offered by his counterparts in Hollywood on both sides of the political divide. Beatty saw himself as more of a strategist than an overt campaigner. McGovern also viewed him as a fount of ideas for communicating with the public, and especially the youth of America. In the event, McGovern did not win the nomination in 1968. It went instead to Hubert Humphrey, who gave Nixon a close run for his money. But from the introduction that summer, Beatty began to amass more influence inside the Democrat camp than any Hollywood figure had ever achieved, and it extended over many years.

This would develop further, and it offered yet another avenue of power and importance, another string to his bow, another element in the complexities of the character of the man himself. Star, sex symbol, rampant lover, successful producer, socialite, millionaire; he was all of those things at the age of thirty. Politics became yet another dimension which helped detach him, Warren Beatty, and allowed him to stand apart from the accepted image of a Hollywood personality.

11
Elizabeth's Game

Beatty's value and standing in Hollywood after the roller-coaster ride on *Bonnie and Clyde* was no better demonstrated than towards the end of 1968. He was approached by Darryl F. Zanuck at 20th Century-Fox in September with a remarkable offer. The story had its beginnings earlier in the year, when George Stevens had been signed to direct Elizabeth Taylor in *The Only Game in Town*, in which she was to co-star with her old friend Frank Sinatra. Originally, filming was to have begun in the summer, but production was held up by Elizabeth's illness, headlined as 'a mystery operation' but which was, in fact, a hysterectomy.

Production was rescheduled to allow for her full recovery from what was then a very debilitating operation noted for having both physical and mental side effects. Sinatra had to pull out. He was already booked for a season at Caesar's Palace, Las Vegas, in November for a fee that was substantially more than he would have earned from the picture.

Beatty found himself being invited as a late replacement, and with all that had gone in the immediate past, he would not come cheaply – that was if he decided to accept. However, the prospect of working with Taylor was especially appealing. It was widely known that when Elizabeth signed to do the picture in April, she had upped the guaranteed $1 million fee that she had been charging for every picture she had made since *Cleopatra*.

The asking price was now $1.25 million and, coincidentally, Richard Burton had demanded the same figure from Zanuck

157

to star with Rex Harrison in *Staircase*, the tale of two ageing homosexual lovers. Thus, that summer Fox had shelled out $2.5 million, plus later percentages, to the Taylor-Burton household, which was quite a climbdown for the man who had served joint writs on the stars at the end of the *Cleopatra* fiasco, claiming they had damaged the picture by their unwarranted off-screen behaviour and demanding damages of $55 million. The case had dragged on for five years, with both having to make deposition after deposition, before it was settled out of court.

Zanuck wanted them back and their fee had risen accordingly. 'The price of bread is going up,' Elizabeth quipped, but added with all due modesty, 'Am I surprised that producers pay me so much to do a picture? They must be out of their tiny Chinese minds.' Perhaps they were. But who else in the business provided such guaranteed publicity, except Beatty himself? But Beatty was the modern man. Taylor and Burton belonged to a fading era and few dared to predict, least of all Zanuck, that the whole movie business was on the brink of a change which would rapidly overtake the Great Star syndrome and render it ineffective.

Barely a week went by during 1968 when the Burtons were not in the news for one reason or another. They had been wallowing in the benefits of their accumulated joint wealth – which Burton estimated would stand at $12 million by the end of that year – in a manner which even Elizabeth conceded in hindsight was verging on the obscene. They'd bought a yacht that cost them half a million dollars in purchase and refurbishment. Then Burton laid out $305,000 to buy his wife the Krupp diamond; they coughed up another million dollars between them buying a Monet, a Picasso, a Van Gogh and an Epstein bust of Churchill, and there was much speculation over their purchase of a $200,000 shareholding in Harlech Television, which gave them two seats on the board.

In June, Elizabeth instigated and paid for a full-page advertisement in *The New York Times* calling for tighter gun laws in America in the wake of the assassination of Robert Kennedy, then she went into hospital with her 'mystery' illness. Interspersed between these events were the usual gossipy headlines, portraying the fiery nature of the Burtons' marriage and the cataclysmic fights which were observed by all and sundry within shouting distance.

By the end of the summer, Fox executives were looking on with gloomy desolation at the start-date for the two pictures which, by agreement, both hung on Taylor's recovery. Beatty, well aware of their plight, wanted $1 million to replace Sinatra. Zanuck, over a barrel for a big star at such short notice, agreed and Beatty stuffed a few clothes into a bag and flew to Paris to enter the new and heady world that surrounded the Taylor-Burton camp.

The location in Paris was, on the face of it, a strange venue. *The Only Game in Town* was set in Las Vegas, and Burton's film, *Staircase*, was set in London. The explanation was that Taylor and Burton would only work in France because of their tax situation, which restricted the time they could spend working in either Britain or the US. They also feared that a lengthy separation might be the final undoing of their marriage, which was being held together more by their extravagances and tensions than by anything else. So Fox had obligingly inserted into their separate contracts agreement that the two films would be made simultaneously in Paris, where they built two sets at very considerable expense, one with a skyline depicting the east end of London, and the other Nevada.

That, as Miss Taylor had previously observed, was power! Or was it? Beatty would glean his first close observation of the Taylor-Burton situation, and it was one that he did not like at all. Power? Freedom? Actually, they were locked in a gilded cage and were far more restricted than even himself. It was a living nightmare, largely of their own making. They peered out at a world which allowed them no real freedom.

If wealth was the indicator, then they had it all. But their lives were filled with their personal traumas; they were confronted by relentless external pressures and surrounded by socialites and aristocrats who sought their company for all the wrong reasons.

Meanwhile, the two production teams were waiting for the off, with George Stevens directing his unit in one studio, and Stanley Donen with his in another. Stevens was Taylor's favourite director. Twenty years earlier, he had steered her over the bridge from adolescent child star to probably the best performance of her early adult years, in *A Place in the Sun*, with Monty Clift. It was the most important picture of her life, and in another way, for the development of the movies.

As Charlton Heston explained to me, 'Stevens was a relentless perfectionist who really discovered the art of the close-up shot. In *Casablanca*, for instance, in the whole movie there are only four close-ups. He began to use this technique of going in close with the camera; the scene of the kiss between Taylor and Clift in *A Place in the Sun* was a stunning use of close-up. It was widely commented upon and he began to use it more and more, as did others.'

Stevens would also become Beatty's model for directing, perhaps because of his penchant for sitting around and tearing a character apart and putting it back together again. On this occasion, there in Paris waiting for Taylor and her new co-star to appear, he was uncomfortably sucking on his pipe, and going into some long silences. He could see the potential of the script, but wondered about its relevance in modern America, or elsewhere, for that matter, and in these doubts he was to be proved accurate.

The Only Game in Town is the story of two sad losers, she a chorus girl unhappily involved with a married man and he a cocktail pianist addicted to gambling. It is an intimate story, closely focused on the two stars and too confined and introspective for the tastes of current movie-going audiences, who were being steered by external events of life itself to an ever-increasing lust for excitement, rebellion, sex and violence.

That was the situation as Beatty arrived in Paris. Stevens, still seeking the route to satisfaction, sat Beatty down in a hotel room with the writer, Frank Gilroy, and made them read the entire script aloud to him. Meanwhile, the Taylor-Burton entourage of so-called friends and hangers-on had arrived in force, and were moving between the two film sets, where Darryl F. Zanuck was desperately hoping that the most famous twosome in the world, filming apart but in parallel, would present him with a double jackpot.

Knowing Beatty's reputation as a Hollywood stud, Burton was not unnaturally nervous about him working with Elizabeth, and in his cups a few nights before Beatty arrived, he and Rex Harrison were reminiscing about the past, and about history repeating itself. Burton recalled the last time they had all been together, himself, Harrison and Taylor, for *Cleopatra*. On that occasion, it had been the beginning of the romance between Taylor and Burton and the end of her marriage to Eddie Fisher. Burton was also conscious of her emotional state following the hysterectomy and told Harrison that he feared she might be building towards doing something dramatic, just to prove a point.

'Wouldn't it be ironic if Elizabeth fell in love with her leading man on this picture? It would be an ironic ending to our love affair, wouldn't it?' Burton added. He took another mouthful of brandy, and said, 'I think I may fire a warning shot over the bows of our young Mr Beatty.'

This he apparently did, with a half-joking but half-serious remark to Beatty when he arrived on the set in October, suggesting that he should be wary about falling in love with his wife. Overnight, Burton had also made a 'kidding remark' to Elizabeth about Beatty. Later, with the benefit of hindsight, she agreed she might well have fallen in love with him at a time when she was 'trying so hard to prove that she was still desirable'. But Burton's remark brought her to her senses. She obviously had not heard about Beatty and Julie Christie.

Unaware of Burton's fears or of Taylor's emotional state or of the intermittent excruciating pain she would suffer throughout the hundred days of filming from her recurring back problem, Beatty walked straight into a situation where the atmosphere could be cut with a knife. He found Elizabeth, whom he had known at a distance for years, exceedingly polite and charming, but coolly businesslike. He stood back and whispered to a production man, 'What have I done?'

Burton was not alone in his anticipation of rising passions. The whole production unit at the Studio de Boulogne, and especially the French technicians, who well knew of Beatty's reputation, were half-expecting it and were certainly hoping for some sparks to liven up the proceedings as Beatty and Taylor began work. In fact, the clinches were acted with clinical professionalism. In one scene, they were to appear apparently naked, side by side in bed. Out of camera range, their bodies were wrapped in towels – and Burton was watching from behind the cameras.

'I say, Elizabeth,' he yelled. 'Don't you think you should be a bit closer to your lover? And Warren . . . you look a touch bashful. Is my presence making you nervous?'

There was, for all the bonhomie, a certain formal coolness between Beatty and Burton which transferred itself to Burton's personal record of the encounters. One entry in his diary for 12 October recalled how he finished early because Harrison had a touch of flu, and so went over to the Boulogne Studios to wait for Elizabeth to finish for the day. 'I saw W. Beatty,' he noted, 'who gave me a drink and was extremely flattering about Elizabeth. He said how remarkably beautiful she was, a great film actress. I replied that she thought similarly of him.'

Burton and Beatty were hardly bosom pals. However, Beatty increasingly found himself drawn into their grand social whirl in Paris. He was no stranger to the scene but was more used to the fashionable *chic* night-clubs and discotheques. The Burtons moved on a higher plane of classy restaurants, populated by old friends and the so-called élite of the day, like the Duke and Duchess of Windsor, who visited Elizabeth on the set; Maria Callas, various Rothschilds and a clutch of French aristocrats.

At dinner one evening, Maria Callas confided to them all that she had had a spectacular confrontation with her lover, Aristotle Onassis, and had finally parted from him. Even so, the news the following week that Ari was to marry Jackie Kennedy came as no less of a surprise. On the night of the announcement, Beatty, Taylor and Burton all went out to dinner with Callas who, said Burton, 'appears to need our company & comfort & perhaps the attention we attract tho' god knows she can attract enough at the moment in her own right.'

'Ari is a peeg,' said Callas, and predicted prophetically: 'He is not in love with that woman, nor she with him. She wants the money and he wants the most sensational partner in the world. It will all end in tears and he will come running back. Ha! Just let him . . .'

Then another of the élite of Parisian society met up with

the Burtons. Prince Philip's startling and stunning cousin, Princess Elizabeth of Yugoslavia, visited both Taylor and Burton on their respective sets. Beatty invited her to dinner, on 5 November, and she accepted in a rather casual, off-hand manner, apparently trying to hide the excitement bubbling away inside. Taylor reported daily to Burton that half the female aristocracy of Paris was sniffing around the Studio de Boulogne hoping for glimpse of Beatty, and perhaps to catch his eye.

There were occasional lapses in filming to accommodate Elizabeth's back problems, which now necessitated her wearing a metal brace almost daily. Zanuck, viewing the daily rushes and rubbing his hands with glee, convinced he had two winners, tempted fate by sending out a round of congratulatory telegrams telling everyone they were doing a marvellous job and what great actors they all were. Then production was halted on Beatty's film, first on 20 November, when Burton had to break the news that Elizabeth's father had died – 'she was like a wild animal even though we've been expecting his death' – and then three weeks later, when she was ordered to lay flat on her back for at least a month.

Filming dragged on into the new year and it was the end of February before Stevens called a wrap and released Beatty to the arms of Julie Christie. As for Zanuck and his two money-spinning movies, he was to be sorely disappointed.

By then, there was news of the competition that would be around, which curiously enough had certain affiliations to the new wave of movies inspired by Beatty himself, with *Bonnie and Clyde*. It included Jack Nicholson, Dennis Hopper and Peter Fonda, spaced out in the superb but dope-drenched *Easy Rider*; Jon Voight and Dustin Hoffman in John Schlesinger's classic, *Midnight Cowboy*, and Natalie Wood, back in the limelight and involved in the current party rage of mate-swapping in *Bob and Carol and Ted and Alice*. *The Only Game in Town*, in which even the sex was low-key and polite, looked a tired rival.

It was all wrong – the time, the place, the story belonged in an earlier decade. Fox did not know what to do with it, and kept it on the shelf until 4 March 1970, by which time it looked even more dated. The movie had cost $10 million to make and took a miniature $1.5 million at the box office, whereas *Easy Rider* was made for less than $400,000 and grossed close on $35 million.

Burton and Harrison's *Staircase* fared no better. Though the sight of two of Britain's greatest screen lovers and hetero-sexual males camping it up had brought howls of laughter from the crew who filmed it, the audiences did not appreciate the joke and stayed away. Zanuck's future as head of the studio looked positively precarious.

Oddly enough, although they panned *The Only Game in Town*, the critics were not unkind to Beatty and Taylor and today, taken out of the context of its release in an era when every convention was being shattered by epoch-making movies, the two stars can be seen to have generated a genuine chemistry. It would prove to anyone swayed by the bad press, the amatory antics and his good looks that Beatty was a very talented actor, especially when challenged by such a script as this. One critic best summed up the problem with *The Only Game in Town* – it was 'old-fashioned, trivial, melodramatic and ponderous. It is also the sweetest, gentlest and saddest film in some time – I loved it.'

Beatty banked his money and flew back to Julie Christie in London. He had seen the Burtons at close quarters, and had probably warned himself never to get like that; the days of such power – if power it was – must surely be nearing an end, for them at least. He could see it then, and he was right. Elizabeth would never command $1 million a picture again. And there was a moral in that somewhere, which he undoubt-edly noted for the future. Actors only have power while they are wanted.

Meanwhile, the $7 million sloshing around in Beatty's bank account from his last two pictures provided him with an unrivalled sense of security and satisfaction. Julie Christie had just finished her own latest film, a joint British-Italian production called *In Search of Gregory* with John Hurt, and the two of them went to ground. Their affair was no longer secret, but they seemed to have decided upon a determined effort to keep themselves out of the spotlight.

Beatty called a complete halt to media interviews. There

was nothing to be gained from them now and he was not about to offer himself for public scrutiny when the only beneficiary would be the newspaper or magazine whose sales he had boosted by cooperating. They bobbed up here and there, in Geneva, in Rome, in Paris, back in Los Angeles and then in London. They travelled the world, unhurried and without purpose, and often with only themselves for company, and this they continued for almost two years.

Producers and directors seeking the services of these two most bankable of modern young stars found them inaccessible and unresponsive, and scripts and books were again being returned with polite but firm 'nos'. At the time, they probably weren't even bothering to read them. The question of who was influencing whom in their disappearing act became a topic of speculation, especially among Christie's friends.

On the one hand, it was being suggested that Beatty was now running her life and that Christie was happy to allow herself to be subjugated by the stronger and wholly greater personality of her lover. The writer Robert Ottaway suggested however that being with Beatty merely emphasised her own fear of fame, because for once she could observe at close hand the pressures that fell upon Beatty because of it.

Beatty was also known to have the quaint notion that he should be the breadwinner, and he had already won them enough bread to survive the immediate future. Those allegedly 'in the know' seemed to believe that Beatty had become her career guide, just as he had been with other lovers in the past, and that it was his doing that she turned down a succession of offers.

In the meantime, he was increasingly elusive to the world outside. When cornered he was charming, intelligent and pleasant to those to whom he wished to be charming, intelligent and pleasant. To the rest he was maddeningly vague, and exceedingly wary of exposing himself to any kind of situation he might not be able to control. Christie had caught on to his style and had become rather proficient at creating her own smokescreen.

Devoid of any words of wisdom from either, the media began to speculate upon the possibility that the couple were preparing to marry. The story, in Beatty's case, was no different than before. Only the name had been changed, and still it wasn't true. They were also said to be searching for a script in which they could both star – just as he had done with Leslie Caron, and with Natalie Wood. There was one other remarkable similarity between this and Beatty's other serious affairs, documented in the preceding chapters.

He and Christie were charged with the same kind of emotions and strengths that sometimes clashed, and when they clashed they did so spectacularly. Julie, in good voice, could be heard through several cardboard hotel walls, and her language was of choice late-sixties vintage which, interestingly enough, contrasted with Beatty's – a person once described, it will be recalled, as a most foul-mouthed young man by an interviewer in 1961. Now, and unlike Christie, he had curtailed his use of the expletive, he did not smoke and seldom drank more than a modest intake of alcohol. He was also the Mr Clean of Hollywood, inasmuch as the only pills he took were vitamins, and he would have nothing to do with the fashionable vogue for marijuana or cocaine. This in itself was once again totally against the grain of things as they were emerging in 1969; indeed, his own efforts in *Bonnie and Clyde* had alerted many movie-makers to the extent of changing attitudes.

Beatty was well ahead in that respect. That Jon Voight and Jack Nicholson should receive Oscar nominations for their respective portrayals in *Midnight Cowboy* and *Easy Rider* spoke volumes. There was Voight charged with the line: 'To tell you the truth, I ain't a real cowboy, but I'm a hell of a good stud,' and Nicholson stating through a haze of good quality Mexican grass, 'This used to be a hell of a good country . . .'

The anti-heroes came of age and the movement of counter-culture was choosing its leaders. In spite of *Bonnie and Clyde*, Beatty was not among them. He stayed on the periphery of these explosions of social behaviour, carried out under a cloud of marijuana smoke. He refused to be caught up in the tide of overt rebellion which had captured the imagination, for various reasons, of many of his colleagues and celebrities from the world of film, art and pop.

Politically, he could not stand aside. He had seen the effects of the Paris student riots in 1968 and, in the same year, the assassination of Robert Kennedy and Dr Martin Luther King, the upsurge of Black Power and police shoot-outs with the Black Panthers, the continuing war in Vietnam, which claimed its 40,000th American victim, and the two million acres defoliated in South Vietnam by the beginning of 1969. They were all issues with which he could identify his support for the Democratic voice when McGovern renewed his campaign for the presidency.

Hollywood was affected both commercially and in its direction by the events of the late sixties and early seventies. Films like *Midnight Cowboy* and *Easy Rider* expanded the boundaries of explicitness and anti-heroism; there was a general air of tension and menace in everyday life, and a certain unreality.

Drugs played their part, not merely by their emergence as an integral part of the counter-culture movement but in the attitudes of plain, straightforward young people, to whom any kind of illicit substance, save perhaps for the odd joint, would have been a complete mystery a couple of years earlier. Now, there was a preponderance of everything from LSD to magic mushrooms. Drugs provided the elements for the suspension of reality as young people were being encouraged by counter-culture gurus to raise the stakes of involvement by the pressures of wars, racism, brutal police and other assorted hostilities as the feeling of impending apocalypse heightened.

Beatty was no less affected by these developments personally than some of his more actively vociferous colleagues, but if he was going to get involved, it would be from a political standpoint, behind the scenes, eventually pushing his ideas on a campaigning model for McGovern. Otherwise, his profile in the counter-culture movement was decidedly low. He did not support extremism.

The feeling was mutual within the counter-culture movement itself. Unlike his Brando-like character in *Splendor in the Grass*, he was not an actor, or even a political activist, who could be seen as an inspiration for youth rebellion, even though he and his movies had quietly been a model of nonconformity all his adult life. The likes of Dylan, Lennon and now Nicholson, and to a lesser degree Roman Polanski, were the darlings of the west coast film and rock music communities. Their message was freedom, and that was music to the ears of those who followed the anti-war, hippy-inspired trend of throwing aside all inhibitions and joining the Timothy Leary edict of 'Turn on, tune in and drop out' or rediscovering the paths recommended by the poet Jack Kerouac.

All of this had its effect on the movies, of course. Audiences were demanding at least a recognition of the times. That did not mean they were parading outside theatres with placards, as they had done outside Nixon's White House, but they were certainly voting with their feet.

All this was emerging in the year of Beatty's new movie with Elizabeth Taylor which, between its inception and delivery, had become remarkably dated in its attitudes. Movies like *The Only Game in Town* and *Staircase* were to be rejected.

Polanski's *Rosemary's Baby*, released around the same time as *Bonnie and Clyde* – and therefore doubling the impact of both – was another movie which was accused of contributing to the liberalising of movie morals. The American Catholic Office for Motion Pictures gave it a C rating – meaning condemned – for its explicit sexual content and perverted use of, and distortions of, fundamental Christian beliefs. In London the British Board of Censors cut a rape scene because it contained elements of kinky sex associated with black magic. Polanski's new wife, Sharon Tate, made her own artistic contribution to the genre in her starring role in the film adaptation of Jacqueline Susann's true-life novel *Valley of the Dolls*, about pill-popping sex-crazed Los Angeles womenfolk, which was an exploitation movie if ever there was one.

The word exploitation cropped up regularly and the debate gathered momentum: was all of this merely a reflection of art imitating life, or was it sheer, unadulterated commercialism? Notable writers such as Stephen Faber, whose review of *Easy Rider* for the respected journal *Film Monthly*, could so easily have been applied to *Bonnie and Clyde*, examined the reasons why young audiences had responded in the way that they had. It was a prophetic piece of writing: 'There is something morbid about this film as a whole – a fascination, almost a wallowing in death and suffering that represents one of the least appealing tendencies in the audiences as well as the film-makers. The people who conceived this film and the people who applaud it take certain masochistic fascination in casting themselves as martyrs, poor innocents slaughtered by barbarians.'

The ultimate slaughter, and in real life, occurred not long after that article appeared. It would send shockwaves through America and scare the living daylights out of Hollywood, and Beatty was caught up in the cross-currents.

At the time, he was staying with Julie Christie in London where Roman Polanski and his heavily pregnant wife, Sharon Tate, had also sojourned. They had all become good friends, and dined together occasionally with Victor Lownes at the London Playboy Club.

Towards the end of July, Sharon left the London scene, and sailed home to America on the QE2 to prepare for the birth of her baby. Polanski himself was still delayed by work on a new project and was planning to fly back to Los Angeles, where they had a rented home, on 12 August. He had already shipped the his-and-her cars, bought from the proceeds of *Rosemary's Baby*, his being a Ferrari and hers a white vintage Rolls-Royce Silver Dawn.

Late in the afternoon of Saturday 10 August, as he was preparing to go to dinner with Lownes, Polanski took a telephone call at the house where he was staying with two friends. It brought news of the most horrific crime, which became known as the Sharon Tate murders: in their house on Ceilo Drive, Beverly Hills, Sharon and three friends and an unconnected young man aged eighteen who had been visiting a caretaker in the ground nearby, lay dead. Real bodies, real blood, and with 115 bayonet wounds and six gunshot wounds between them.

Polanski collapsed. Victor Lownes was contacted, he telephoned Warren Beatty and they both went to the house where Polanski was staying. He had to go to America as soon as possible, and was in no state to travel alone, the doctor having given him a heavy dose of sedatives. The two men arranged for first-class seats aboard a PanAm flight, and for an airline car to pick them up in central London and take them directly out to Heathrow Airport. Beatty and Lownes assisted him aboard and escorted him back to Los Angeles.

Beatty had telephoned ahead to arrange for some accommodation, a suite at Paramount Studios, where Beatty and other friends of Polanski took it in turns to stay with him as the true horror of the murders began to unfold. Charles Manson, whose drug-crazed disciples carried out the killings, was not merely a symptom of the drug age; he was the epitome of a sickness that gripped sections of society by whom he was exalted after the killings.

This fact, and the responsibilities of film-makers, would not be allowed to pass by the media once the shock and sympathy of the killings had passed. *Time* magazine, whose proprietor, the Luce family, believed it was the true voice of America, recorded: 'It was a scene as grisly as anything depicted in Polanski's film explorations of the dark and melancholy corners of human characters... the most likely theory is that the slayings were related to narcotics.'

Newsweek took it further: 'Almost as enchanting as the mystery [over the deaths] was the glimpse the murders yielded into the surprising Hollywood subculture in which the cast of characters played. All week long, the Hollywood gossip about the case was of drugs, mysticism and offbeat sex, and for once there is more truth than fantasy in the flashy talk of the town.'

Hollywood was scared all right, but not merely in their panicky thoughts for self-preservation. The stinging media criticism of 'new Hollywood' highlighted the questions of moral responsibility, and that film-makers who promoted the current genre of movies must accept some of the guilt for the social reaction which followed. The question was not new and is to this day a debatable topic, with nineties violence being taken to new, explosive proportions.

In the sixties, when films like *Bonnie and Clyde* and *The Godfather* were being produced, they were a target for the kind of criticism that might be expected of the establishment. One such feeling was that Polanski had brought trouble upon their heads and that he should be removed as soon as possible. This was eventually achieved by Polanski's own actions a few years later, when he drugged and raped a thirteen-year-old girl in Nicholson's house on Mulholland Drive (Jack was away at the time). He was released from a custodial probation and fled to Europe and effectively to exile. A warrant was issued for his arrest, and he has not been back to the United States since.

These events undoubtedly had an effect on Beatty himself. With his own film being listed among those which had aided the breakdown of boundaries to what should or should not be shown in the movies, he reflected upon this accusation at length. His conclusions were apparent. Unlike Nicholson, who was also deeply involved in the scene, Beatty stayed out of violent scenarios for many years, until the nineties. If indeed movies could influence, as well as reflect, social attitudes, then he would not take the risk with violence. Sex . . . yes.

12

Meeting Jack

'I don't do a lot of movies,' said Beatty once again. It had become a sort of catchphrase that he trotted out whenever he was momentarily cornered by a passing journalist. The weeks of inactivity turned into months, many months, and there were rumours as to why Julie Christie had disappeared from the scene and so totally immersed herself in Beatty's life. There was no secret reason; they had simply decided not to work. No one was especially surprised about Beatty's lack of appearance before the cameras. One of his favourite anecdotes concerned the fabled producer Sam Goldwyn, who had taken a shine to Beatty – as he later did to Jack Nicholson – soon after he arrived in Hollywood, and the contact was maintained for years. He would invite Beatty to the Goldwyn studios for lunch, instructing him to be there at one o'clock sharp, and would berate him if he was a minute late.

The point of the story, though, was this: if he had time for lunch, it meant he wasn't working hard enough. Goldwyn would say, 'Warren, you're not working. Why not, Warren? Make a lot of movies and make a lot of money. Don't wait around – look, you haven't done a picture in two years.'

When eventually his next project was announced in the trade papers, Goldwyn called him at eight that morning. Beatty thought it was to congratulate him on going back to work. 'No,' said the old mogul, 'I just wondered if I could rent you some space!'

When he wasn't working, he was assumed to be cooking up some new deal somewhere, and a couple of projects which would become major events in the future were already in the embryonic stage – *Shampoo* and *Reds*. For the time being, they were no more than ideas, along with others which never came to fruition.

Life and travel were inspirations to his ideas and thoughts. He was a known early participant of the jet age, clambering aboard a plane in London, and spending twelve pampered hours in the first-class cabin over the pole and into Los Angeles, where he might stay for hours or days at his suite in the Beverly Wilshire. Then, he might go to New York, or back to London, or Mexico, or anywhere. He would wake up in the middle of the night sometimes not knowing where he was, and his world was one where the names on the towels in hotel bedrooms identified his position, and where telephone was his contact with those he wished to speak to.

In 1969, he was in Moscow when *Reds* began to bubble as a project. He'd always been interested in the story of John Reed, the dashing young writer from Portland, Oregon, who joined the Greenwich Village radical circle of the early 1900s when there was much talk of revolution. Reed discovered Pancho Villa's struggle in Mexico in 1913 and then just happened to be in the right place at the right time to view firsthand Lenin's rise to power in Russia. His book on the Russian Revolution, *Ten Days That Shook the World*, made him internationally famous, and he became the only American to be buried within the walls of the Kremlin after his death from typhus at the age of thirty-three.

During Beatty's sightseeing visit to Moscow, he turned over in his mind the prospect for the Reed story. He spoke with Russian film-makers and writers, though expressed personal doubts that the Russians would allow him to make the film in the way he would wish. Beatty, under the watchful observation of the KGB, was able to conduct sufficient research to decide, at that moment, he wanted to make the movie, although the world would have to wait more than ten years before he was ready to begin what would become one of the epics of his career.

More travelling back and forth across the Atlantic, and in the new year, he and Julie began to get serious about a new film which would be *their* picture. Getting a commitment was another thing. Making a commitment was difficult for both. It wasn't just for films; it was for anything – dinner, parties, appointments at a specific time of day (one Hollywood hostess would only ever put on a buffet meal when they were invited because she never knew when they would turn up); even the fitting for a new suit was a commitment. One day, walking down New Bond Street in London, Beatty passed a tailor's shop with a friend and paused. 'What's up?' said the friend.

'Err . . . it's my suit.'

'What about your suit?'

'I'm due for a second fitting.'

They walked on past the shop. The friend was curious and asked if the suit was ready. They walked on another fifty yards before Beatty replied. 'No. About a year ago, I went in for a first fitting and I haven't been back. Somehow . . . I just can't.'

They strolled on. 'Are you going back?'

'Nah,' said Beatty. 'A second fitting will mean a third . . . and . . .'

The moment passed and the fate of the unmade suit remained for the moment unresolved.

Robert Altman, the director of current acclaim, was looking for a commitment. He was fresh from directing *M*A*S*H*, which would become the hit of 1970 and earn him an Oscar nomination for best director and best picture. *M*A*S*H* was a classic of the era and, just as Beatty and Arthur Penn had done with *Bonnie and Clyde*, Altman had cloaked the blood and gore and bitterness of war in humour and sexual slapstick. Altman admitted that without the influence of *Bonnie and Clyde*, perhaps *M*A*S*H* could never have been made.

Beatty's admiration for Altman and a script that offered exquisite potential for himself and Christie convinced him that they should co-star, subject to a few 'minor' script amendments that he would like to make. These turned out to be a major rewrite, but since Altman and screenwriter Brian McKay were already having a problem raising funds for the picture, they were happy to let Beatty influence the outcome, since he would also attract backers.

The movie had suddenly become very attractive to the backers, doubly attractive. For Taylor and Burton, read Beatty and Christie. They had the publicity and the modern appeal of beautifulness that had long ago deserted the Burton partnership and, in terms of couples, there were barely any rivals on the horizon.

The project had the working title of *The Presbyterian Church Wager* – later changed to *McCabe and Mrs Miller* – and was based on Edmund Naughton's novel, *McCabe*, which Beatty had read. Filming would not begin until autumn at the earliest, on location in Canada. Julie, meanwhile, had also been approached by British producers Norman Priggen and John Heyman, who were packaging a film based upon L.P. Hartley's classic period novel *The Go-Between*, for which Harold Pinter had written a screenplay.

Julie, the producers admitted, was pretty off-hand about the project to begin with and it seemed likely that a refusal was on the cards. Word was that she just wanted to be left alone and lived her life in the privacy of her Malibu beach-house with Beatty, or in whichever penthouse suite he was currently occupying. 'It was a very private world,' said one of her friends of the time. 'We never knew much about her lifestyle because she was so secretive. As far as we could tell, when she wasn't travelling with Warren she spent her time making little glass ornaments and figurines which she carefully wrapped and sent to her friends. You would see them everywhere.'

However, Priggen and Heyman had more luck than they had hoped. Julie read the early pages of the screenplay in Los Angeles, and came back on the telephone insisting that she must do it, especially since Alan Bates was to be her co-star. She flew to London and rented a house near the sea in Norfolk, where the film was to be shot on location. She purchased a bicycle on which she used to travel to work each day, and naturally became the focus of intrigued local attention. Any hopes of retaining anything near normality had already been eroded by media attention, which merely heightened to a further bout of breathless speculation when Beatty arrived to join her. The peace and quiet of the typical English countryside was suddenly alive with telephoto lenses and cameramen hanging from trees.

Christie, whose months away from the limelight had done nothing to improve her inherent shyness, was besieged, and the film publicists, feigning sympathy, were in reality having a ball. They put out one of those statements which they said was aimed at relieving the pressure but which merely heightened the interest: 'Julie tries her hardest to accept that success means inconvenience. That means battalions of admirers following her around. She tries, yes. But she will openly admit that it is all a great burden and honestly she'd rather do without it. You could say she is a girl in a whirl of torment. That is why she is so seldom seen on the screen.'

The 'I want to be left alone' retort of Garbo was never more applicable. She would say to inquiring writers from Fleet Street and the fan magazines that she did not give interviews and then spend half an hour explaining why not. Typical responses could have been scripted by Beatty himself: 'It's a waste of time and energy to feed curious minds . . . curiosity is never satisfied. I know how I'd like to be thought of: scintillating, witty, intellectual and gracious, which I am not. I haven't got control over what people think so there is not much point caring. And anyway, if I give you my character, it then has to be filtered through various people who haven't been through my experiences. So there's no point to that, either.'

The press, at this point, usually turned nasty. The attitudes of Christie had not changed, merely hardened, during her time with Beatty and their dual penchant for negative responses to the media's requests for insight brought a rash of new headlines suggesting they were to marry, or that they may even be already married, to which question Julie tantalisingly replied: 'If we are, we are; if we are not, we are not.'

If nothing else, this continued to guarantee them exactly what they purported *not* to be seeking – an array of publicity that matched Taylor and Burton's, minus the booze, the screaming matches and the overt extravagance. The renewed vigour of media attention made Christie ratty and on edge; occasional tantrums on the set were stoutly defended by Alan Bates, who said that no great artist was devoid of temperament, and he could not find enough good things to say about her.

The film was finished by early summer of 1970. Those close to the couple noticed a degree of coolness in their relationship and at that point, bets might have been taken as to whether it would last out the making of their new film. Most doubted it. The filming period would be filled with their personal tensions. Anyway, Beatty's eye was already roaming again.

A brief interlude followed . . .

Britt Ekland first met Beatty some years earlier at a dinner party in London, when she was married to Peter Sellers and Warren was with Leslie Caron. Britt said she was so much under her husband's influence as to be immune to Beatty's charm, but 'the situation was remedied when we met again in the lingering summer of 1970' at a dinner party in London for Roman Polanski.

With Christie tied up on post-production work and retakes and, as Britt put it, often foolishly absent, an affair developed. They would dine in some secluded restaurant in London's west end, or find a dark corner in the fashionable night-spot, Tramp. 'Then he would drive me back to my studio,' Britt confessed, 'where we would make love until sleep came from sheer exhaustion.'

Britt's account of their two-month liaison is as colourful as Joan Collins' descriptions of bedroom vigour a decade earlier. No man, she said, made her happier. He had an affection which flowed as generously as his passion and she fought hard to entice him away from everyone else.

Her hopes rose when she flew from London to Los Angeles to appear on the *Dean Martin Show*, and Beatty followed. The relationship began to take a more serious note, away from the close proximity of Christie. She moved into his penthouse at the Beverly Wilshire, where 'we would sprawl about naked for most of the day, or sunbathe on the terrace . . . he was a divine lover.'

At nights, they would venture out into Los Angeles night-life, but Beatty was apprehensive about being spotted by the paparazzi, fearing that Christie would get the gossip in the next day's papers. One night, they went to a sleazy fleapit of a cinema, because she said she had never seen a porn movie. They slipped into the back row, unrecognised, when the lights were down. And they laughed and joked, and went back to the penthouse for the real thing.

A call from London ended the affair. Britt was needed for a television play and Beatty, she said, seemed relieved that she was leaving. She added the postscript that she realised Warren was incapable of lasting love. When he picked a bloom it was only for a season. As he kissed her goodbye, she knew that the affair was over, but she did not have the courage to say, 'Thanks, Warren . . . it was nice while it lasted.'

Britt moved out, and Christie came back, ready to begin work on their first movie together.

Just as *M*A*S*H* was like no other war film, Robert Altman's *McCabe and Mrs Miller* – with a heavily rewritten script not bearing Beatty's stamp – was like no other Western and, now that Altman had cast Beatty and Christie, they became integral to his thinking so that the movie is as much about them, or at least their relationship, as the story. Beatty plays a gambler, with bushy beard and bowler hat, who turns up in a town called Presbyterian Church and decides to build a whorehouse.

It was a Beatty as never seen before, or since. Christie is a tough Cockney madam who persuades him to take her on to manage the place. She has her own reasons; she wants to leave this dump of a town and go back into city life where she belongs. He agrees and she delivers what she promises, a flourishing business which attracts the attention of the local big businessmen. They demand he sells out; he refuses and ends up dead while Christie (Mrs Miller) has sought relief from the pressures of life in the Presbyterian Church and gets high on Chinatown opium. There were messages and explorations galore, and Altman's style of directing almost allowed them to develop naturally.

He had a way of letting things happen in the making of the movie, almost as if they were unplanned, as indeed some were. It was a very intimate film, very much like the personal relationship of the two stars.

They rented a house at Horseshoe Bay, seven miles from Cypress Park, in the bitter December cold of West Vancouver, Canada where they were on location. For some of the time they actually lived in the buildings specially erected to look like a mining town. One of the production team likened filming to being a peeping tom; he actually felt as if he were looking through a window at the couple; it all seemed so private and intense.

The Canadian jaunt was to have a number of repercussions, not least the friendship that began there between Beatty and Jack Nicholson.

By coincidence, Nicholson was working not far away with Art Garfunkel on locations for the filming of *Carnal Knowledge*, written by Jules Feiffer, then famed for his satirical cartoons and commentaries on modern America in *Village Voice*, and as a playwright of note and notoriety. The movie was being produced and directed by Mike Nichols, and Beatty, an old friend of both director and writer, went out to see them. Jules introduced him to Nicholson, and the two men struck up what was to become an enduring friendship.

Some intriguing discussions began which went on into the night, and then on into the next twenty years, about sex, women and making movies. At the time, Nicholson was right in the thick of controversy, and Beatty became fascinated with his work. Not least, Beatty wanted to know about *Drive He Said*, the movie for which Nicholson had taken a leaf out of Beatty's book by co-writing the screenplay, co-producing, directing and taking the starring role.

From Nicholson's point of view, it was a dramatic attempt at a movie and Beatty admired him for his courage, especially since it was made immediately after the international success of *Easy Rider*, when Nicholson's future as a major star was by no means assured. Also, Nicholson's movie had political undertones beneath the sexuality, and Beatty enjoyed the premise of political message in artistic work.

Based upon the novel *Drive* by Jeremy Larner (who had since achieved additional fame as speechwriter for the anti-war Democrat senator Eugene McCarthy), the film tells the story of two college students, one a radical anti-war activist, the other a basketball student with no political convictions. Theirs is a story of sexual interaction with campus women which deals explicitly with rape, drugs and venereal disease. There was one particular scene of full-frontal nudity, mostly of men, which Nicholson knew might cause some trouble, though he never imagined how much trouble.

When the film was shown at the Cannes Film Festival, Jack was sitting in the back row and was shocked by the reaction. First there was cheering, and then jeering and conflicting views led to a fight, then a riot. Nicholson felt flattered that his film had caused such a stir. 'But then,' he told Beatty, 'I realised the riot was going to hurt the picture. It was a disaster and I knew it was going to set me back.'

A permissive age it might have been, but still not *that* permissive. In the US, the film was given an X rating; it was banned in Canada unless he made forty-five separate cuts and he faced similar problems in Britain.

Nicholson had taken up where Beatty left off in *Bonnie and Clyde*, first with *Easy Rider*, which was a natural successor with its theme of slapstick mixed with issues of sex and violence. Now, in *Carnal Knowledge*, he was to establish a reputation that would rival, if not overtake, Beatty's as the Great Seducer, and their meeting together in Canada would have a number of implications. Apart from their developing personal friendship, they would also work together in the future, with Mike Nichols, who was directing Nicholson in *Carnal Knowledge*.

Nichols, acclaimed for revitalising the careers of Elizabeth Taylor and Richard Burton, was no stranger to controversy himself. He had already done much to extend the boundaries of artistic licence in the use of sex verging on obscenity. The rating SMA – Suitable for Mature Audiences – was introduced in the US especially to deal with the blitz of four-letter words in *Who's Afraid of Virginia Woolf?*

Now, in *Carnal Knowledge*, he and Nicholson were in the process of delivering a movie that contained all the sexual promise that the title suggested with a cacophony of adventures in lust and love. Nicholson saw it as a career turning point: 'Occasionally you play a character that creates such an impression with the audience that suddenly you are affected by the feedback and it can change your life.'

His role of Jonathan, the mindless sexual malcontent, would do exactly that and, apart from putting his own sexuality under the microscope, it would also put him in line for considerable abuse, appearing as it did at a time when the feminist movement was growing.

So, there they were in Vancouver, Beatty with Julie Christie and Jack with his co-star colleagues, Art Garfunkel, Candice Bergen and Ann-Margret, turning out two films that would have varying impact upon audiences in the months to come, in one of which Nicholson established himself as a major force. His acclaim would eventually outstrip Beatty's in both personal and professional controversy.

Nicholson, rather more open in his interviews with the media than in later life, by which time he had discovered the same problems Beatty had experienced, was quite happy to talk about the movie in relation to his own sexual activity. 'If you look at the real facts of life,' he said in the *Playboy* interview, 'you'll find that if you've not released your sexual energy you're in trouble. If you take a trip and you're away for three days and you don't relate to a chick then pretty soon that's all you think about; three days in a new town and you're thinking, "Why can't I find a beaver in a bar?" It's not that sex is the primary element of the universe, but when it's unfulfilled, it will affect you.'

This revelation of his own views would be run alongside Beatty's when, in future years, they became the most notorious of Hollywood *boulevardiers*, although their similarities in most respects, other than women and politics, were actually negligible.

Carnal Knowledge provided sufficient controversy for the American judiciary to become involved. The film was banned in the state of Georgia and the producers fought all the way to the Supreme Court to get the decision overturned. It went on to become one of the big box-office successes of the seventies.

Beatty's picture had far less impact. It was an exceedingly good movie, in which Altman's ability to exploit the actors for their talent rather than their fame shone through. They were two members of a community, and the movie is about a particular period and a number of people, but the focus is on Beatty and Christie. Critical reaction was, in many ways, like that he got with *Bonnie and Clyde* – it was either strongly for, or strongly against.

Pauline Kael in the *New Yorker*, who gave him such a boost with *Bonnie and Clyde*, said this one was a beautiful pipe-

dream of a picture, a fleeting diaphanous vision of what fron-
tier life might have been. *McCabe* was a testimony to the
power of the stars, Beatty and Christie, who seemed to take
over the screen by natural right. Alternatively, *Films in
Review* blasted it as cinematic incompetence, with Beatty falling on his face and Christie worthy of better things. Beatty
went out on the road to pump up the action. Whatever the
financial outcome, it was Christie's finest, most powerful performance to date, which had much to do with the chemistry
between them.

By the time these reviews appeared, whatever chemistry they
had had disappeared like a puff of smoke. The showbusiness
couple of the late sixties drifted apart. All the promise, all
the intensity of their relationship ended almost as casually
as it had begun. Those who retold stories of their private
rows would add that they knew all along it would never work.
Beatty had been cast as the man who tamed Christie – and
vice versa. Neither had done either. They had worked at com-
patibility but perhaps because of the similarity of their underlying needs and desires, they could never remain together.

Christie was too shy and retiring. Robert Altman recalled
how she would sit on the edge of movie parties, and would
be ready to leave just as soon as it was possible. She only
got interested when there were political conversations, about
which she held decidedly leftish views. Beatty was here and
there, talking and bustling with the crowds. The gossip among
their circle was that Beatty wanted to marry her, but she
turned him down.

She did not enjoy the extrovert meanderings and would
have preferred to settle for a quiet cottage in the country, far
from the madding crowd – which is exactly what she eventually did. Before and after Beatty her relationships have
been strictly monogamous. She set great store by faithfulness,
and when she and Beatty broke up, she was heard to say
angrily, 'Infidelity destroys love. If you love someone and it's
good, you've got to have the sense to stick with it. This doesn't
mean you will never be attracted to another living soul. But
if you give in to that attraction, then you risk losing the
person you're in love with. You can't just go swanning off with

everyone who attracts you. It's greedy and selfish. It sounds great to do whatever you want at a given time. But it never works out in real life – only in the movies.'

The moment of separation is hard to pinpoint. After filming *McCabe*, they went back to Hollywood for the revelries and then he went straight into another film, and perhaps an excuse to work.

There must have been some reason why he agreed to appear in *Dollars*, a fairly ordinary caper movie written and directed by the much-admired Richard Brooks. On this occasion Brooks, famed for such works as *The Brothers Karamazov, In Cold Blood* and *Cat on a Hot Tin Roof*, had a screenplay so trite and unimportant that it would need two major stars to rescue it from total oblivion. Beatty and Goldie Hawn, recently endowed with an Oscar for her performance in *Cactus Flower*, obliged.

It is hard to understand why Beatty would turn down several movies which became major hits and then turn up in one that barely challenged his ability. Capers were fashionable, and this one had the benefit of an ingenious plot to rob a bank, but it was frivolous and lightweight, a repeat of *Kaleidoscope*, only worse. The critics poured scorn on him for wasting their time, not to mention his own. He too seemed to have coasted in it, treating it as nothing more than a paid vacation, and rarely mentioned the movie in his retrospective conversations on his work.

Still, it brought Goldie Hawn temporarily into his life and they spent much time together while filming. Julie Christie's presence declined daily, and she stayed most of the time at her home in Selwood Terrace to avoid any repeat of the attention she and Beatty had attracted while she was filming *The Go-Between*. Then she too flew away, to Venice to join Donald Sutherland in Nicholas Roeg's *Don't Look Now*, which finally consigned the Beatty-Christie affair to history.

Not long afterwards, he was back in the arena, squiring more voluptuous ladies, including the actress Liv Ullmann. He and Christie would resume a platonic friendship and they were destined to have two more memorable screen encounters, but the reunion lay in the future. For the time being, Beatty took himself out of the Hollywood spotlight, and *Dollars* would be his last film for almost three years. Frivolous it might have been, but now he returned to an altogether more serious project. Politics.

13
McGovern's Man

As a boy brought up on the edges of the world's most virulent political capital, Washington, Beatty had toyed with early ambitions of becoming President, which later tapered off to a period of disenchantment with the way the country was being run, even during the Democratic reign of Lyndon Johnson. However, he was a student of politics as well as one of the Democrat backers, and never wanted to be viewed as a mere liberal-minded actor giving his vocal support to his chosen candidate. It went much deeper, and had done for years. His long-standing study and fascination with John Reed, who became embroiled in the birth of American left-wing politics, had caused some right-wing journals to accuse Beatty of Communist sympathies, mistaking interest for active involvement in communism and the rising American New Left of the early seventies.

By then, Hollywood's political activity had hardened, polarised and was subsequently under the microscope. The intimate connections between Los Angeles and Washington had long been established, but in the raging arguments over the Vietnam War and the inner-city problems on the American home front, positions were being taken and voiced loudly. Beatty's interest, like that of a number of his fellows, was intellectually based upon what could be done to help the liberal cause of the Democrats.

In years past, moguls like Louis B. Mayer and Jack Warner had toyed with political propaganda movies, especially during the war years. For two decades after the war, many stars fought shy of politics after the hysteria surrounding Senator Joseph McCarthy and the inquisitions of his Committee on Un-American Activities which resulted in blacklists of suspected Communist sympathisers and the jailing of the Hollywood Ten.

Right-wingers, like John Wayne, James Stewart, Charlton Heston and Ronald Reagan, had no compunction about putting their weight behind the Republicans, and with the Hollywood blacklists still within recent memory, those who supported left of centre causes needed to have courage in their convictions. The threat of damaging their careers, even in this so-called enlightened age, was still present, especially if they became involved in overt support for the anti-war and anti-racist campaigners of the late sixties and beyond, as did Jane Fonda, Jean Seberg and others who suffered intensely as a result.

The ghost of McCarthy still roamed the corridors of the FBI and the CIA, and stars who involved themselves in the protest movements of war, race and urban blight at the start of the seventies were prone to heavy investigation, constant surveillance and smear campaigns. Jean Seberg's former husband, author Romain Gary, claimed that it was the FBI smear tactics, spreading rumours that she was pregnant by a leader of the Black Panther movement which she supported, that drove her to suicide. John Lennon was under intense surveillance in 1971 by the FBI and the CIA for his support of the anti-war lobby, and J. Edgar Hoover alerted his agents that year to try to arrest Lennon in possession of narcotics so that they could legitimately throw him out of the country.

Julie Christie was also a known political thinker and a supporter of left-wing politics in Britain and was on the FBI surveillance list, as indeed was Beatty, and thus, they too became a subject of scrutiny. Mutual studies during her time with Beatty kept him abreast of the rising tide of left-wing protest at the continued fighting in Vietnam, though unlike the vociferous Jane Fonda, he had seldom ventured to the soap box after his involvement with the Democratic campaign in 1968.

However, he was astounded by the turn-out of the anti-war demonstration in Washington on 15 November 1969, when three-quarters of a million people marched through the streets to the Washington Monument in what was the largest single protest in American history. There they cheered their great white hope for change, Senator George McGovern, and listened to songs by John Denver, Arlo Guthrie and the touring cast of *Hair*, and then Pete Seeger led the throng in *Give Peace a Chance*. As breakaway extremists battled with police, hurling smoke bombs, the US Attorney General, John Mitchell, gazing out upon this spectacle, observed to his boss, Richard Nixon, that it looked like a scene from the Russian Revolution.

By early 1971, McGovern had launched himself on the campaign trail for the 1972 presidential election with his assurance that he would pull America out of the Vietnam War. Beatty argued with himself – and others – on the question which faced many of his actor colleagues engaged in political campaigning: should an artist apply himself to commenting on the social issues of the times through his work, or should he actually participate in events of the moment?

Art was a powerful enough medium, but few had the power or ability then to portray through the movies a sufficient response to the Vietnam War, Black Power or inner-city turmoil. Serious exposés of those issues on film lay far in the future.

Beatty made his decision to step out of Hollywood for the duration and donate his entire time and energy for the next eighteen months to the task of attempting to get McGovern into the White House, and his involvement became a crucial element in McGovern's bid for power. It was by no means certain then, indeed it was pretty well uncertain, that McGovern would get the Democratic nomination. He was outsider to the front-running Edmund Muskie, until Nixon's dirty tricks campaigners brought Muskie down.

Beatty joined the McGovern campaign from the beginning and travelled with the senator in the early primary states of New Hampshire and Florida. His famous face opened many doors. He spoke at private gatherings, public meetings, labour halls and college campuses. He was a competent enough public speaker, and quite compelling with his Hollywood aura, but he looked uncomfortable and did not like reeling off political platitudes. At the University of Wisconsin, Beatty declared that McGovern 'has a greater degree of foresight than anyone I know. He is eight to ten years ahead of everyone else in what he perceives the truth to be, and if we can't deal with the truth then what the hell are we doing?' The audiences reacted badly. A rowdy group of students taunted him and forced him to reconsider the issue of whether he should go out up-front as a campaigner.

At first, he wondered whether it was a personal attack, that they did not take kindly to this young multimillionaire from Hollywood who had it all, whose reputation was largely to do with being a great romancer. Would they have done the same to Redford or Newman? He hadn't really considered it, but now he would. The students had a point. It was one thing to impose himself on an audience just because he was who he was, Warren Beatty, movie star; it was quite another to expect them to listen – or accept – anything he might have to say on burning political issues. 'It was not only an embarrassing encounter,' Beatty recalled later, 'but it made me think about my role in the campaign. I came to the conclusion that some members of the public, and especially younger people, were innately suspicious of the motives of some capricious artist attaching some mood of seriousness to his persona by participating in public affairs.'

His sister, Shirley MacLaine, whose private life was far less spectacular, had a far better reception. As they travelled back from Wisconsin, Beatty made a conscious decision to extricate himself from the public side of the campaign and take up a less visible role at the heart of the machine, where he came into close contact with McGovern's youthful campaign manager, Gary Hart, then thirty-two and a former Colorado lawyer. They were immediately compatible; they were about the same age, and were interested in each other, Beatty in Hart's radical ideas and Hart drawn to Beatty's star quality. They even looked alike. This alliance was destined to blossom further in future times, but then, in 1971–2, they had but one aim, which was to get McGovern into the White House.

Beatty assumed the role of political strategist, rather than outgoing activist. He regularly sat in on campaign planning meetings and other more seasoned political advisers found his ideas often unconventional but interesting. The difference was that, not having been there before, he knew no pre-set boundaries. He had the notion that there was a great mass of people out there in the United States of America who were waiting to be motivated into voting Democrat. Beatty admitted that his ideas were 'aimed at the very flexible mass of public opinion which is dangerously changeable.' He conceded, too, that he was full of theatrical, often bizarre ideas as to how McGovern could enlist this silent mass.

But, aside from what some viewed as initial naïveté towards the tough cut and thrust of political campaigning, he was carving for himself an unprecedented role as a Hollywood personality who was at the heart of a party machine, from which he would grow in status and power in the years ahead.

One of his most profitable ideas for the cash-starved McGovern campaign was a model for the future – he suggested a series of coast-to-coast rock concerts to raise money and spread the message. The latter was more of a subliminal aspect initially, since the aim was to boost the McGovern campaign funds and they did not want to scare away customers with political campaigning. There was doubt expressed about this form of electioneering, but Beatty persisted. He actually knew little about rock music himself, though he had many friends in the business. He went on to enlist some top names to join him for five concerts starting in Los Angeles in April 1972. 'He really invented the political concert,' said Gary Hart. 'What he achieved was quite remarkable.'

Beatty rounded up just about every liberal in Hollywood. Stars like Barbra Streisand and Carole King performed at his Los Angeles gig and he persuaded Jack Nicholson to come along with Gene Hackman, Julie Christie and Sally Kellerman to act as ushers, showing the richer supporters to their seats. It was a 16,000 seat sell-out. For the final, and biggest, concert he hired Madison Square Garden in New York, which scared the pants off some of the more nervous among the McGovern campaign team. Would they fill it?

Tickets were up to a hundred dollars each. But he had captured a reunion performance by Simon and Garfunkel, and the supporting acts included Peter, Paul and Mary, Dionne Warwick and Mike Nichols and his former writing partner, humorist Elaine May. Equally attractive was another line-up of celebrity ushers – announced well in advance – which included Candice Bergen, Julie Christie, Bette Davis (who dropped out with a poison ivy rash), Tammy Grimes, Jack Nicholson, Gene Hackman, Goldie Hawn, Dustin Hoffman, James Earl Jones, Stacy Keach, Shirley MacLaine, Paul Newman, Ryan O'Neal, Jon Voight and Raquel Welch. Beatty stayed in the wings directing the show, and never made an appearance. That one concert attracted 19,500 people and raised $450,000.

Not to be outdone, the Nixon camp laid on its own much-photographed celebrity gatherings, with an altogether older and quieter bunch, including John Wayne, James Stewart, Jack Benny, Bing Crosby, Charlton Heston, Eddie Fisher and even Frank Sinatra, who had deserted the Democrats after Kennedy.

Much was made by the pundits of the McGovern in-crowd, and the Republican supporters in the media were not slow to draw comparisons between the contrasting line-ups – Beatty's young and beautiful people, who had been portraying on screen of late all the things that middle-class Americans feared in their confused society, drugs, violence and sex, against Nixon's supporters, heroes of the good old days when traditional morality meant something.

Beatty's concerts were attacked, of course, as liberal rabble-rousing, and even some of McGovern's supporters refused to join in. Robert Redford, who took a far more jaundiced view of politicians was, like Beatty, uncertain that people wanted to listen to what he had to say; they merely wanted to peer at a movie star. So what was the point? He eventually channelled his energies towards environmental issues but, again like Beatty, he adopted a less visible approach and went for greater access to the seat of power.

George McGovern, however, remained ever grateful to Beatty's efforts: 'He took two years out of his life; he travelled around the country making speeches, debating issues, interpreting me to the public and the public to me. He was personally responsible for raising more than a million dollars.' McGovern needed the profile and the money, and he got both. He also won the Democratic nomination and took Missouri senator Thomas Eagleton as his running mate. However, Eagleton was discovered to have suffered from mental illness some years earlier and had received electric shock therapy. He was unceremoniously dumped, and in the ensuing débâcle of choosing a new vice-presidential candidate, the power of Beatty's voice was displayed in a bold political move.

He saw the search for a vice-president as a way of finally consolidating the Democratic Party leadership behind McGovern. There were many party elders in the camp who were lukewarm towards the candidate, to say the least. Beatty took it upon himself to visit the former presidential candidate Hubert Humphrey and, after four hours of debate, persuaded him to accept the nomination as McGovern's running mate if he was publicly summoned. Beatty wanted the party to call a meeting of the Democratic National Committee to formally nominate Humphrey.

He was negotiating at the highest levels in the Democratic Party to influence the selection of a politician who could conceivably become the next Vice-president of the United States. In the event, it did not happen. Those in the smoke-filled rooms accused Beatty of backing Humphrey into a corner, and McGovern settled for Kennedy's brother-in-law, Sargent Shriver.

Still, he was taken seriously enough never to be merely cast aside as a naïve and meddlesome actor tampering with politics. People in high places listened. But his efforts were in vain. America, torn by so many conflicts at that time, was not ready for the liberal policies of McGovern. Nixon's landslide victory – 502 votes in the electoral college against McGovern's paltry seventeen – was so great that it went into the record books.

McGovern was devastated, and many expected that Beatty would slink off back to Beverly Hills and never return to the political arena. Far from it. He may have been disappointed, but he was not disillusioned, and the fact that the Watergate scandal lay somewhere in the background, to emerge in sensational manner the following year, rather put some perspective into McGovern's abysmal poll showing.

Beatty, who had not given a substantive interview to the press for years, allowed himself to be drawn into the open on his political thinking, and especially on Watergate, which concerned the break-in of the Democratic Party headquarters during the election campaign. 'Given the enormity of the Watergate phenomenon,' he said, 'it is hard to evaluate in terms of a single campaign, but I do think that had the public been aware of it before the election, McGovern might have won.'

As far as his own political connections were concerned, he repeated his preparedness to work for the Democratic Party but did not believe he was generous enough to run for public office. He did not rule it out, but at that point in time, he could not see himself running. 'My two years with McGovern were worth it,' he declared. 'I gained a great deal of confidence in my currency. When you participate heavily and keep a low profile – as I did – you learn. Right now, running myself is unattractive. The silly ego rewards in movies are as great as the ones in politics, but the insults to a movie actor don't approach the insults to a politician. Movies are also more fulfilling. Politics is a constant compromise. Art should never be...'

However, politics remained a vital interest and in spite of his denials that he was interested in candidature, there was continued speculation that he might make the move into the front line himself. When Ronald Reagan left the Californian State House a couple of years later, a private poll was conducted for the Democratic Party to assess their man – as yet unnamed – to succeed the Republican Governor. Beatty topped the list of potential candidates. He was said to be mildly titillated by the idea, but held back. He remained more interested in a behind-the-scenes role and was still unconvinced that, in spite of Ronald Reagan's political aspirations, the public was interested in what 'mere' actors had to say.

Not long afterwards, there was also talk of the Democrats attempting to woo him into entering several presidential primaries. He never took it seriously, not least for the fact that he would have presented the media with a golden opportunity of running scandalous headlines from his past. He remained a discreet political force, talking quietly into telephones at the ears of the powerful. Still deeper involvement lay in the future, and especially a decade later, when Gary Hart made his bid for power.

His time out with McGovern was to influence his work in the near future. Three of his forthcoming films had associations with politics: *The Parallax View* concerned a presidential assassination, *Shampoo* was set on election day 1968, and *Reds*, which was still years away from coming to the screen, would be the culmination of his extensive study of the life of John Reed.

Beatty took a year off after the election. He toyed with the John Reed project, and tinkered with a script that would become *Shampoo*. He also rejected various proposals that in the end did much to enhance the career of Robert Redford, including *The Way We Were*, in which Redford starred with Barbra Streisand, *The Sting*, for which Redford received an Oscar nomination, and *The Great Gatsby*, in which Redford was better than the critics gave him credit for.

Beatty also turned down one more controversial film, Bernardo Bertolucci's sexually explicit *Last Tango in Paris*, which eventually went to Marlon Brando – rumour had it that he did not care for the sequence involving a half-pound of best butter. When Beatty did finally settle on his next movie, it would mirror the political intrigue that had engulfed him since the assassination of Robert Kennedy, although he and the producers of *The Parallax View* were quick to point out that the film was not based upon the Kennedy murders.

There were, however, certain obvious parallels which intrigued Beatty although, again, he insisted that he decided to do the movie not because of the politics of the issue – at a time when he was still a high-profile voice in the gun control lobby – but because he admired the producer-director, Alan J. Pakula. The movie tells the story of a presidential candidate who is assassinated and, rather like the inquiries which followed the death of John F. Kennedy, an investigating tribunal announces that the murder was committed by one deranged individual not as the result of a conspiracy. A number of witnesses are systematically killed and a news reporter, played by Paula Prentiss, voices her suspicions to a colleague, Joe, the small-time reporter played by Beatty. She, too, becomes a sudden-death victim.

He begins his own investigation and, in a stylish thriller, packed with suspense and action, concludes that a powerful combine named Parallax has developed a system of setting up puppet-assassins to carry out their murderous activities, during which a second senator is killed later in the movie. The story was based upon Loren Singer's novel and toyed with an idea to be explored in a number of movies, notably *The Manchurian Candidate*, that brainwashing techniques had been employed in a spate of political killings.

Alan Pakula, who produced and directed *The Parallax View*, had recently brought Jane Fonda to her Oscar-winning performance in the thriller *Klute*. He had long discussions with Beatty on his intentions with the film. He explained that he did not want it to appear as a documentary. 'It is not an exposé of what happened in the Kennedy assassinations. I have deliberately set out to stage a fictitious story which takes account of American myth, the fears and suspicions we may have of what might have happened.'

Beatty had his own views on the issue since he had been deeply ensconced in the political scene at the time of Bobby Kennedy's murder. Reviews of the film credit Beatty for a fine, if low-key, performance which was integral to the psychological theme that Pakula was attempting. Paul Zimmerman, in *Newsweek*, praised the director as 'a first-rate stylist whose professionalism and technical acumen – backed by a superbly chosen support troop – characterises American film-making at its best.'

The movie ended as it began, with a remote tribunal dismissing the assassination of a second senator as the work of a single, crazed killer. The issues were so effectively dealt with that some critics believed that audiences would wonder whether it was sufficient for them to be explored in mere melodramatic fiction and Beatty, in his heart, knew it wasn't.

These were unsettling questions which were to remain a burden on the American conscience, and which its establishment has consistently refused to recognise or pursue. They remain unanswered to this day, in spite of continuing attempts by Hollywood, and pretty well everyone else who has tried to unravel the Kennedy killings through the years, most recently with Oliver Stone's controversial movie *J.F.K.*

There was another side issue to *The Parallax View* that was noticeable to Beatty observers. His screen personality –

as opposed to the rather more frivolous one that the tabloids still seemed intent on portraying – was taking on a particular life of its own. Those movie-goers who had disliked Beatty's early style were taking a second look. With the financial freedom that came with *Bonnie and Clyde*, he had made some surprising choices of roles. His choices, sparse though they were in comparison to those of many of his colleagues, were not always popular roles, or even successful movies. He was able to choose a route to satisfaction through a combination of careful selection and business acumen.

The result was a diversity of characters which really defied any accusation of typecasting. He seemed intent on reminding his audience that he was not just another good-looking actor, and plans were already well advanced for his consolidation of his career as actor-impresario. As he helped *The Parallax View* promotional activity with some interviews about his political interest, there was yet to be one more overhang from that era of Bobby Kennedy's assassination.

His next movie, which he had been working on as a writer for some time, was set on election day 1968, and whereas *The Parallax View* explored those darker areas of American myth, his new project was to examine in quasi-Freudian terms the 'age of groovyness', in which he would push back further a few more boundaries and reflect some of the remaining sexual and four-letter reticences in art's playback of life.

14

Shampoo

The edges of explicitness were being pushed ever outwards. Warren Beatty had already made his contribution, but was ready to extend them further. To the more cautious and concerned among the Hollywood élite, and especially those whose roots lay in the old days of studio control, there appeared to be a contest in progress amongst a cabal of film-makers, but largely directors and actors of the so-called new, new wave, who were intent on capping the last example of extremism in sex, bad language and violence with a new and more definitive example.

It was done in the guise of satisfying public demand, demonstrated by the fact that audiences responded whenever the movie promised any of the excitement mentioned above. As the movie industry prepared to enter the decade of the seventies, best summed up by the phrase 'letting it all hang out', literally, the moral code to which it was allegedly supposed to adhere for the U, A or X ratings was looking past its shelf-life.

In November 1968, the old production code which had set the guidelines for sex in the movies since 1930 was finally scrapped. It no longer had any relevance to modern times. It still included such restrictions as 'lustful kissing', sexual perversion or any implication of it, obscenity in word, gesture or reference and complete nudity, and insisted that bedroom scenes be filmed in an aura of 'good taste and delicacy'.

For years this code had produced those coy Doris Day-Rock Hudson-type love scenes where husband and wife usually had separate beds, were always covered by sheets and kept one foot on the floor in any embrace. The code demanded such innocence, and by the mid-sixties it was being broken and ignored, especially by Continental directors who did not recognise it. The new system classified movies with new initials: G for general audiences, PG to be watched by the young at the discretion of parents, R to denote an adult picture which no one under seventeen could see without an accompanying adult, and X for adults only.

The gates had already been prised open. In 1966 Antonioni's *Blow Up* lured huge audiences with flashes of nudity, as did Sidney Lumet's *The Pawnbroker*, although that was an excellent film even without it. As we have seen, Mike Nichols had to secure a special rating for the four-letter words in *Who's Afraid of Virginia Woolf?* Beatty's slow-motion, machine-gun carve-up of Bonnie and Clyde gave a meaning to the label of 'violent' like nothing else had, and when the old production code was dropped at the end of the year of *Bonnie and Clyde*'s massive success, that movie naturally established the level to beat.

Directors like Francis Ford Coppola and Stanley Kubrick capped it with their direction of *The Godfather* and *Clockwork Orange* respectively; Clint Eastwood made his contribution in *Dirty Harry*, while on the front line of sexual boundaries, Mike Nichols faced the wrath of the Supreme Court of Georgia – not to mention the collective might of censors in the United Kingdom, Italy and Canada – slung against Jack Nicholson's sex scenes in *Carnal Knowledge*.

Jack Nicholson was in trouble again in 1973 in the Hal Ashby direction of Robert Towne's screenplay of *The Last Detail*, on account of the fact that the word 'motherfucker' was used on forty-two occasions at a time when a four-letter word broadcast over public airwaves would cause an absolute furore and heads to roll. In fact, expletives often caused more trouble than nudity. Towne refused to cut, stating that the objectors would feel just as badly about twenty-one motherfuckers as forty-two.

Studio bosses cautiously allowed the new wave cabal to continue its revolution and the courts did nothing to hinder the progression, either. A new genre was jostling itself into

position – not to mention a whole new industry of sexploit-
ation pictures which sprang up, ranging from soft porn which
would be permissible in the family cinemas to self-styled tri-
ple-X-rated, hard-core movies designed for the specialist
houses.

All of this might never have come about but for the introduction of the new classification system, and certain films,
such as *Last Tango in Paris*, would never have got past the
old code. Certainly Warren Beatty would have had very considerable trouble with his newest project, *Shampoo*. Commercial viability remained the buzz-word, and anything that
bolstered profits was to be welcomed. As *Variety* reported in
1973, between 1969 and 1972, the major Hollywood studios
had lost $600 million between them, and the latest surveys
showed that annual attendances had fallen from 4,060 million
in 1946 to 820 million in 1972.

Yet 'the deal' for a movie became harder and harder to
make. Faceless executives in far-off conglomerates often held
sway over a project, and more and more, 'packaging' – where
a producer puts together a package of director, script, stars
and distribution – became the all-important factor in obtaining backing.

Beatty had undoubtedly studied the scene with great care
and deliberation and, while he continued to recognise that
projects had to be commerce-led, he refused to bend on the
creative aspect. 'It came out of the discovery,' he explained in
a trade interview, 'that if you were to mass-release movies
and pump a tremendous amount of advertising money into
television marketing – which was finally happening – you
could make a hell of a lot of money. We all attempted to cash
in on the commercial possibilities of the movies and so we
moved into an era of what we now call "high concept". Can
you tell what this movie is about in a thirty-second spot? If
so, we can make a lot of money. The trouble was that eventually people who wrote about films began to evaluate a film
on its business and not its merit.'

He had decided the direction of what he perceived as his
next great coup, which he intended would emulate the success
of *Bonnie and Clyde*. He had to make an impact, cause controversy, stir up some interest and get the punters punting,

which is what every maker of mass-market movies sets out to do although few, perhaps fewer than one in ten, succeed.

In 1973, when he was ready to move, it was no mere chance that he involved himself with the duo which had brought us Jack Nicholson in *The Last Detail*, writer Robert Towne and director Hal Ashby. He had approached other directors from the mainstream but few were interested in his new producer-actor venture. Towne and Ashby were fresh from the market-place of controversy, well-versed in the field of doing battle with the establishment. They would need that experience, because Beatty was aiming to stretch a point with the new ratings, and to jack up what was permissible in a 'PG' film to previously unattainable heights.

To be absolutely truthful, although *Shampoo* would be dressed up as some kind of social discourse on the morals of the late sixties, it was also a sex film, almost soft porn, whose content would be sure to attract publicity because of its explicit nature. The trick was to achieve this level of publicity without actually getting it banned or X-rated.

Warren Beatty was nothing but certain of the route to com-mercial success, and when it was his own film, he had few qualms about exploiting it, but in a very special way – like opening with an orgasm being interrupted by a telephone call and having Julie Christie going down under the table moan-ing, 'I want to suck your cock... oh God, I must suck it.' Such an approach not only broke new ground, it tapped into the gossip market for publicity purposes after the charming twosome's five-year affair.

In terms of work, Beatty was due a spectacular movie. Hollywood was expecting it of him any day now, after his casual coasting over the past two and a half years, during which time he had done nothing but travel, write, talk on the telephone for hours on end and date girls, and more girls. Names now mentioned included Carly Simon, Joni Mitchell and Dennis Hopper's ex-wife Brooke Hayward, daughter of Margaret Sullavan.

Occasionally there was a difference. He rescued Natalie Wood's sister Lana from a violent relationship when she tele-phoned him seeking a quiet haven. She was broke and had recently been estranged from Natalie. Beatty sent a car to

202

collect her, provided her with a suite at the Beverly Wilshire for herself and her baby and Lana, who used to hate him when he was with Natalie, found him 'thoughtful, considerate and supportive' and, when she had settled down, 'a passionate and inventive lover.'

Beatty reached the summer of 1973 with his script for *Shampoo* pushing him towards activity. *The Parallax View* was awaiting release, which would be inexplicably delayed until the summer of the following year, and in the meantime Beatty's screen role of investigative journalist was being played out in the real-life exposé of Watergate, which was tearing the heart out of American political life and leading to Richard Nixon's resignation. By then, he would have been off the screen for almost three years.

Even the story of *Shampoo* had been loitering. It had begun six years earlier, when Beatty was in London after the release of *Bonnie and Clyde*. Robert Towne, who had been his script consultant on that movie, was also in England, and they began toying with a new screenplay based on the life and times of an inveterate womaniser. The inspiration for the plot had a number of influences, but it vaguely originated from a script Towne had written for television a few years earlier, called *Breaking Point*, which explored the dilemma of a modern Don Juan with 'so many pretty girls and so little time'.

The idea was further enhanced when Beatty and Towne went off to the Chichester Festival Theatre, where they watched a performance of William Wycherley's coarsest and strongest play, *The Country Wife*, written in 1675 and partly founded on Molière's *Ecole des Femmes*. Maggie Smith took the lead at Chichester as the seduced wife whose lover hides behind the pretence of being homosexual to ward off the husband's suspicions.

As the script gathered momentum, the central character, the roaming rake, was fictionally transposed to modern Los Angeles as a campy hairdresser with a voracious sexual appetite, which he sates under the guise of being gay. Beatty and Towne wrote a script of more than 200 pages under the working title of *Hair*. This was superseded by the arrival of the musical play of the same name which momentarily shocked even swinging London in 1968 because of its nudity.

Other influences in that same year included two best-selling novels, Gore Vidal's *Myra Breckenridge*, the notorious 'exposure' of sex in Hollywood which Mike Sarne turned into a pale shadow of a movie, and John Updike's *Couples*, which also followed the theme of America's obsession with sex and was based upon the spouse-swapping activities of a Connecticut village.

Along the way, Towne and Beatty had a falling-out over the plotting of the script and they barely spoke for six months. Towne says later that it was like two brothers quarrelling: 'Although I don't know anyone who's a bigger prick, there's no one I love and admire more.'

The project was set aside and nothing happened until the autumn of 1973. Beatty, still taken with the idea, wrote his own draft script, which was influenced still further by Jean Renoir's *Rules of the Game*. He reckoned no movie about hypocritical, sophisticated fools having a good time and being funny in the middle of a social catastrophe – which is how he assessed Richard Nixon's 1968 election victory – could fail to be influenced by *Rules of the Game*, unless the writer had been asleep for the last half-century.

Towne checked into a Beverly Hills hotel for an eight-day huddle with director Hal Ashby and produced a new version of the original he had written with Beatty. Eventually, the two scripts were merged and rewritten, with Towne and Beatty sharing the credit, and *Shampoo* was finally born.

There was another similar story around, too. In 1971 retired manicurist Bernice Mann, an unpublished writer from Los Angeles who had spent twenty-five years working in swank Beverly Hills salons such as Pagano's, had sent a twenty-nine-page outline for a movie to Columbia. She called her play *Women Plus* and registered it with the copyright office the same year, but received no other word than a rejection slip. When *Shampoo* was released in 1965, Bernice screamed blue murder and accused Beatty and Towne of plagiarism.

The fact that Columbia was distributing *Shampoo* seemed more than a coincidence, and eventually her lawyers filed a claim for damages. Towne responded angrily and said he had never heard of the woman or her script. He said his own was 'the most personal screenplay I ever worked on because of the people I knew and the events that had happened to me.'

Beatty made similar protestations and said he assumed that it was 'a nuisance suit'. Lawyers for Columbia, Beatty and Towne decided however that to avoid any costly litigation they were prepared to dispose of the 'nuisance' by offering an out-of-court settlement of $17,000. Bernice refused, and the issue went to a fifteen-day hearing before the Los Angeles Superior Court where a jury agreed that there were a number of similarities and awarded her $185,000. The judge, however, did not accept the verdict and the case went to the Los Angeles Supreme Court, where the decision was reversed. Bernice therefore lost the $185,000 and faced heavy legal costs.

Beatty remained adamant as to the origins of his idea, which went back into the late sixties, and he had carefully chosen the moment in which the story of *Shampoo* was set, during the US election of 1968. 'It was the moment when this country came face to face with the hypocrisies that *Shampoo* represents – the day we turned to each other and realised that we had elected Richard Nixon with Spiro Agnew as his number two. George, the central character, is like the country, a guy who looks like he's got the world by the tail one day and next morning he realises he hasn't.'

The *Shampoo* story revolves around barely more than a day in the life of George Roundy, the agile and much sought-after star of a Beverly Hills hair salon, who is aiming to start his own business. His subjects are women preparing themselves for one of America's social rituals, the election night party on 5 November 1968, when mini-skirts and Richard Nixon are in fashion.

Beatty assembled old friends and past lovers and his coup in getting Julie Christie was one more example of his uncanny ability for keeping past lovers as friends. Julie and Goldie Hawn completed the now all-important movie 'package' that Beatty would sell to a studio, retaining a percentage for himself as producer, co-writer and star. He was working on a budget of less than $5 million, which was chickenfeed compared to the cost of some contemporary movies, but in spite of his recent track record, he had to trail around Hollywood to secure the finance and a distribution deal with Columbia.

The casting was brilliant. His co-stars Julie, Goldie, Lee Grant and Carrie Fisher first of all guaranteed an abundance of gossip, speculation and publicity but also assured him of superb performances in the key female roles. Of this there is no question from the opening sequence of the coitus inter-ruptus with the most voracious of his clients, Lee Grant, whose husband (Jack Warden) is the Republican fat cat who is convinced that Beatty is a homosexual and thus no threat. He is also involved with Warden's daughter (Carrie Fisher) while Warden himself has a mistress (Julie Christie), who also happens to be George's former girlfriend. Goldie Hawn plays his current girlfriend, and she is demanding more of his time and affection. He roars from body to body on his motorcycle, but as the election night party approaches, so does the updated Don Juan's chastening.

The party brings matters to a head. With a tipsy Christie wishing to apply her mouth to his genitalia as they slither under the table, his betrayals of all three women are realised and he loses them all, even Goldie, who goes off with a richer and older man. The last scenes, where he realises that he, not the women, has been used, and which leave him in the depths of self-pity, are important.

Years later, in conversation with Norman Mailer, Beatty laid much of the credit at the door of his co-stars. 'I felt Julie, and Goldie also, made the picture work for me, and particularly the ending of *Shampoo* with Julie – that was after our relationship. The integrity on that face. That person. It's never faltered.'

Activity on the set was, as usual, frenetic. The production schedule and the budget demanded completion in sixty days. Beatty, working eighteen hours a day, converted his dressing-room into his apartment for the duration. His thirty-seventh birthday occurred during filming. The cast threw a party for him and just as he cut the cake, blushing and shy, a hired redheaded go-go dancer streaked into the midst of the celebration to present him with a birthday kiss. He was locked in an embrace before he realised she was naked and he went red in the face.

Back at work, he was rehearsing a scene in the hair salon

and he gave advice to director Hal Ashby on how he saw the scene being played. 'I'll show you,' he said, straddling himself across the lap of a brunette so that his groin was touching her lower regions while he caressed her hair with his hands, like hairdressers do.

Shampoo went much deeper than sex. There were political undertones, though the Nixon-Agnew jokes were somewhat contrived, and the comedy was excellent, with some classic one-liners. But the commentary on the flotsam and jetsam of life in Los Angeles was more devastating than most of its period. The movie is typically sixties, and with all the influences gathered in the script it becomes another Beatty exploration of human frailties and one which, in the end, puts the producer (Beatty) in a rare light as the confident, artistic motivator of what is a very good film. The portrayal of George, who ends up baring his sensitive, desperate soul, could have been more clinical and harder in the final analysis of his actions, but then perhaps Beatty was subconsciously swayed by other considerations.

George, the heterosexual stud always on the move and constantly engaged in urgent copulation, would naturally be seen to bear some resemblance to the star himself, and few writers could resist comparing his own rich, complicated life with that of hairdresser George. Was the screenplay a warning letter to himself, about the risks of burning out? Either way, it made for plenty of publicity.

Beatty would, for a change, answer frankly and willingly the press inquiries on the glaring similarity of his film role to some of his own alleged activity. 'People can make what they want of it,' he said without the bat of an eyelid. 'There's a lot of me in every character I play, and I think that all of us have to close out that promiscuous phase in our lives. But in a lot more important ways, George is simply not me.' Neither did he feel embarrassed about the homosexual connotations. It seemed a good thought, he said, to upset the conventional idea that hairdressers were homosexual, as well as the Freudian assumption that all Don Juans were latent homosexuals.

For all the discussion of Freudian subliminals, *Shampoo* divided the critics on how the movie should be perceived – as a significant satire or exploitative frippery. Actually, it was both, carefully and meticulously scripted by Beatty and Towne to cover every angle. As Charles Champlin's review in the *Los Angeles Times* pointed out, '*Shampoo* will be worth studying a century from now to know what part of our times was like ... Its images manage fairly ingeniously to keep a few letters east of X and the combination of word and half-seen deed makes *Shampoo* seem more explicit than *Last Tango in Paris* ... Warren Beatty out-reveals Brando by a few square inches of sacroiliac [flesh].'

Occasional adversary Stanley Kauffman, writing in the *New Republic*, was in a spitting rage when he came out of the theatre, and penned his reactions accordingly: 'It is disgusting! Fake porno of the most revolting kind.' The US Catholic Conference weighed in with similar disapproval, giving it a C rating, as being morally objectionable to Catholic society, with a conceded beautiful cast nonetheless acting out the most ugly scenes of sex shown outside of hard-core theatres.

It was all music to the ears of the theatre managers, who watched the queues stretching around the block and counted their takings with glee. If there were now any doubts about Beatty's ability as a film-maker and producer with a clear eye on society, then *Shampoo*'s commercial success would banish them. It was a huge bonanza at the box office, grossing more than $45 million worldwide from the outlay of less than $5 million, and everyone concerned reaped a rich harvest. Robert Towne, who took a flat fee of $125,000 for his work on the script, also had five per cent of the profits. Beatty's share was substantial, said to be in excess of $8 million in the first year alone. No actor had ever made so much from a single film.

The control Beatty was able to exercise over the outcome of the movie was important, from scripting to the final cut and even on into the promotion, involvements which he demanded as part of his contract, keeping his hands on the creative element. As the hype for *Shampoo* was being prepared, not a word of promotional copy escaped from the press office or the advertising people without his approval. That was his power, and what other actor in Hollywood held such sway?

He had by then decided that he would prefer to make no

other movies as merely an actor, unless the role was so incredible that he could not turn it down. A pattern was being established and his future was as producer-actor, the line of pursuit he had been working towards since *Bonnie and Clyde* and which had provided him with his greatest successes. There was still one commitment as an actor which he had made to director Mike Nichols soon after they'd met in Canada, which was to star in a film with Jack Nicholson.

Mike Nichols could seemingly do no wrong. He had four films in the seventies list of 'all-time rental champs' produced by *Variety* – *The Graduate*, *Who's Afraid of Virginia Woolf?* *Carnal Knowledge* and *Catch 22*. They were all significant movies, breaking moulds and providing signposts for the future. He was seen to have won the day over the critical arguments which raged about his handling of the sex scenes and bad language that were a feature of his biggest successes, arguing that the inclusion of scenes which reflected true social behaviour were made artistically and not for exploitation purposes.

It was a debatable point, but the reaction of contemporary audiences supported this notion, though detractors in the Bible Belt would say, conversely, that it demonstrated exactly the point they were making – that explicitness was merely a commercial ingredient which would prompt mimicry in society, especially amongst the young. Looking back from a vantage point in the 1990s, it might be said that they had a point!

Professionally, Nichols gained the respect and friendship of many Hollywood stars of the day. Anyway, the new movie which would bring Nichols, Nicholson and Beatty together was not a sex film. It was a romantic comedy set in the 1920s, written by Nicholson's pal, Adrien Joyce (a pseudonym for Carol Eastman), who had written Nicholson's successful *Five Easy Pieces* in 1970.

Nicholson took the script to Nichols, and after meeting Beatty in Canada, asked him if he would care to join in. They read the script and agreed that they could have some fun. The plot was a story about an heiress who had to go through a marriage of convenience, weds the Nicholson character but prefers Beatty, who is already married. The most encouraging aspect was the introduction of a new actress, Stockard Channing, who played the heiress.

They gathered on location in the summer of 1974, when Beatty had just finished filming *Shampoo* and Nicholson was receiving massive acclaim for *Chinatown*, the quintessential seventies movie directed by Roman Polanski, and for which Robert Towne's screenplay won an Oscar. The hype for *The Fortune* therefore centred on the fact that the two hottest male stars in Hollywood had finally come together.

Publicity material surrounding its release in May 1975 suggested more than the film would deliver, and critical reaction was cool. One of the problems was that both men were committed scene-stealers, Nicholson by his natural presence and Beatty by his devices and intensity.

Although the reviews of *The Fortune* were mixed, Nicholson went out on the road to rustle up some media support and the audiences responded to the intriguing prospect of seeing these two mercurial and much-publicised figures working together. That was the trouble with this movie – it wasn't big enough for the both of them. Certainly the critics expected something far more spectacular. They needed a much stronger vehicle and lines which would spark off each other. It was unsatisfactory, and a movie that Beatty seldom spoke of in the future, and one was left with the impression that he only did it because of his new friendship with Nicholson.

Off screen, the closeness of the two men had also developed towards a relationship that would inspire legendary accounts of their joint excursions down the boulevards. In reality, their meetings were not as frequent as the media was inclined to suggest, two raunchy males out on the town every Friday night, or whenever, picking up whatever stray girls they could meet or having model acquaintances flown in from various parts of the globe. The latter happened and they were good buddies, though they might not see each other for long periods of time.

Nicholson, far more open about his personal life to interviewers than Beatty, was asked during a long interview with *Rolling Stone* in 1986 to explain what attracted him to Beatty as a friend. He replied: 'The noncommunicable things about an unusual circumstance in life that we have in common.

He's very smart, very free of bullshit and emotionally unde-manding. I haven't seen Warren for months but he is the type of person that if you don't hear from him for a year, it doesn't shake anything. He can say no simply, and I can't, while I can say yes simply and he can't. He can presume he knows better for you than you do yourself, and he's right. I can never presume I know better than anybody, and I'm wrong. I tease him about being a pro. Warren would never relate to this . . . I take a reverse narcissistic pride in not over-tarting it up as an actor. He knows this is my narcissism and I'm comfortable when he says it. I always tell people a little too much that I don't wear make up. But I don't because I look bad . . . but I got some tricks from Warren that he learned in the English theatre. If you're going to be lit for a photograph you put dark powder here [pointing to his hairline] because it keeps the light from making the hair you do have disappear. There are certain things Warren is just not ashamed about, but I am. Other than that, if I don't know what I'm thinking and I've got to talk sense, I talk to Warren. He can also, however, bore the shit out of me!'

There were not many other similarities between the two men, apart from their penchant for the chase. Their lifestyles ran in a sort of parallel as far as women were concerned, but Nicholson was a far more outgoing man who was surrounded by close friends who had been with him since he was a nobody, and who mingled with his new and powerful intimates like Robert Evans, the head of Paramount, Robert Towne and, lately, Roman Polanski. It was said that if you had Nicholson as a friend, he was there for life.

Beatty had many, many acquaintances. His head was filled with hundreds of memorised telephone numbers that he could recite without reference to a book. He could call anyone, any-where at any time to do with anything. He had friends in the highest of places, not merely in America but in Europe, Russia, Japan and pretty well every other important inter-national centre. But who were his true friends? Who were those who even had his trust of friendship? Very, very few people in reality. Because of his mobility, few people would see Beatty on a regular basis unless they were living and travelling with him. And he travelled light.

One friend of both Beatty and Nicholson observed: 'Warren and Jack? They were like Neil Simon's odd couple – Lemmon and Matthau in the movie. Jack was blowing grass and walking around in a crumpled suit and scruffy sneakers, not bothering about his looks or whether he was getting wrinkles or if his hair was falling out. Warren, on the other hand, kept himself in pristine condition, worried about his appearance, never used hip language or current slang expressions, checked himself regularly in the mirror, no drugs or booze – just sex and talking quietly into the telephone, which was his second most important appendage.

'I suppose they shared the same attitudes about life; they were both utterly dedicated to the sexual act as the greatest form of pleasure and both are extremely intelligent men. But Jack was always Jack like we know him today, super cool behind the black shades, super hip and really laid-back. That's what made him the hero of the college kids and the campuses – and they didn't go for Warren at all. In fact, they used to boo him. Jack never ran anywhere, except on Bob Evans's tennis court, but Warren was always bouncing, perhaps not physically, but you always got the impression of movement . . . nice to see you, must fly . . . you know, impromptu. Jack always had a gathering of friends around him. His house, which he bought before he could afford it, was his pride and was open to all who knew how to get past the security gate. He began collecting works of art, which Warren seemed to have no interest in, and he had this bowl of money, just plain dollar bills, on the coffee table – just to make a point; he'd made it but it could easily blow away.

'Warren seemed to me to be the proverbial rolling stone. He gathered no moss; nothing. He had no possessions to speak of, nor at that time even a house he actually lived in. The only thing that would slow him down was if you got him on to politics or the movie business or Julie Christie. Then he would talk and talk, especially about politics, when you would feel your eyelids uncontrollably snapping shut.

'There was another distinct difference. Jack would help any friend in distress; you could actually depend on it. Money. Car. Girls. All you had to do was ask. Warren was charming, of course, always. But you never got the same vibes from him.

212

You speak as you find. I once heard Lillian Hellman call Warren her foul-weather friend, the first person to call when you were in trouble. Lillian was a good friend; Warren and Julie when they were together would spend Christmas at her place. Conversely, I have heard people say that Warren wouldn't walk across the street to help you. I think that is a bit extreme. You see, he was always in such a hurry that he could not stop to consider the problems of others – unless they affected him, too.'

This was perhaps his Achilles' heel, that he could never quite appreciate the needs and expectations of others around him, and one of the reasons why his previous relationships had stalled. One more was about to be added to the list.

15

Michelle, Briefly

At its highest point, Mulholland Drive looks down on a spectacular night-time vision of a hundred-mile carpet of lights in the San Fernando Valley. It was here that Warren Beatty bought a house which he had, as yet, hardly lived in. The sunny living-room with its polished oak floors and ceiling-to-floor windows overlooked this amazing panorama, and among the sparse furniture and possessions he had a telescope that he used to look down into it more closely. It was once the cherished home of opera singer Lauritz Melchior, set in acres of pinewoods above Beverly Hills, not far from Nicholson's house. It was the house he was looking for when he planned to settle to domestic bliss with Julie Christie before they drifted along their separate ways. As he and Nicholson finished making *The Fortune*, it became the home of Michelle Phillips and her daughter China, then six, who had recently moved out of Nicholson's life and into Beatty's.

The story of Michelle's periods of residence at Mulholland Drive, first with Nicholson and then with Beatty, went back three years or more, and although the story represents a diversion from the chronology of Beatty's movements, it paints a vivid portrait of Hollywood not far off the one Beatty had just captured in another way in *Shampoo*.

Michelle Phillips, the former singer with the Mamas and Papas, had come through a divorce from the group's lead singer John Phillips. They wrangled over the custody of their daughter when Michelle became involved with Dennis Hopper, Nicholson's good friend and co-star in *Easy Rider*. Hopper was himself once talked of as the potential second James Dean. He appeared with Dean in *Rebel Without a Cause* and *Giant*, and was in Dean's circle of closest associates.

Hopper had long ago brought the wrath of the Hollywood establishment down upon his head. 'Come the revolution,' he would retort, stoned, at posh parties, 'this crowd will be dead.' At that time, in 1970–71, Hopper had an experimental appetite for chemicals and drugs of every permutation, which led him to erratic behaviour. He was also affected by various traumas in his life, such as the divorce from Brooke Hayward, whose parents were the epitome of Hollywood establishment, and the tragic burning down of the mansion he shared with her, in which he lost much of his written and painted work.

In 1970, John Phillips was not pleased about this man becoming a possible stepfather to his daughter. However, Michelle moved in with Hopper while he was working on his own new picture, *The Last Movie*, which was being shot on location in Peru. Hopper's film was a disaster, not so much because of the movie itself but because of its message, which berated the Hollywood system and the people who ran it. Universal, who provided the backing, refused to release it and he was in the depths of despair. In the meantime, he and Michelle Phillips decided they were in love and were married; they invited 200 guests for the ceremony and Hopper built a nursery for China at his ranch.

Eight days later Michelle, anxious to resume a career of her own, went off to Nashville for a singing engagement, and that weekend she and John Phillips were reunited briefly for a concert at the UCLA in Los Angeles. Dennis had been warned he'd better not turn up because John was there. He decided he was going and arrived indignantly at the hall, but was refused entry because there were no seats. He said he would stand, but the attendant said no and Hopper punched him in the mouth and kicked the door open.

At the interval, he went backstage where he was confronted by two policemen who wanted to question him about the incident earlier. They were about to arrest him when Joan Baez came out of Michelle's dressing-room. She explained who he was and they straightened things out. Dennis went into Michelle's dressing-room where a crowd of people were drinking champagne. John Phillips asked him to pay the bill for the drinks because he was short of money, and then they all went over to Phillips' house for a giant party.

'I spent the whole evening going from room to room trying to find Michelle,' Hopper recalled. 'At the end, when I had sort of given up and was watching television, she turned up. So we went off to bed. Now, you've got to know I was really in love with Michelle. Devoted to her. She's a very sensitive person, too, and I can't paint her black. But anyway, I went home and she called me up the next day and said she wasn't coming back. Click! We had been married eight days . . . eight fucking days.'

Michelle called Nicholson, who was a good friend to both, and told him she could no longer stand Dennis's terrible depressions and the temperament. Dennis was a lovely guy and all that, but the marriage was the biggest mistake of her life. Jack offered her comfort and accommodation. Later they became lovers, and Nicholson telephoned Hopper and said that out of politeness he was letting him know he and Michelle were together. 'Best of luck, man,' said Hopper. 'I still love her, but it's over between us . . .'

Michelle eventually moved into Jack's new house on Mulholland Drive, next door to his idol, Marlon Brando. It was a pleasant and multi-faceted house and Bruce Dern said that Nicholson thought that they were *the* couple; they had it all.

Everything went well for a year or more, and then the relationship began to become strained. Michelle was seeking her own career and the pressures of two professionals, one working and one not, increased the strain. After years on the road with the Mamas and Papas, Michelle was definitely not the slippers-and-fireside home-maker. There was talk of her being cast in a movie project Hal Ashby was putting together with Nicholson, a remake of *The Postman Always Rings Twice*, but MGM pulled out because they did not think she was a big enough name (Nicholson later made it with Jessica Lange).

Anyway, things did not improve and Jack even bought a smaller house next door to his in the compound to try to keep Michelle with him. His pal Harry Dean Stanton said, 'He thought that by giving her some space she would stay, but come the spring of 1973 Michelle was away.'

Not long afterwards, Nicholson met Angelica Huston at a party given by her father, John, who was working with Nicholson on *Chinatown*. In the movie Faye Dunaway was Huston's daughter, and one of his lines to Nicholson was, 'Are you sleeping with her yet?' which had off-screen connotations lost on the audience. By then he was, and Anjelica moved into the Mulholland Drive residence, sharing the bedroom recently vacated by Michelle.

Beatty, who according to his associate Dick Sylbert, liked to be kept informed of splits, matrimonial crises or divorces 'because he was great with wounded birds', had his house not far from Jack's. Simply buying the house was a traumatic move; he just did not know how to live in one. His life, as we have noted, had been spent in hotel suites. Food was room service or restaurants; cars were standard models or rented; clothes were what he carried around in his holdalls or bought at his destination. He had no wardrobe to speak of and no belongings, no works of art, no collections other than piles of books and old scripts.

What would he do with such a house? He eventually spent months trying to decide the décor and remodelling. He spent years trying to decide upon the furniture and rented some for so long that the store eventually gave it to him. He would forget to switch off the lights, and leave them burning for days; and then in the autumn of 1974 he installed his latest love, Michelle, and her daughter China.

Nicholson denied any hand in these developments. 'Michelle and Warren's relationship was nothing to do with me,' he said. 'I was going with Anjelica Huston when they got together. Warren's high-school-principled parents would have been proud of the way it was handled. Michelle, being the lady she is, took the trouble to call me and ask if I had any feelings about them getting together, which I did. I thought it was fabulous because I like them both very much. Michelle's a real stand-up woman. You can't get her to do anything dishonourable. And . . . she can move it!'

The house was the house of a bachelor, and a home envisioned without a woman's influence. Both Beatty and Michelle stood to glean new experiences, especially Michelle after her recent experiences in the rough-and-tumble world of two of the great heroes of counter-culture. Hopper, a generous friend and lover, had taken a violent swerve in life which led him to his years of drink and drugs from which he did not emerge until the eighties. Nicholson, never a user of hard drugs, made no secret of the fact that he supported the legalisation of pot and had admitted in his *Playboy* interview that he was a regular user of marijuana. Who wasn't in Hollywood?

Well, actually, Beatty wasn't, and for years Michelle, through her time in the music business, had been surrounded by the sweet smell of smouldering grass and people who not only resented authority, but kicked against people who thought they were *it*. In Beatty, she would find a man who rarely smoked even ordinary cigarettes and even then did not inhale. His drinking was moderate to low, and when he was working he drank only milk. He chose his food carefully and stuck to a routine designed to take care of his body and his looks. He also had a technique which was like no other lover she had ever had; the whisperings in the ear, promising her anything and telling her how much he loved her, and her child, were music to an unsettled, perhaps rather vulnerable Michelle Phillips. It had the makings of an interesting relationship.

By the time *Shampoo* was premiered and opened at the Coronet Theatre, New York on 11 February 1975, the Beatty-Phillips liaison had not only become common knowledge, but was achieving the usual kind of will-he-won't-he-marry-this-one speculation which was becoming somewhat tiresome. New and upcoming gossip columnists seemed to believe they were breaking new ground with their revelations that Beatty was intending to wed. Hedda Hopper, Louella Parsons and Sheilah Graham had written identical stories a decade and a half earlier and repeated them through the years. Only the names changed. Was there a chance of this affair resolving itself in any way different to the last?

Michelle said she was in love with him and they lived like a family; sometimes he would drive China to school. Then he would revert to bachelorhood in the seclusion of the Beverly Wilshire penthouse, where he would go to work and make telephone calls. Beatty tried to keep Michelle in the background, knowing the kind of media pressure to which she would be subjected, and when they flew to England for the London premiere of *Shampoo* in April, he wanted Michelle kept out of sight of the strident British tabloid press. She protested her displeasure at being shut away by day and having to be most discreet about their ventures out into the London night-life.

Rows ensued. Then Michelle hopped on a plane back to Los Angeles, leaving Beatty to tour on, promoting the hell out of *Shampoo*. Neither did it slip the attentions of the pursuing and competing reporters that he had dined with Russian actress Viktoria Fyodorova in between visits to Paris, back to New York, Los Angeles and London again in August.

Julie Christie, who had locked herself away for months, surfaced at the same time and on 25 August 1975 they were observed dining at Leith's, a fashionable gourmet restaurant in Notting Hill, London, where Beatty refused a secluded table and chose one of the most visible, situated under a spotlight where he, dressed all in white, and she in gypsy clothes replete with large shawl, conducted a dignified argument during most of the hour-long visit.

A week later they both left for Los Angeles, Christie returning to the Malibu house and he to the Beverly Wilshire, and later Mulholland Drive, where Michelle still lived, though not for much longer. As with most of his past encounters, their relationship did not end with a huge bust-up, merely a parting of the ways. She admitted not long afterwards that she, of all people, there in the thick of Hollywood, should have known better than to move in with him in the first place. Hopper was a life-curdling experience, Nicholson was just too good to her, but also promiscuous. Beatty . . . well, he was something else. She was in therapy for two years after leaving him, trying to get over his technique. She said it took her that long to realise that when he said, 'I want to marry you . . . I want you to have my babies', he was just saying the things she wanted to hear. 'I don't think he felt that marriage was either a happy or productive way of life,' said Michelle. 'He preferred not to be involved. What satisfied him more was a shallow, meaningless relationship which he believed was healthier. Perhaps he meant they were the only kind he could have.'

After so much media coverage about the prospect of a marriage at last, the discovery of the split came as a shock. Opinions were canvassed, as always, but public analyses of Warren Beatty the man were meaningless. Privately, his acquaintances were split over his motives and intentions – was he using his romances with high-profile women (as opposed to the lesser known, of whom there were many, and who no one ever heard about) as a career move, milking the publicity that comes with such alliances, or was it, as Michelle suggested, that he was unable to contemplate a serious and absolute commitment? It was a fashionable dinner-party topic: 'Heard the latest Beatty story . . .?'

What was it that made him, and Nicholson for that matter, speak as if they distrusted marriage and women? Was there something in that noncommunicable fact that Nicholson talked about – which presumably meant that three strong women had played important roles for both in their childhood years? Had they recognised a starting point? *Playboy* tried to pin Nicholson down on the subject when they interviewed him during his time with Michelle Phillips. He replied that marriage was not on his agenda; nor would it be. He spent the next seventeen years after Phillips unmarried to Anjelica Huston, until he began his relationship with Rebecca Broussard, who had the first of two babies with him in 1990.

Beatty, on the few occasions he could be pinned down on the subject, invariably prised himself off the ropes by some obscure comment, sometimes joking that if he ever got married he would do it before noon, then if it didn't work out the whole day wasn't ruined. Or, more seriously, he would say that the marriage contract had serious flaws and so many loopholes that you could drive a coach and horses through it. Whimsical locution was an easy route to fending off the unwanted.

As we have already seen, he had this uncanny knack of retaining old friendships, but how did women at large view him in the mid to late seventies, when feminist groups were surging and women's voices were being heard? In my biography of Nicholson, I suggested that if a special court were constituted to hear accusations against men who had sinned against the rights and dignity of women, someone, somewhere would make the charges stick against Jack, the Great

Seducer. The same would undoubtedly apply to Beatty, and it was perhaps an apt time, so soon after his split from Michelle Phillips, for a women's group to summons him before them and demand that he account for himself.

It was not intended as a personal interrogation, although that is what it became when, in 1976, he agreed to join a panel of speakers at the Second International Festival of Women's Films in New York. One suspects he looked at the invitation with some bemusement that he should receive it. Let's see how things developed . . .

For the women who organised this event, the motives were very serious. It was staged first to exhibit and discuss women's films that might not otherwise get shown because of their lack of commercial viability, and secondly to discuss issues concerning the American movie industry which had in recent years moved entirely to large-scale productions leaving no room for middle-ground or art films, and virtually no opportunity for women's films or women producers, directors or writers. When did anyone ever see a major American-made film directed by a woman? It just did not happen, whereas there were far greater opportunities in countries like France.

All of this was important to those interested in the women's film movement. The organisers also had five panels arranged to discuss with the audiences various topics of film-making, and the one to which Beatty was attached was called, aptly but without Beatty in mind, 'Where is Love?', which offered considerable potential for debate.

Alongside Beatty, the organisers had booked his old friend and controversial director Arthur Penn and two prominent female stars, Dyan Cannon and Jeanne Moreau. Beatty made it a condition of his appearance that there should be no advance publicity so as to avoid a media circus. The names of the panel should merely be pinned on the festival noticeboard shortly ahead of the meeting, which was held in a school hall on West Seventieth Street. This was done, and actually there were a few seats not taken when the panel assembled – minus Cannon, who had had to cry off at the last moment.

Was Beatty at last to meet his match, confronted by rows and rows of serious, intelligent women with pinned-up hair and intense, bespectacled faces, ready to put him on trial for all those past misdemeanours they had been reading about for years?

Would he be lynched and strung up from the nearest lamppost?

Would he, at the very least, be stripped naked and tarred and feathered, with particular reference to his genitalia?

No.

For one thing, the ladies of the Second International Festival of Women's Films were not in the mould of serious-minded harridans, as Hollywood might have cast them in a film. Molly Haskell, who convened and chaired this particular panel, reported:

'I as moderator tried desperately without success to hold the discussion to ideas that obviously nobody was interested in, with an audience who had come for names, addresses and phone numbers ... preferably Beatty's. And Beatty, with a sexual cunning one had to admire, for all its transparency, galvanised the love-hatred in the room, incited the rage and the tears ... and he had them eating out of his hand.'

The bedlam that developed was slow in starting, but it was Beatty who gently, almost covertly, lit the blue touchpaper and stood back to await the fireworks that followed. First, as Molly Haskell introduced the panellists, Beatty took Jeanne Moreau into his arms for a long and passionate embrace, explaining that he had not seen her for many months. Then, he coolly leaned towards Molly, took the corner of her flowered corduroy jacket in his fingers and began cleaning the lenses of his spectacles on the cloth – a cool, calculated and cheeky move if ever there was one. Molly explained afterwards that she was so stunned by this provocative act that all she could do was ignore it, although with hindsight she would have loved to have made some witty quip, or cut off the corner of the jacket which Beatty had fingered and auctioned it off.

But she proceeded, somewhat nervously clearing her throat, and announced that the topic for discussion would be: 'Where is Love – meaning where is love in the movies? Where is boy-girl love in the movies? We've had plenty of boy-boy love and boy-girl sex but where is the boy-girl love?'

A long discussion followed, with Penn and Beatty attempting to blind them all with science, talking about the effect of sexual repression on narrative film, until Moreau stepped in and said they were basically talking intellectual crap and suggested they got back to real life.

There were more exchanges and Moreau continued to spout her one-liners until someone in the audience got up and said the panel sounded like a comic collective who had escaped from the *Johnny Carson Show*, and why didn't they all shut up and let the audience speak? 'We have feelings too, you know.' Loud cheers drowned the conciliatory attempts of Haskell, and she had to give way to questions. Beatty spotted this changing mood immediately and, knowing how to get an audience on his side, announced that he was bored and embarrassed by his fellow panellists (loud cheers).

Arthur Penn, attempting to bring the discussion back to earth, suggested that the story of Patty Hearst's love for the man who kidnapped her was a love story which had been overwhelmed by the political aspects. Moreau, furious at 'these men ... talking about Patty Hearst ... what kind of story is that?' flung her red-lined black cape around her shoulders and stormed off, leaving Haskell to lie that she had to leave for another appointment.

Attentions focused directly on Beatty. He was to answer for the sins of the movie industry, not his own, and he blandly responded, 'That's what I am here for. And I'll tell you this, there are actresses going begging for decent screenplays.'

'Who, who?' the audience shouted in unison.

'Jane Fonda. Goldie Hawn. Glenda Jackson, Faye Dunaway. That's who.'

'But they only do men's screenplays,' a woman in the front row retorted.

'That's because women's screenplays aren't as good.'

Loud boos and uproar. Beatty had taken a calculated risk and now wondered if it would come off; had he underrated the seriousness with which some women treated this topic? A woman at the back, with tears streaming down her cheeks, launched into a tirade. 'Perhaps if I met you face to face I might like you ... but right now you piss me off. I've got clients (reeling off several names) who have sent screenplays and don't even get replies ...'

Another woman said, 'Jane Fonda bought my screenplay ...

but men wouldn't allow her to make it.'

And so it went on . . . with Beatty toying with them right to the end. Then there was a moment of true realism as the audience began to drift off, and Beatty was still at the dais, talking. The woman who had cried came up to meet him, and he put his arms around her. Now she had stars as well as tears in her eyes, and Beatty, patronisingly, said to Haskell afterwards, 'They always do . . .'

Haskell admitted they loved him, and he'd done his bit and now he could return to being a male chauvinist, pure and purified. To give him his due, he did telephone Haskell the following day to ask if he had made a sexist remark to her. Jeanne Moreau clearly thought he had. She also telephoned and apologised for leaving the meeting early, and blamed her departure on the attitudes of Beatty and Penn. Beatty himself emerged unscathed. Nothing, not a sea of initially hostile women, could make him falter, it seemed.

Beatty was by then used to having people theorise about him and his views. It mattered, inasmuch as he disliked theoretical comment in major magazines and newspapers if it began to damage him, and he might call up the author and explain, off the record, why he or she had got it wrong, insisting that he never, ever spoke about them for public consumption. 'As for my love life,' he told Frank Rich, 'I know that movie actors are over-rewarded in our society and that the press has to cut people like me down to size. They make me into an insane eccentric with an incredible fear of losing my youth who lives in a bomb shelter, who contemplates or is going through plastic surgery and who has devastating relationships with women. It goes through cycles . . . my tide goes in and out.'

Could Beatty really complain at this perception of eccentricity when we know from true accounts of his ability, for example, to select a table in a popular restaurant under a spotlight and totally visible, he in his white suit, and, after all these years, expect *not* to be noticed? The eccentricities were only usually portrayed in the extremes he mentioned in the more scurrilous tabloid magazines.

So long as these extremes are recognised, it is easier to identify the point where fact has been stretched into fiction and deal with it accordingly when making an objective study. And then, when you have dismissed them and given him the benefit of the doubt, you hear a story like the one from Paul Schrader, author of the acclaimed Martin Scorsese film *Taxi Driver*, which starred Robert de Niro and Jodie Foster, who went to Beatty with a dramatic script which was eventually to be filmed under the title *Hardcore*.

Schrader's story was of a middle-class businessman from Michegan whose daughter simply vanishes while away on a church trip to California. He sets out on a personal mission to find her, hiring a private detective to discover the clues, and the trail ultimately leads them into the seedy depths of hard-core porn movies, where the daughter has become a celebrity.

Schrader, who at first had it in his mind to direct the film himself, showed the script to Beatty, who began suggesting changes to accommodate his own interpretation and indicated he might even want to direct it himself. The most dramatic change was that the central character, the father, should be changed to a husband. Schrader said that Beatty felt he was not an appropriate age to play a father of a girl in her late teens. 'I then went through the Beatty shift', he said, 'visiting the Beverly Wilshire where he was living every day, two hours a day, for a month.'

According to Schrader, the experience was educational, but not very rewarding, especially as Beatty's comments about the script, in the author's view, set in motion a series of changes which softened it. He described Beatty's grinding assertions difficult to handle. He presented his objections in such a clever way that it was difficult to argue, and slowly he asserted his power and control. 'He will always win,' said Schrader, 'because he wears you down. If you have a particular disagreement, say on an artistic issue, you can sit and argue for two hours and think you have won. One week later, he will bring it up again, and you are back to square one. In the end, you never really convince him; he has his own ideas which in my particular experience were virtually immovable.'

In the end, and after all that had passed between them, Beatty pulled out of the film. Eventually, Schrader secured a deal with Columbia, with himself directing and George C.

Scott taking the role of the father.

Beatty talked vaguely of his continuing obsessions with the story of John Reed and the life story of Howard Hughes, who had died in April 1976, and who once occupied a penthouse atop the Beverly Wilshire. He also stated it would possibly be vastly incorrect to report that he was contemplating a remake of the 1941 movie, *Here Comes Mr Jordan*. In the event, that is exactly what he did ... although the audiences would have an even longer wait, this time, before Beatty finally brought himself back to the screen.

16
Heavenly Bodies

Although Warren Beatty may have been vilified for his patronising air by some of the less starry-eyed members of the audience at the 1976 conference on women's films, the impassioned tears of the agent who could not get her clients' work on screen made some sort of impression. That and his long friendship with the writer-director Elaine May must have been a factor in rescuing her from the depths of despair and from the swirl of derision that had surrounded the release of her own movie, *Mikey and Nicky*, that year to begin an important collaboration which would last for his next three major projects.

Beatty's professional admiration for May dated back to the early sixties, when she and her partner Mike Nichols were at the height of their fame as humorists. Nichols was already moving on to his second career, which would see him emerge as one of the leading directors in both theatre and film, while May was regarded as a comic genius, although plagued by a reputation in Hollywood as a difficult perfectionist. She and Beatty shared the same disdain for many of the projects they were offered, and she could match him any day in their discussions about the need to go off the track and excite audiences with different, even quirky, movies. She also shared his dislike for talking to the media and, unlike most of her contemporaries in Hollywood, she positively shunned press attention. She rarely gave interviews, never came out in public herself, shied away from the glitzy parties and kept herself off the credits.

She wrote two successful movies, *A New Leaf*, in which she also acted, co-starring with Walter Matthau, in 1970, and the satirical parable *Such Good Friends*, with Dyan Cannon, in 1971. Her direction of *The Heartbreak Kid*, a Neil Simon screenplay, was widely applauded in 1972 and the following year she was engaged in her second, *Mikey and Nicky*, which is where the explosion of her 1976 troubles really began.

A technician who was working on the film recalls a moment which typified her desire to inject the unexpected into her work by improvisation. It was well past three in the morning when they were shooting a scene in a Los Angeles Street with the two main stars, John Cassavetes, a crook with a contract out on his life, and Peter Falk, his friend, who had been charged with the task of killing him. The cameras had been running for ages, with the two men talking to each other about whatever came into their minds. It is a technique that Cassavetes would use in his own pictures, and one which several directors had tried. But suddenly, the men stopped talking, and wandered off the set.

May continued filming, although there was no one in shot, until a cameraman took it upon himself to call 'Cut!' May, angry that her directorial authority had been usurped, asked why he had done this. He replied that there was nothing to film. The actors had left, gone away. 'Yes,' replied May, 'but they might come back.'

Improvisation is one thing, but the amount of film it takes can be awesome, expensive and confusing. May spent the next two years editing her movie, until Paramount began to get nasty and issued lawsuits demanding she hand it over immediately, pointing out that she had gone way over budget and the movie was months behind the agreed delivery date.

Eventually, Paramount released it into a few cinemas and then canned it. It was shown long enough for Stanley Kauffmann to write in the *New Republic* that it was one of the best ten movies of the decade, although others, like Frank Rich in the *New York Post*, took the alternative view that it was an 'unendurable mess'. Eventually, Paramount gave the movie back to May, and it was reissued in 1986.

Back in 1976, when all this had come to a head with writs flying, May had difficulty in getting new work as a director.

'I think they thought I was sort of crazy,' she admitted in one of her rare appearances in public when her movie was honoured at the Museum of Modern Art in the autumn of 1986. 'And then I wrote *Heaven Can Wait* for Warren Beatty ... and everything was all right again.'

For Beatty himself, the arrival of *Heaven Can Wait* to the stage where he was ready to make the movie give a fair indication of his current mood, and his lack of haste to rush into a new movie, or indeed into anything at all. It had developed over the previous few years and was to become the pattern of his work, which would become even more spasmodic in the coming decade.

He had toyed with *Hardcore*, he had looked again at the possibility of a biopic on Howard Hughes, which he had partly scripted, but in the wake of the reclusive tycoon's death on 5 April 1976 there had been much television and media coverage, and various Howard Hughes projects had been rapidly commissioned. So Beatty put it to one side. He was also still pursuing his interest in John Reed and *Ten Days That Shook the World*, but few in Hollywood were as aware or appreciative of the story as Beatty himself, and eyes glazed over with disinterest whenever he mentioned it.

Then he became interested in *Heaven Can Wait*, which at that point still languished under its old title of *Halfway to Heaven*, a play by Harry Segall which became the 1941 hit movie *Here Comes Mr Jordan*. It won an Oscar for Segall and an Academy nomination for best picture. It starred Robert Montgomery and Evelyn Keyes in the story of a prize-fighter who crashes his private plane and goes to Heaven by mistake. He is supposed to have survived, and lived for another forty years, and so the administrators of Heaven send him back to earth in another body.

The rights to the Segall play had, by 1975, been passed to the former stage director Jed Harris, then seventy-five, unloved, unheard of for years and dying. He wanted sufficient capital to keep himself in moderate luxury until his own call to the hereafter arrived, which he imagined would not be long considering he smoked three packs of cigarettes a day, and agreed upon a fee of $25,000, for which Beatty wrote out a cheque instantly.

Elaine May got the call while gloomy and out of sorts from her recent traumas and began writing the script, and Beatty himself joined in, thus giving himself a list of credits as producer, co-writer and star. To this was eventually added the word 'director', and thus he became the first Hollywood actor since Orson Welles to assume all four major roles in the making of a movie. His decision to direct came after months of the usual procrastination. He approached Elaine's former partner, Mike Nichols, and then Arthur Penn, but both were busy on other projects.

He had given the completed script to Peter Bogdanovich, then one of the hottest new directors in town after *The Last Movie Show*, *What's Up Doc?* and *Paper Moon*. Bogdanovich went through the now familiar debates in which Beatty indulges prior to a go situation, but as the discussion proceeded, the calls from Beatty became fewer, until Bogdanovich realised things were leading nowhere and cried off.

Beatty named himself as director, with Buck Henry, who was also listed among the acting credits, as co-director. There was to be no doubt who was in charge, however, and so Warren Beatty, producer and movie star, now added director to his status. Barry Diller, who had recently replaced Robert Evans as head of Paramount, was to receive the proposal, and Beatty began his astute negotiating technique for which he was well-known to those who had dealt with him previously. He would have the conversation pre-planned; he would say this, they would say that, he would counter, they would offer, he would stand firm and finally give way only when he had to, which now wasn't often.

He ended up securing the best deal he had ever made for a picture, which provided him with an up-front fee of $3.5 million, payable in three stages in advance, plus a percentage of the gross, with elevators at agreed levels of profitability. More than that, he asked for – and got – the supreme power of creative control, to an extent virtually unheard of in Hollywood, assuring him of absolutely no external interference while he was making the movie, the final cut and even a say in the promotion and marketing. The importance of the deal, and its value to Beatty personally, would not become apparent until later, when it became far and away the most financially successful movie Beatty had made.

He began casting, and once again gathering some old friends. His co-star was to be Julie Christie, but she did not know this until she got the call at her new hideaway, a large grey farmhouse which she had bought at Cefn-y-Coed, Montgomery, Wales. She had moved there after *Shampoo* and was joined by a pair of artists from San Francisco, Leslie and Jonathan Heale. There, reclusive and retiring, she had angrily rejected a succession of tarty roles in exploitative sex movies which flooded in after *Shampoo*. She, like Beatty, had turned away script after script and then settled on a surprisingly bad one, *Demon Seed*, which brought her briefly back to America in 1976 but did nothing for her career.

Beatty's offer revived her declining fortunes and, temporarily, her preparedness to work in Hollywood. The rest of the casting was done with his usual meticulous thought. In the original film, Claude Rains had played the administrator from Heaven who guides the hero back to earth. Beatty wanted Cary Grant but settled for James Mason. Jack Warden, who had worked with him on *Shampoo*, came in as his old football coach, and his pals Dyan Cannon and Charles Grodin completed the main roles.

For a time, Beatty had considered making the film without himself in the lead. He had toyed with the idea of making his good friend Muhammad Ali into a movie star, in the leading role – the original play called for a boxer. Ali had other commitments and anyway, although it was not a demanding part, he might well have found it beyond him. Having reached the decision to star, Beatty had written the script with Elaine May around a footballer, which called upon his own skills from his schooldays, and in spite of his approaching fortieth birthday, he played most of the scenes himself.

It is a fun comedy, but there is also great poignancy, especially in the final scenes between himself and Christie, when their communication is through intense eye contact which became an essential part of their performance. Beatty the director insisted on numerous retakes to get it right and it became a routine aspect of the production that he would go back over scenes where, on viewing the rushes of the day's shooting, he would want to do them again and again.

His style and pattern of workmanship had become established, working all day, and then well into the night viewing the result, marking out areas for retakes and adjustment, polishing the script with Elaine May and giving his co-director Buck Henry a hard time. Henry, who also appears briefly in front of the cameras as the escort from Heaven who collects Beatty before his time, found him a tough taskmaster. 'We had plenty of disagreements,' said Henry, 'but they weren't violent. Whenever Warren wants to do something his way, he's already got it figured out in his mind. So you better be goddamned sure that when you have a difference of opinion, you can argue your case.'

Heaven Can Wait took on a life of its own. It was not a spectacular film by any means, and no one was really expecting it to take off. Beatty worked round the clock in the post-production stage of editing and music. He delved into every aspect, designed the posters which showed himself with a pair of wings, he examined the publicity material and the promotional hand-outs. Even in the last hours before it opened, he was visiting cinemas in New York, listening to the sound quality of the speakers, and giving advice to the projectionists about lighting.

He would explain to these mystified technicians, who had seldom in their lives been confronted with such advice, 'It is not realistic for any producer to ignore this final phase. You can put great effort into a particular scene, and then have it erased by a wrong light bulb or bad projection.'

Reviewers were generally kind, and even his old adversary from years back, Rex Reed, who had written a particularly stinging profile of Beatty for *Esquire* in 1967, which Beatty hated, now set his work favourably against a background in current trends: 'At a demoralising time in movie history when trash like *Jaws 2* and *Grease* still sucks in the suckers, *Heaven Can Wait* is all the more winning because it doesn't leave you heavy-hearted, depressed or frightened out of your wits; it lifts the spirit and makes you feel good about life on earth and beyond.'

Molly Haskell who, it will be recalled, had been chairperson of the panel at the women's film festival in 1976, found herself reviewing the film for *New York* magazine, and was unmoved by the fact that he had taken on a woman writer for his new movie. She concentrated on Beatty's chauvinism and made it plain that while admiring his abilities, she still refused to be smitten by him or his goddamn charm. She made a point of letting her readers know what she knew – that he was an ace at self-promotion. 'His ultraphysical presence dominates the film,' she wrote, 'in an ego trip in which Death, like everyone else, is on the Beatty payroll . . . As a sex idol, Beatty is too calculating to have the direct appeal of the old stars (as a fantasy lover, you'd want to kiss him only with your eyes open). But watching him apply the hard and soft arts of self-merchandising is a dazzling spectacle in its own right.'

The movie opened at showcase theatres in New York and simultaneously at 625 cinemas across America. Beatty toured around, talking technical matters, gauging public reaction and talking it up in media interviews. Business was brisk, and it was soon clear that *Heaven Can Wait* was going to be a massive hit, so great that it could not go unrecognised by the Academy awards.

On its first US release, *Heaven Can Wait* took a princely $48 million in rentals alone, and went on to record grosses in excess of $120 million worldwide, from which Beatty's slice was reported in the trade press as exceeding $15 million. This was his biggest box-office success to date, and his earnings from the three major movies which he had both produced and starred in, *Bonnie and Clyde*, *Shampoo* and *Heaven Can Wait*, eventually provided him with a personal income in excess of $50 million.

A Beatty movie was now recognised as a superb exercise in Hollywood aggrandisement; few could now argue with that. The power, the ability, the mystique and the enigma of the man himself could no longer be ignored. When Oscar time came around at the beginning of 1979, he was ecstatic to discover that his movie had received an incredible *ten* nominations, including Jack Warden and Dyan Cannon for best supporting roles. Beatty himself was nominated for four Oscars – as producer of the best film, best actor, best director and best screenplay (with Elaine May). He was the first man to be nominated in four separate categories since Orson

Welles' great triumph with *Citizen Kane* in 1941.

Competition was fierce in 1978, however, and even *Superman*, tipped for something big, managed only to secure nominations for technical merit. The best film line-up included *The Deer Hunter*, which won the award, while the best actor category had seventy-one-year-old Laurence Olivier (*The Boys from Brazil*), Robert de Niro (*The Deer Hunter*) and Jon Voight, who won it for his performance in *Coming Home*. Beatty had to sit through the tension of the awards ceremony, biting his lip and adjusting his spectacles nervously, and realised that being up for multi-awards could also mean multi-disappointment. Each category came and went, 'And the winner is . . .' as Beatty remained seated. *Heaven Can Wait* converted only one of the nominations – for best art direction and set decoration.

There was some consolation in this highly charged and emotional scenario. Throughout the glittering evening, as Beatty edged about in his seat, twitching, rubbing his nose and performing all those other little mannerisms that came with the Method years ago and which subconsciously come back under duress, Diane Keaton was clutching his hand.

Diane Keaton was no stranger to this experience herself, and was in his life at an opportune time. Leslie Caron once said the Oscar presentation nights were very special to him, and were usually marked by his arrival with a new lady on his arm. It happened with Natalie Wood in 1963, Leslie herself in 1964, Julie Christie in 1966. There were others, fleeting and passing, in the meantime – and now it was Miss Keaton, who had won her own Oscar for best actress the previous year, when among those she beat were Shirley MacLaine (*The Turning Point*) and Jane Fonda (*Julia*).

There they were, holding hands and making small talk as the cameras panned down upon them, and especially when Shirley MacLaine, there to make a presentation, told sexy jokes about her brother at which he smiled nonchalantly and looked a trifle embarrassed. And for those who hadn't caught up with his movements of late, Diane was – according to Nicholson's phraseology – the 'current model'.

Keaton was another deep and interesting character actress

whose involvement with Woody Allen had made her a star, but also in a curious way had held her back. Like others before her in Beatty's mind's eye, she possessed a rare screen presence which invited both interest and sympathy. The natural expressions of her face gave the impression of normality so that her lines were very believable.

Her rise to fame had been rapid. The eldest of seven children of an Air Force family from southern California, she was basically shy and worried about her weight, but arrived in New York when still a teenager, full of ambitions, rather like Beatty a couple of decades earlier. She landed a role in the stage version of the musical *Hair*, and became known as the only member of the cast who refused to disrobe for the final nude climax.

From *Hair*, she gained a place in the first theatrical staging of Woody Allen's *Play It Again Sam*, and went on to co-star with him in the 1972 film version. In the same year, she landed the part of Al Pacino's second wife in *The Godfather*, which would have meant an earlier encounter with Beatty had he not turned down the role of Michael. She adjudged her performance in the movie to be 'background music', and to a degree this was to be her fate in future movies with Woody Allen, with whom she had now become romantically involved. After *Play It Again Sam* she was his straight man in *Sleeper*, the story of a man frozen to awake 200 years in the future, and again in another comedy fantasia, *Lovers and Death*, in 1975.

Only in *Annie Hall* did Allen allow her to blossom. By then, she had adapted to his muddle-headed neurosis on and off screen, and the play *Annie Hall* was in part based upon their own relationship. Their affair played a crucial part, because it led Allen to a new dimension when dealing with women in his films, so that they became as important to the plot as himself.

The comic-straight man syndrome at last disappeared and Allen presented both his own character and that of Keaton in a new light. He created the role of Alvy Singer, a neurotic, romantic night-club comic, in his own image. He has a complicated relationship with a night-club singer, Annie Hall, played by Keaton, which was in many ways a mirror of their own affair. Finally, in the Keaton-Allen partnership, she was allowed to come into her own, and the portrayal won her the Oscar.

Annie Hall was a funny, sad, sentimental story that strikes a jagged nerve about the search for relationships – it was as much a reflection on Allen himself, and led to his now famous remark that maybe he should never get into a relationship in which one of the partners was himself.

The comedy was one string to Keaton's bow. In drama, *The Godfather II* provided her with a much meatier role than the first outing and she also starred in Richard Brooks' sexual nightmare, *Looking for Mr Goodbar*, and again with Woody Allen in his dullish psychodrama, *Interiors*, in 1978. By then, the relationship between Keaton and Allen had already peaked and was on the downward slide. Life with neurotic, insecure men could become very boring. She had stuck, like a damaged record, in the groove of playing women who sought the companionship of insecure, even immature, men – as in life, to a degree.

Then along came Beatty, captivated by her performance in *Annie Hall*, and whispered his charm and passion into the mouthpiece of the telephone in the autumn of 1978. The seduction had begun; the calls became more frequent. Beatty was in love again, and he did not mind who knew it.

Keaton, like others before her in his life, was a special product of her time, a role model for modern women, just as Natalie Wood had come from the crazy mixed-up fifties, Caron from the realism genre of the early sixties. Christie was the epitome of the beautiful people, Michelle Phillips was from the hip era, while Keaton was the heroine of the neuroses of the late seventies. Beatty would not care to have categorised his women in that way; he may not have even realised that his romances had coincidentally encompassed the beginning and passing of eras of sociological change and attitudes which he himself had adopted for his work, and his life.

It was a curiosity that he attempted to explain once when he was asked why he seemed to fall in love with all of his leading ladies. He replied that it was far more complicated than a mere falling in love, as indeed it was, and as Leslie Caron confirmed. Apart from Joan Collins and Natalie Wood, he had begun a relationship *before* his women became his co-stars. He was already deeply involved with Leslie Caron when they decided to make a film together, as he was with Julie Christie.

The same would now apply to Diane Keaton who, by the spring of 1979 when they turned up arm-in-arm at the Oscar ceremonies, was already earmarked to become a key figure in his life, and in his next major project, which would be the story of John Reed, *Reds*.

Another similarity between all of his most famous liaisons, though, was that they were all with women of their time who in each case had reached a certain pinnacle in their careers, which in turn would punctuate his own rambling life. The timing of each involvement also tended to be significant, and one wonders whether it was entirely coincidence. When he began seeing Keaton, he had already begun serious work on the back-burner project of *Reds*, and moved into top gear once the success of *Heaven Can Wait* had become assured.

The intriguing question as to his true motives behind these developments lay in the 'complicated' foreplay to work and love about which he had spoken. Did he make a move towards Keaton because he was attracted to her in real life, or was he already thinking of his next movie? Was romance a pre-amble to everything, to ensure some electricity and fire between them as the cameras were running? Did he view personal involvement as the ultimate casting couch, a pre-requisite to a magical duet on screen?

It is an interesting thought which only he could answer, and never has; but there are some clues which may throw light on his intentions, perhaps even subconscious ones. Although the plots of his movies have been cast in wide and various settings, entailing all measure of sex, violence and social upheaval, they basically boil down to relationships between the two leading characters. There are usually other characters on the periphery, and supporting actors who may shine. Looking back over his collection of work, it is possible to see the pattern emerging almost from the beginning, when Elia Kazan threw Natalie Wood into his arms and admitted, 'I knew they had become lovers – and I didn't worry because it helped their love scenes.'

239

Did Kazan tell him that or did Beatty work it out for himself? Vivien Leigh gave a better performance because of his flattering attentions, and thereafter, whether it was with Leslie Caron in *Promise Her Anything*, Julie Christie in *McCabe and Mrs Miller*, *Shampoo* and again in *Heaven Can Wait*, the fierce white light shone ultimately on himself and his co-star, exploring the relationship and prodding around amongst all the hidden facets of human souls.

The movies, as was Beatty's private life, were filled with his search for relationships and, at the end of the day, he seemed to be giving out the message that although life without relationships is unthinkable, it is also foolish to imagine that they can, by and large, be uncomplicated or even enduring. So far, with one exception, his loving relationships on screen had come to grief and the consistency, if not persistence, of many of his screen characterisations centres on the irony of the situation – when a relationship could have been good, if it wasn't for something else – and it was all shaping up like an episodic adventure; art and life, once again.

And here was Diane Keaton, and a whole new set of ironies were on the brink of emergence.

17
Reds

The relationship, once again, was at the heart of the matter. And now, for Warren Beatty and Diane Keaton we substitute the names of John Reed and Louise Bryant, an almost forgotten encounter of two vital young things of American radicalism of the early 1900s, whose romance was played against the monumental and exhilarating story of a revolution which would dominate events of the twentieth century.

The very idea was daunting. In an age of multi-million budgets in which even one bad picture could bring a studio to its knees, Beatty's project required a sense of unbridled adventure and courage. Careers had foundered and sunk on far lesser projects.

We need to recap to appreciate the full sense of drama in Beatty's fulfilment of the project that had been in his thoughts for almost a decade, and first we must look at the inspiration, John Reed, who had become Beatty's fascination and obsession. Aligned to that was the connection of Reed's friend, and Beatty's boyhood hero, the playwright Eugene O'Neill, on the one hand; and on the other Beatty's own friendship with some of the American writers who had taken him back in time through personal reminiscences of the era, people like Clifford Odets, William Inge, Henry Miller and the controversial playwright Lillian Hellman, who counted Beatty among her closest supporters during the last years of her life.

In a nutshell, John Reed (1887–1920) was a dashing young all-American from Portland, Oregon, who came to New York after Harvard in search of intellectual stimulation and con-

241

sorted with like-minded leftists, of whom the young playwright O'Neill was one, and fast-talking anarchist Emma
Goldman another. Reed made a name for himself reporting
the Mexican Revolution in 1913. Back in America, he became
a hero among the Bohemian and socialist circles where the
talk was of freedom from capitalism, of Bolshevism, Marx
and Lenin.

Reed, author, journalist and revolutionary, became involved
in the competitive socialist factions of Greenwich Village,
where arguments raged over all manner of new thoughts
emerging with the new century. He was considered by some
to be too much of a playboy, especially for his ability to sweep
women off their feet – there were numerous brief affairs –
and this made him worry about ever being taken seriously, a
thought which had dogged Beatty for half of his career.

Reed's companion, Louise Bryant, was the wife of a home-
town dentist whom he met while revisiting Portland in 1915
for some anti-war activity. Herself a radical thinker, she was
captivated by this romantic young man and waved goodbye
to her husband to become Reed's devoted supporter and his
lover for the rest of his life, apart from a brief interlude
when she had an affair with O'Neill and the painter Andrew
Dasburg in New York while Reed, conversely, became involved
with a girl of sixteen in Russia.

Reed's interest in Russia and the mounting unrest inspired
by the Bolsheviks led him to travel to Europe and onwards
to St Petersburg and Moscow, and the action of the film alter-
nates between his journeys to Russia and his political debates
in New York.

In 1917, he happened to be in Moscow for the start of the
Russian Revolution, which enabled him to write the book for
which he became famous, *Ten Days That Shook the World*.
Reed met the leaders of the revolution, and was fêted there
as a great American writer who had come to report with
sympathy and understanding the sweeping movement that
would change the face of human society across Europe and
later elsewhere in the world.

Beatty knew well enough that a movie about American
Communists and the Russian Revolution would hardly be
welcome at that tense time in the western world. So his

is centred upon the characters, and on their feelings and relationships. In another age it might have been billed as a great love story set against one of the greatest events of world history, and one in which there was a final twist of fate for his story.

Reed, travelling back and forth, had become disillusioned by the great new Communist system and may well have turned his back on Russia, had not tragedy struck in 1920. He contracted typhus, died of kidney failure at the age of thirty-three and became the first and last American citizen to be buried in the Kremlin Wall – the highest honour the Soviets could provide for their wayward American supporter.

His friend Lenin did not of course live to see the fruits of the revolution, either, and perhaps, had he survived the illness brought on by an assassination attempt in 1918, it might all have been different in the remainder of the century. As it was, when Lenin died in January 1924 the rise of Stalin, which Lenin had sought to halt before his death, became unstoppable. That was the basis of the story of *Reds* – tracking the upsurge of the American Communist Party and left-wing groupings through to the death of Reed and beyond. It was a true story, and Beatty had every intention of presenting an accurate picture of events as they happened.

His personal interest in these events began almost half a century after they happened, in his early days in New York, when he came into contact with the American literati, some of whom had held strong socialist sympathies in the thirties. Lillian Hellman herself had made visits to Russia during the great Stalin purges, and was among the early Communist apologists in America. She had been at the centre of a hotbed of unshakable Stalinist fidelity which eventually became the subject of Senator Joe McCarthy's scrutiny, as indeed did Hellman herself.

Hellman, who became a close friend of Beatty's in the sixties, later recanted her support of Stalin, but remained sympathetic to the Communist cause and was the subject of investigation by the CIA and the FBI. Beatty, by his mere contact with this sphere of writers and artists who were known sympathisers, past or present, to the Communist cause, would have been monitored in his contacts, as were many others in the literary and acting world on whom J. Edgar Hoover kept voluminous files.

Mere visits to Russia by American citizens were noted, as doubtless was Beatty's trip in the early sixties with Natalie Wood, whose parents were Russian. His associations with Soviet personalities whom he might encounter on his travels in Europe, or when they came to New York, would likewise have been recorded. Any events that put Russians and Americans together – however innocent the circumstances – in a social setting on USA territory would be spied upon by both the CIA and the FBI and the KGB.

These social spies would certainly have been present when, a couple of years after his visit to Moscow, he joined a gathering at the New York penthouse apartment of Mr and Mrs H. J. Heinz, overlooking the East River. The guest of honour was the Russian poet Yevtushenko. Mrs Heinz, known to her friends as Drue, was a socialite of standing as well as being editor of a literary review magazine. The party was a large affair, with many representatives of the art of film present, as well as some 'translators' and other curious hangers-on whom one present identified as informers for both the CIA and the KGB. Sensitivities in the era of the post-Cuban confrontation still ran high, and all present were no doubt duly accounted for by both sides.

Beatty had a brief conversation with Yevtushenko, who had been giving his party-piece performance with due melodrama, intensity and conceit. Beatty said, 'I think you are the greatest poet in Russia.'

The poet, a tall man dressed in baggy trousers and a sloppy sweater, looked up, apparently offended by this remark: 'No, *du monde*! I am also the greatest living Russian actor. They want me to give a prize as the greatest actor, but the government says no, Zhenya . . . a prize for the greatest poet, yes, Zhenya. But as an actor too? That would give you too much power . . . the people love you too much.'

Beatty pulled on his left earlobe, and scratched the back of his head while Drue Heinz announced that there was some specially imported Russian vodka on ice if Yevtushenko would care for some. 'Champagne!' he bellowed. 'French. Brut!' and then, turning back to his assembled admirers, he said, 'You

Americans. It is so simple for you. You do not understand us. You know little about survival.'

So Beatty's fascination for the left-wing politics of the previous sixty years went beyond the story of John Reed. The romance of being among some of the great American writers during the late fifties in New York and in his early film career in Hollywood would make an impression on any young mind. The mere recollections and thoughts of such people, whether Communist-leaning or not, was of no mere curiosity value.

When they talked 'old days' talk about the pre-war debates of communism versus fascism in Europe and the rise of new socialist groups in America, the scenario mirrored John Reed's own discussions in Greenwich Village in the early 1900s, though Beatty did not know it then. There were numerous other similarities. In 1913, for example, Reed staged a huge pageant with a cast of hundreds at Madison Square Garden to raise money for the International Workers of the World, who were on strike. It was at the same venue, almost sixty years later, that Beatty staged his most spectacular concert in aid of George McGovern's presidential bid, and at which the end of the conflict in Vietnam was promoted.

These associations, like Beatty's fascination for O'Neill, which also began long before his better knowledge of Reed, were only realised when he set about the task of researching Reed as a subject for his *big* picture. This began in earnest back in 1969, when the Russians themselves suggested he would make an excellent Reed. The state film company of Moscow already had a screenplay written for a major epic. When they saw Beatty in *Bonnie and Clyde* contact was made, and that year he went back to Moscow, where serious discussion was planned. Beatty wondered from the outset if the Russians would allow him to make the film the way he would want to tell the story.

He was right to wonder. The Russians wanted to do the story of Reed their way, which was hardly a perception that could be either sustained or appreciated in the West. Beatty knew immediately they began talking about it. The script was not unnaturally filled with Soviet propaganda, which hung over the whole project like a lead balloon. They asked him what he knew of Reed, and he told them of his knowledge.

He was interested in discovering if there were actually any survivors from the era who knew him. There was one, he was told, but she was very old and he gained the distinct impression that they did not wish him to meet her.

Beatty persisted and was eventually escorted to a high-rise apartment building on the outskirts of Moscow, there to discover Eleanora Drapkina, who had been a beautiful sixteen-year-old when she met the American in 1918. The gravel-voiced woman in her tiny apartment was reticent at first, owing to the presence of an interpreter who was also a KGB spy. 'So you knew John Reed?' Beatty asked. 'Were you in love with him?'

'Love? What is love? I fucked him, if that is what you mean, then he was gone and I too.'

Under Beatty's questioning she revealed she had been in a labour camp.

'How long?'

'Sixteen years.'

'My God,' said Beatty. 'What did you feel about Stalin?'

'Hate. But of course the revolution was in its early stages.'

At that moment, Beatty realised he had to make the movie – but not with the Russians and their propagandist script. It was boring, and anyway simply not feasible in those politically acute times when the US was at war with communism world-wide and when the threat of nuclear war between the two great superpowers still cast a shadow over humanity.

Beatty returned home, and in the intervening years studied his subject in minute detail, personally scouring the boxes of archive material in the John Reed collection at the Widener Library at Harvard. He had hired students to research the American political left, and to write their digests and theses, and he prepared 300 pages of draft material.

In 1976, he was at Mike Nichols' wedding in New York and shared a car with English playwright Trevor Griffiths. Not long afterwards, back in England, Griffiths received a tele-phone call. It was Beatty asking what he knew about John Reed; Griffiths said enough, and Beatty commissioned him to prepare a screenplay. Eight months and 1,000 transatlantic telephone calls later, Griffiths delivered a script with the working title of *Comrades*!

Beatty began the rewriting procedures to bring the screen-play into line with his own thoughts on the way the story should be presented. He would spend hours with Lillian Hell-man, trying to establish the philosophy of the piece, to capture the mood of communism as it existed in the earlier part of the century. Hellman's condonation of or silences on some of the worst sins of Stalin angered many of her friends. The very mention of her name still aroused fury among her enemies, of whom there were many still alive, but she had apparent instant recall of the radical old days.

Her memory, however, was somewhat flawed by her adjust-ments to meet what she believed history ought to have recorded. Many a night, perhaps not until late in the evening, Beatty would arrive and their conversations and readings would go on into the night.

By 1979 Beatty had decided to return again to Moscow. He now had his script and his potential leading lady to star as Louise Bryant in Diane Keaton, who was by then his own lover, and she agreed to accompany him, as did his confidant and set designer, Dick Sylbert, and his cameraman Vittorio Storaro. In many ways, it was like the return of John Reed and Louise Bryant all over again.

From his previous visits, Beatty was well aware of the bureaucracy and it had not eased in the interim. Nor had the political sensitivities. Indeed, they had heightened of late with Ronald Reagan's tough electioneering for the forthcoming presidential race, when he would uncompromisingly brand the Soviet Union 'that evil empire'.

Beatty would be campaigning for the re-election of Demo-crat Jimmy Carter, despite personal misgivings about the man, but this would cut no political ice in Moscow, where the temperature of Soviet-American relations was decidedly chilly. He had enough contacts to cut through some bureauc-racy and hold talks with the ministry of culture to discuss his project, and they gave him a guarded reception. One day, he wanted to visit the revolutionary museum which was in Leningrad. They travelled to the city under escort and checked in at a hotel, but then the guide informed him that the museum was closed.

Beatty replied that they would wait until the next day and

they arranged for a car to collect them and drive to the museum. Once again, the guide told them the museum was closed. However, Beatty got out of the car and walked closer to the building; it was open. The guide could not explain his instructions not to take Beatty and his party there and ultimately, he was refused permission to film in Russia at all unless they agreed to give the ministry script approval. He refused point blank, and was shown the door.

Keaton, by this time, was getting nervous. She had been quietly astounded by her lover, by the charm he exuded and his handling of difficult people and by his bravado and sheer confidence. What a difference she found in Beatty from the neurotic fearfulness of Woody Allen, who was like a shy mouse. Beatty excited her, and then calmed her fears and said there was nothing to worry about. He was intent on making the movie, and he would not be put off by the Russian ban. They flew home, and he began in earnest to get a workable script that might turn the dream into reality.

He would be questioned, of course, on why he wanted to revive an old and half-forgotten story of a man who preached communism and hated capitalism, to be presented in an age of emerging ultra-conservatism in which the fullest extremes of a capitalist economy were flourishing, led by market forces and monetarism, populated by whizzkids, dealmakers and yuppies whose champions would be Ronald Reagan and Margaret Thatcher. Why indeed?

Jet-lagged and with images of Russia swirling around his head, Beatty was now unstoppable in his quest. He stayed that first night back in Los Angeles not at his apartment in the Beverly Wilshire, nor at his home on Mulholland Drive. He swung into that renowned house of pleasure and relaxation, Hugh Hefner's Playboy mansion on Charing Cross Road, Bel Air – a million refreshing miles from the repressive air of Moscow he had just left – where people like him, famous people, beautiful people, influential people, could repair at will to replenish their minds and souls, or anything else that was physically or mentally lacking.

It was something of a paradox that his thoughts for telling this story of an American Communist should be forming one night in the confines of one of the world's most overt settings

Politics first took on a significance in Beatty's life in the 1972 Presidential campaign for George McGovern. Beatty was a major backroom player and fundraiser, and called upon many of his Hollywood stars to help, including his co-stars from *Shampoo*, Julie Christie and Goldie Hawn who joined him at a major celebrity concert

Later, he was a key figure in the abortive bid for the Presidency by his close friend Senator Gary Hart whose affair with a model caused him to pull out, in spite of frantic efforts by Beatty personally to save him

Moscow bound: The story of John Reed, author of *Ten Days that Shook the World* and the only American buried in the walls of the Kremlin, became Beatty's ten-year obsession and resulted in his epic *Reds* in which he co-starred with Diane Keaton, pictured with him, above, when they visited Moscow in 1979 to survey locations. But the Russians refused to allow filming unless they had a say in the script, and thus it was mostly shot in England (*Syndication International*)

Left, with Keaton in a scene from the film which won nine Oscar nominations (*Yardley Collection*)

The action in *Reds* was dramatic, often of epic proportions, as in this scene, and though a very good film, never quite made the list of all-time classics, as he had hoped (*Yardley Collection/Columbia Pictures Industries Inc*). True, it received a bagful of Oscar nominations, but only two were converted into awards: his own for best director (pictured with the award, below) and the second for Maureen Stapleton as best supporting actress

Brief encounter: After her eight-day marriage to Dennis Hopper, Michelle Phillips of the Mamas and the Papas pop group, moved in with Jack Nicholson, and later with Warren Beatty after his relationship with Julie Christie ended

Family matters: From the beginning, they kept their careers apart, and were never professionally linked, nor traded on each other's names. But Beatty and his big sister, Shirley McLaine, remained, as always, the best of buddies

Song and dance: The movie *Ishtar*, a light comedy set in the desert, has been Beatty's only major failure to date. The movie, co-starring Isabelle Adjani (above) and Dustin Hoffman, was a box office dud. Beatty· did not make another film for almost six years (*Columbia Pictures Industries Inc*)

Dick Tracy: The movie which brought him back to the screen was the comic strip hero Dick Tracy which he once again produced, directed and co-starred (© *Touchstone Pictures. All rights reserved*)

Though not such a huge success as *Batman*, in which his pal Jack Nicholson appeared as The Joker, *Dick Tracy* achieved respectable notices, not to mention massive hype which centred on Beatty's relationship with Madonna with whom he is pictured here with Al Pacino as the crook, Big Boy Caprice (© *Touchstone Pictures. All rights reserved*)

The hottest couple around at the time – not just for their respective roles in
Dick Tracy with all its sexual connotations – but offscreen, too, they were
for a while the most talked-about duo in showbiz (© *Touchstone Pictures.*
All rights reserved)

A circle is completed. Warren Beatty and Annette Bening, met when he interviewed her for a starring role in *Bugsy*. She became pregnant while filming, and they married soon afterwards (*Associated Press*)

of capitalist freedom. The Playboy Organisation was at the zenith of its post-sixties sex boom, and in fact on the brink of sliding down the other side of the mountain. The mansion was one of the most exclusive settings for the Hollywood in-crowd. The great house, set in five and a half acres of lush gardens, provided an oasis of Polynesian-style opulence for guests personally approved by Hefner, who could come and go as they pleased. Its main building was surrounded by pools, exotic saunas, bars, games-rooms and a theatre. There was a massive jacuzzi behind the mansion itself, and guest bungalows were always available. Life at the mansion went on *ad infinitum*. Guests could, and would, arrive at any hour of the day or night, for champagne and breakfast, or dinner at nine, or a party at 2.00 a.m., and playmates abounded.

All of this has no real bearing on our story, except to note that Beatty was among those of the so-called Hollywood élite who could use the place at will (and did), the point being that on the night of Beatty's return from the East, actor George Plimpton had just got out of the pool at the Playboy mansion. It was between three and four in the morning, and he trailed back into the foyer of the mansion, dripping wet, where his eyes fell upon a body, which appeared to have collapsed over a day bed.

Further investigation revealed the prostrate form of Warren Beatty, who appeared to be in a coma. Plimpton shook him, and inquired, 'Warren . . . you all right?' There was no movement, and Plimpton shook him again.

Warren opened his eyes and blinked, and then mumbled, 'Whigham. You're Horace Whigham . . .'

'No, Warren. It's me. George. George Plimpton.'

'Goodnight, Horace,' said Beatty, and went back to sleep.

Some weeks later, the telephone rang at Plimpton's office, where he was busy writing. It was Warren Beatty, on his car-phone, announcing – as he always did – that he would be there in precisely two and a half minutes to talk about the part.

'Part? What part?' said Plimpton.

'Horace Whigham – you know, in my new movie.'

Thus Plimpton discovered that he was Horace Whigham, the millionaire publisher who figures in the John Reed story, and had presumably been selected the night he disturbed Beatty from his jet lag recovery mode in the foyer of the Playboy mansion. Between that night and the point some weeks later when he was finally casting, Beatty had been involved in his usual amount of horse-trading and going into huddles for the writing and casting. The question of finance had been ongoing, and it ought to have been more of a problem.

He had offered the project to Paramount, who had just seen their cash reserves pleasantly improved by the returns from *Heaven Can Wait*. Beatty sent the script to the studio head, Barry Diller, who said he liked it; it would have to be trimmed back, of course, because it was a huge tome, a double-epic. But the crucial question was, 'How much is it going to cost us?'

Beatty was evasive. He had not completed a budget but thought it would be in the region of $20 million, certainly no less. Diller said he would have to bring in Charlie (Bludhorn, head of Gulf Western, Paramount's owners), and fixed a meeting for a round-table discussion. The length needed to be cut back, and at various times Beatty recruited Elaine May and Robert Towne to assist with reworking some of the scenes and with the cutting.

Diller and Beatty flew to New York to meet Charlie, who seldom read scripts himself but liked to have the outline read aloud to him. On listening to the outline, he sat back, pondered and then spoke. 'What we've got here,' he said incisively, 'is a story about an all-American boy who turns Communist and goes to Russia, becomes an idol of the Reds, has a love affair with a dentist's wife, gets sick and dies and they bury him a hero in the Kremlin. And you want me, who raises money through the supreme channels of the capitalist system, to back it?'

'Right.'

'This is a very iffy subject, Warren. How much are we talking?'

'Charlie, I can't say for sure.'

'Twenty-five million dollars?'

'Around that figure.'

'Do me a favour, Warren . . .'

'What?'

'Take the twenty-five million dollars; go down to Mexico and spend some on making another picture and keep the rest for yourself. But just don't make this picture.'

Beatty explained that he had got to make the picture. He had lived with it for ten years, and he woke up every morning with a feeling of self-disgust that he hadn't done it yet.

'All right,' said Bludhorn. 'Make the goddamn picture. Twenty-five million. Right?'

They shook hands and Beatty had the commitment; all he had to do now was make the picture, and considering the idea had been around for so long, it all happened in something of a rush. He'd already begun casting. He'd tricked Jack Nicholson into playing Eugene O'Neill by calling him up one day and pleading, 'Hey Jack. I'm desperate. I'm looking for the right actor to play the part of O'Neill. Any ideas?'

Beatty got the response he'd hoped for, which was: 'It's got to be me.' That way, there isn't too much of an argument over money.

Maureen Stapleton was suggested by Keaton for the role of Emma Goldman. Keaton and Stapleton had worked together on Woody Allen's psychodrama *Interiors* the previous year, for which Maureen had been nominated for an Oscar for best supporting actress. Stapleton, who had known Warren for years, had also been close to the hotbed in her early days around the Actors Studio – 'My room-mate in New York in the forties used to take the *Daily Worker*' she told me – and there were plenty around who were left-wing. She already had a feel for the piece, and it was the kind of role that she could get into, anyway.

Jerzy Kosinski, the Polish-born novelist who had fled the Eastern Bloc, like his friend Roman Polanski, years earlier was another recruit to play the evil Gregory Zinoviev, a leading member of the Russian government in the twenties whose alleged letter to the British Communist Party in 1924 was used in the general election campaign to defeat Ramsay MacDonald's first Labour government. His was one of the show trials of the mid-1930s when he was accused of plotting to kill Stalin.

George Plimpton, meanwhile, had received his visit from Beatty, accompanied by Keaton. He was nervous about the reading, and it did not go well. Suddenly Beatty flung the script on the floor and said, 'Forget the lines – improvise. You know what kind of person you are, put the make on her ...' He nodded towards Keaton, who was sitting on the green couch in Plimpton's office, observing but saying little.

Plimpton made his move and sat beside Keaton, watched by the eyes of Ernest Hemingway, photographs of whom adorned the walls, and the face of a dead zebra, whose skin lay on the floor in the form of a rug. The improvised acting out of a seduction scene went on for some seven or eight minutes before Beatty called it to a halt: 'That's enough George. Stop it ... you got the part.'

Finally, Plimpton realised who Horace Whigham was. Next, Edward Herrmann, best-known for his television mini-series portrayal of Franklin D. Roosevelt, got the call. He was summoned to Beatty's mountain-top, the eyrie high on Mulholland Drive. Margaux Hemingway was there too, but had nothing to do with the picture or this story. She was watching *Rebel Without a Cause* in Beatty's private cinema in the basement.

They discussed Beatty's new movie. Beatty wanted him to play Max Eastman, a magazine editor for whom Reed once worked. As they strolled casually through the house, a photograph pinned to a bulletin board caught his eye. He peered closer. It was his wife, the actress Leigh Curran. Herrmann was surprised and stopped short, wondering what a photograph of his wife was doing on Beatty's wall.

Beatty noticed. 'Do you know her?' he asked.

'Yeah, I know her.'

'Could you work with her on this picture?'

'Yeah ... of course I could.'

Beatty threw back his head and laughed. He was teasing Herrmann. He knew Leigh was his wife, and had pinned the photograph there to get his reaction. He would hire them both, Herrmann as Eastman, and Leigh to play Ida Rauh. The cast was coming together. Beatty was as meticulous as ever in his selection, collecting his people who would become a supporting cast. He warned each one to be on standby to travel across the world.

'The travel was half the problem with this movie,' studio head Barry Diller would say later. 'There had been no real

pre-production work and the costings were not properly calculated because of the time factor. We needed to move quickly
for a number of reasons, including such incidentals as avail-
ability of actors, and even the weather.'

Filming began in the late summer of 1979 and there was
a long hard winter ahead. Beatty was once again all things
to all men (and women) – producer, director, writer and star.
He was also the only man with the script fully in his head. He
had two other copies, which he held back and gave to Keaton
and Nicholson as filming approached, but no other actor in
the cast ever saw a complete copy. This technique, used by
director Richard Brooks, is to encourage both freshness and
natural improvisation. The actors are shown their lines the
night before they are to shoot the scene and come to it without
heavily preconceived notions of how they are going to play it.
Herrmann said Beatty was *mysterium tremendum*. They could
have been shooting *Casablanca* for all they knew.

Herrmann and others moaned. 'This movie is too big to do it
without a script,' he said. But perhaps he was wrong; perhaps
because it was so big, it would be too much for any actor to
take in at a one-sitting read. Anyway, a script wouldn't have
helped. 'It's all in Warren's head,' said Keaton. 'Sure, I've got
a script, but it changes every day.'

They did some preliminary work in New York and then
moved on to Europe. There would be filming mostly in
England, but also in Spain, which possessed countryside similar to the Baku region of Russia, and later Finland for its
close proximity to the Soviet scene. England, though, provided
the bulk of the settings, and there were some major logistical
works to contend with, such as arranging for authentic buildings, cars and trains, not to mention hundreds of period costumes, backdrops and extras. Dick Sylbert who, as production
designer, had to contend with many of these problems, likened
Beatty to a field marshal running a war. 'He was into everything,' said Sylbert, 'and working all hours of the day and
night. But, of course, that was nothing unusual for Warren –
and especially not on this picture.'

So they began, and had been filming several weeks when
Beatty cried out, 'Where the fuck is Maureen?'

Someone explained that she had not yet arrived from

America, Maureen Stapleton did not enjoy flying. She did not want to fly the Atlantic and had hitched a ride on the only vessel she could find going across to England from Baltimore at that time, a smallish Polish freighter named the *General Poplawski*, which at least gave her the flavour of the era she was portraying, since the ship was quite old. When she saw the size of it, her first notion was to back out of the deal altogether, but she did not want to let Beatty down.

The captain set sail, promising to deliver her in five days' time. Unfortunately, one of the engines seized up two days out and they floated powerless, bobbing about in the middle of the Atlantic for two days while repairs were carried out. 'I was going crazy through all of this,' Maureen told me. 'I mean, I was frantic. The last time I had crossed the Atlantic was to play in a television version of *Cat on a Hot Tin Roof*, with Laurence Olivier and Natalie Wood and Bob Wagner (they had remarried by then, of course; lovely couple to work with and she was so much better). On that occasion I travelled on the QE2 and the damned thing caught fire.

'As I was bobbing about in the ocean, going crazy and wondering what choice adjectives Warren was calling me, I thought to myself, "Maureen, I reckon God is trying to tell you something." I vowed then that, though I love England, I would never work there again.'

Because of Beatty's secrecy on the project, the media had taken a particular interest, and were giving a regular commentary on progress. As the days and weeks of shooting rolled by, rumours began to fly in the trade press that Beatty had over-extended himself this time, that he was heading way over budget in his quest for his dream project, and in his perfectionism. With carping glee, those with axes to grind were grinding them, and how. Stories surfaced about Beatty, Keaton and Nicholson flying around in helicopters for filming in various parts of England while the large cast followed on behind in first-class rail compartments. It was true, and no different to any other time, but with nothing to write about in terms of the actors and their creativity, media interest focused largely on the money.

Nicholson was fascinated to watch Beatty work, and had nicknamed him the Pro. Others were less complimentary as a certain tenseness gradually overtook almost every filming session, with Beatty ordering retake after retake to get a particular scene exactly the way he wanted it. Nicholson was his closest ally on the set; the two of them would often disappear for a script revision or discussion but it certainly did not cut down the number of takes.

Maureen Stapleton, a veteran of so many excellent characterisations, was normally a jovial, happy-go-lucky soul. She could get on with anyone and always tried her hardest; she was also never one to hold back her feelings, as we have seen. She is well able to express herself in a clear and vocal manner. 'By the time I arrived in England,' she explained, 'Warren had been filming for quite a while and had got into the habit of doing take after take – you know, "Maureen, sweetheart, not quite right . . . let's try it again." ' In one particular series of retakes, she had become frustrated and felt unable to offer a better or different interpretation.

Take twenty-two . . .

'Cut,' Beatty shouted. 'Sorry – again.'

Take twenty-three . . .

'Cut . . .'

'For Chrissakes, Warren,' Maureen cried, 'I don't know how else to play this scene!'

Keaton, too, was put through her paces. But like Stapleton she could handle herself, although at times, she collapsed into Nicholson's arms, crying, 'There is no such word as perfection.' Like Nicholson, Keaton was a voice of independent reason, a comforter when things went wrong and a carer when Beatty was exhausted, and sometimes she looked at him, dashing between camera and set, working himself into a frazzle, and wondered what she had got herself into.

At that moment Jack Nicholson could have taken advantage of the situation. He found himself attracted to Keaton, and let his feelings develop 'to help my scenes with her.' There was one where he, as O'Neill, had to hand Bryant a poem he had written for her during their brief affair. She opened it, and discovered it was one which he, Nicholson, had written for her, Keaton. As for a developing romance, he would report later, 'I don't want to hide behind this, but during the production, that's the way I began to feel . . . Nothing happened as a result, but there's something actorish about thinking, "My God, I've got a real crush, and holy fuck, this is my best friend and his girlfriend." But that was also what the movie was about. My character was attracted to Keaton's.'

Nicholson did not pull back because of his personal attraction to Keaton. He said he allowed passions to become 'over-inflamed' in front of Warren just to see what would happen, and whether it would help his scenes with her. 'But nothing happened between Diane and me,' he said afterwards. 'I'm not an asshole.'

Other tensions arose, and not least was the distraction caused by memos and telephone calls from head office as costs began to mount. Barry Diller, as head of the studio, wanted to know what the hell was going on. The press was becoming hostile, and talking down the picture; someone had written that it was *Cleopatra* all over again – which it was not; not quite.

Diller admitted that no one had really calculated the heavy cost of the logistical movements. The movie was budgeted at between $20 and $25 million and should have been $30 million or more. 'I felt I was understandably correct in querying the costs,' he said on reflection. 'At the end of seventy or so days of filming, when very much less than a third of the picture had been shot, it was apparent that the film was going to cost vastly more than contemplated, and my knee-jerk reaction, naturally enough, I suppose, was to get angry with Warren.'

Beatty defended his position in the way any artist would. He simply wanted to make the best picture possible. Diller suggested he might be too close to it, too involved. Beatty laughed. Diller put down the telephone and decided he would let Mr Beatty stew, make him feel guilty. For six weeks, Diller would not talk to Beatty, and refused to accept his transatlantic telephone calls. He might have known he would not win, because Beatty has that way with people – the charm and the resolve to turn all to his advantage – and it was odds on that one day soon, it would be Diller who would end up feeling guilty, for having presumed to treat him such a way. Because if Diller wouldn't talk to Beatty, then Beatty wouldn't talk to Diller.

So Diller relented, and in November caught a plane to the UK for an on-the-spot pow-wow. He met Beatty in London, and all but apologised, admitting his behaviour had been unfortunate. He was impressed by the set-up, liked what he saw and went back to report to his board.

He returned just before Christmas for further observation and found a package waiting for him. It was a five-hour segment of film, mostly of Keaton's scenes, and he sat and watched it. Diller thought it was 'terrific'. He flew to Manchester, where Beatty and the crew were filming, and told him it had the potential for greatness. The disagreements over costs were by no means settled, nor was Diller happy, but they returned to fighting in a rather more civilised manner than plain not talking.

There was another curiosity which cast members began commenting on as the picture moved into its final stages of filming. Beatty had been taken over by John Reed. He had begun wearing the clothes of the man on screen and off. Jerzy Kosinski thought his acting out of Reed's physical problems was good, until he realised that Beatty was suffering. He was tired, and coughing from the flu and damp of the British winter. He looked sick and emaciated, just as Reed had done in his final weeks. When they moved on to Spain, Beatty shared a three-roomed house with Kosinski and his girlfriend.

'I promise you,' he recalled later, 'it was as if we were transported back in time. He was Reed and I, in a peculiar way, had become Zinoviev. Warren was in this house with me and I am reliving my past, I am living the revolution with hot days and cold nights. I am cynical about John Reed and this thought is transferred to Beatty and I laugh at him daily. I, Kosinski, become as impatient as Zinoviev because I, like him, have begun to ask the question, "Why is this crazy American doing this thing?" The personalities had become so interchangeable that it was uncanny.'

There was a further poignancy about one crowd scene in Spain, where they were recreating Reed's speech to the multitudes in Baku. Beatty got on the podium and made a speech to the extras, explaining what the scene was all about and providing a summary of John Reed's life and times – which was all duly translated for the Spaniards pretending to be a crowd of Russians. He explained that he wanted a sea of upturned faces peering at him with admiration, perhaps wonderment. But before the scene was finally shot, there was a strike.

Extras revolted over pay and conditions, standing around for hours on end in temperatures exceeding 110 degrees. Beatty said he quite agreed with their stance. Was this John Reed striking against Beatty? Or Beatty against himself? Or all against Barry Diller? Pay was increased by twenty dollars a day, Diller checked the number of his local heart clinic, and the whole unit then moved on to the frozen wastes of Finland before returning to America. The cost was being estimated at more than $30 million – and it would go higher, for although the main location work was in the can, *Reds* was nowhere near finished. Would it have that greatness Diller had forecast? Or would it be seen as one man's obsession taken to a worthless extreme?

18

Enter Gary Hart

Warren Beatty had been sensible and cautious about the ideology of *Reds*, and that was good, because all around him a furore was growing. His film would be caught in the midst of dramas breaking out all over the place in the politics of world domination. In the early spring of 1980, when he returned to America, Lech Walesa's Polish miners were talking revolution, and the Soviet leaders eyed their unrest with increasing impatience. The Russian dissident Andrei Sakharov had been arrested by the KGB and exiled to Gorky, against US President Jimmy Carter's protests over human rights, but he in turn looked nervous and apprehensive as one attempt after another to free fifty-three American diplomatic hostages in Iran failed.

Britain had agreed to become the first NATO country to accept the deployment of 160 cruise missiles, to be aimed at the Soviet Union. Brezhnev, meanwhile, was dying and the turbulence of international politics had never been more acute in recent times.

It hardly seemed an opportune time for Beatty to come flying home with his epic production, portraying the ideology and life of an American Communist sympathiser. He had built his story with warmth and feeling around its people, yet there was still much work to be done to point up the history and the accuracy. This would include the filming of statements from thirty-two real-life 'witnesses', Socialist veterans whose testimony would be interspersed in his story. Many others were interviewed, and some were filmed for up to two hours, although their contributions would be edited down to mere seconds.

He avoided promotion of Communist ideals, but at the same time the film would have been sunk by a wave of noisy derision if it had been historically incorrect or given the Hollywood soap treatment. The left of American politics would be pleased by his attention to their views, but in 1980 the Left was a diminished clan, a voice hardly heard above the clatter of Reagan's rattling sabres, so he had to counteract possible hostility from public and critics by demonstrating that the Russian Revolution disintegrated into a corruption of itself, that the communism which Reed and his colleagues avowed was not that which transpired under Stalin.

Paramount studio executives were not least among those who viewed the whole thing with unease. They saw potential problems of attitude, exacerbated by mounting costs, although that was the lesser of their considerations. Barry Diller was frank enough to admit that there was concern that the movie 'could have brought shame and degradation on the company.'

There were months of work ahead. With so much footage – 140 hours from 240 days of filming – the task of editing to bring the film into a viable length of under three hours was immense in itself. Beatty installed himself in a studio in New York where he worked day and night with an editing team, often sleeping on the floor. Editors Craig McKay and Dede Allen were now his key people.

Their work was completed nine months later, by the early summer of 1981, when Beatty emerged into the sunlight, looking tired and drawn, with a film 200 minutes in length. Executives of Paramount – not to mention the British financiers, Barclays Mercantile Industrial Finance Ltd, who put up much of the finance and were listed as owning the copyright – had chewed their fingernails down to the quick.

The first viewing was arranged for the key triumvirate of Beatty, Charlie Bludhorn and Barry Diller. Bludhorn's reaction was crucial. When the movie was finished, he sat back and congratulated Beatty. He had enjoyed the film. He liked Beatty's performance. He enjoyed Keaton and Nicholson. He approved. They had dinner in the viewing room, and sat talking until the early hours. Diller, talking frankly, said there were still problems ahead. Not one writer in the media coverage, which they had closely monitored, not even a liberally minded commentator, had so far pointed out that Beatty and Paramount had unearthed a story which had been hidden from America; the hidden story of American left-wing politics sixty years ago. No one had said, Diller pointed out, that Gulf Western might be 'rat bastards but at least they did that.'

This fear was echoed when the lower echelons of the Paramount executive were given a screening, and the tough Frank Mancuso, head of distribution, openly voiced his fears of a backlash against the film's political overtones, suggesting that it should be sold as a love story. Screenings for exhibitors threw up further considerations. The film was 200 minutes long – too long, in their view, for the urban cinemas where they relied on continuous showing. They could screen it only once a night instead of the normal twice with a shorter hour-long film.

Beatty would not want to cut it, of course, and he possessed the contractual right of veto. The editing had been a painful and tedious experience and he believed he had cut the movie to the bare minimum. He also argued against selling the film as a love story. He even went so far as to commission a private poll to gauge street reaction to the story of *Reds*, and it confirmed his belief that audiences were just as intrigued by the politics of the piece as by the story of Reed.

The Paramount marketing people remained unconvinced, and as there were no orders from on high to counteract their contention, Beatty had to settle for the compromise of a vague and romantic theme for the publicity campaign. *Reds* was released on 3 December 1981 and was, at the very least, assured of acres of review. But it was already being written off as a commercial failure in a very public debate over the cost of production. Official estimates from Paramount put the film's final budget at $32.5 million, but trade press rumours reckoned this would escalate further to exceed $40 million when all the post-production costs of promotion and distribution had been added in. It would require box-office grosses well in excess of $100 million to draw level.

Neither was critical reaction in New York glowing in its assessment, although many reviewers praised Beatty for his tenacity and courage. Rex Reed, a Beatty commentator for almost twenty years now, writing in the *New York Daily News*, was among those who seemed more influenced by the cost and the hype of the film than by its artistic merit. 'It bored me senseless,' he wrote. 'A tremendous amount of money has been wasted on a project that has no commercial appeal whatsoever. I cannot imagine the average Joe sitting through this polemic for a minute. I respect Warren Beatty for following his dream, but what good does it do when you end up talking to yourself?'

It was a review which pandered to the debate of finance. Others congratulated Beatty on his recreation of great moments of history, like the take-over of the Winter Palace in Petrograd, and Vincent Canby in *The New York Times* insisted that it was a large, remarkable, rich, romantic film that dramatised the excitement of a young and idealistic man in an age when everything still seemed possible.

Everyone knew too well that this was Warren Beatty, the quintessential player of a certain reputation. John Reed had trouble being taken seriously among his peers back in 1915. Upton Sinclair, the novelist and social reformer, described him as a playboy of the revolution. Beatty, in 1981, faced much the same problem. He was a master tactician, but could anyone, at that moment at the beginning of the eighties, really believe this man was prepared to die on the barricades? It became possible only with the passing of time.

Diana Keaton was excellent, and could not have been bettered by any other supervision. She actually acted Beatty out of some of their scenes. Nicholson was good, but not brilliant, and the physical differences and his laid-back approach to everything were at variance with the character of the real man. On this occasion Jack the Lad, as was his popular screen image now, was miscast as the sad and alcoholic figure of Eugene O'Neill. However, Nicholson researched the role in his usual thorough style by reading everything he could find on the writer, discovering his tempestuous relationships with women, especially his last wife, with whom he fought some epic battles.

Although the part was not large, Nicholson listed it among his favourite roles, and the reaction – which included a nomination for best supporting actor – astounded him. Probably the best compliment came from Eugene O'Neill's daughter, Oona. She wrote explaining that her father had never spoken to her from the day she married Charlie Chaplin at the age of eighteen. 'After a lifetime of acquired indifference,' she wrote, 'the inevitable finally happened. Thanks to you, dear Jack, I fell in love with my father.'

Nicholson was full of praise for Beatty: 'The guy goes out and makes a movie that is so huge, without idiosyncrasy, sort of like him. It's unpretentious, which is hard to do with an epic.'

Although immensely detailed, *Reds* was a good film but one which would not go down in Hollywood history under the heading of 'classic'. It was before its time – a decade later when Gorbachev was releasing eastern Europe from its Communist shackles would have been better. 1981 was the wrong year. It was a tense time, with too many points of reference against which it could be held as a dubious political statement.

Beatty was surely disappointed by the events which surrounded the opening, coming on top of his exhaustion from the two years of solid grind. The battles at Paramount over the promotion and distribution, the whines of the theatres over its length, carping comments about the cost and some back-biting criticism undoubtedly spoiled the aftermath of what had been, by any standards, an achievement. But achievement in Hollywood is, in most eyes, a line of figures at the bottom of the page. The bottom line. The term 'blockbuster' had entered the vocabulary, and it was not a description that fitted *Reds*.

Beatty became reclusive and reluctant to speak about his movie to the media, and it seemed that now he had finally lifted that burden of obsession from his mind, he could no longer even bring himself to discuss it. After the opening, he did not view the film again for many years. He would be criticised for not doing more to help the promotion at the time *Reds* was released and later, would admit that he should have been more active, especially as there was some big competition in the market which would be vying for the upcoming Oscar nominations, including Fonda and Hepburn in *On*

Golden Pond, Steven Spielberg's *Raiders of the Lost Ark*, Dudley Moore in *Arthur* and the highly praised *Atlantic City*.

He could have fought harder, as he did to revive *Bonnie and Clyde* from its critical mauling, but he was strangely reticent. Even so, *Reds* topped the box-office charts for two weeks before being knocked off its perch by *On Golden Pond*. This was an impressive tally since it could be shown only once a night. By March 1982 it had grossed over $30 million before it began to lose cinemas and drop out of the ratings. It would take some time to break even.

For once, however, Hollywood seemed to have great sympathy for him and rewarded him with accolades that can only be demonstrated by the nominations for awards. In January, he was cheered and overjoyed by the news that *Reds* had been nominated for twelve Oscars, historically topped only by Mike Nichols' *Who's Afraid of Virginia Woolf?* which won thirteen nominations in 1966 and Joe Mankiewicz's *All About Eve*, which had fourteen nominations in 1950.

Close rivals to Beatty's film – each with nine Oscar nominations – included *On Golden Pond* and the surprise outsider *Chariots of Fire*, the British film made on a shoestring budget and produced by David Puttnam. Beatty was once again nominated in four categories personally, as producer of the best film, as best actor, best director and for best screenplay (with Trevor Griffiths). Other nominations included Keaton for best actress and Nicholson and Stapleton for best supporting actor and actress.

The competition was strong, with Henry Fonda, Burt Lancaster (*Atlantic City*), Dudley Moore (*Arthur*) and Paul Newman in the best actor category and Katharine Hepburn (*On Golden Pond*), Susan Sarandon (*Only When I Laugh*) and Meryl Streep (*The French Lieutenant's Woman*) lining up for best actress.

In the event, *Reds* converted three of its nominations into actual Oscars – Beatty for best director, Maureen Stapleton for best supporting actress and Vittorio Storaro for cinematography. Recipient of the Oscar for best film was David Puttnam, producer of *Chariots of Fire*. The moment of the announcement would bear a special poignancy for Beatty; it was the one he had been waiting for and he had lost it. He and Puttnam were destined to meet in the future and the moment would be remembered.

Reds had held his attention for too long. After almost a decade of contemplation and four years of preparation it was finished, but not out of his hair or mind; indeed the end of the *Reds* saga was nowhere in sight. It dominated the whole of 1982. The accolades he had received from within the industry gave him renewed heart to go into battle once again, just as he had to resuscitate *Bonnie and Clyde* from sudden death. *Reds* was nowhere near that situation but he felt something had to be done to achieve some better ending to these years of involvement.

He went to Europe and then on to Japan to help promote overseas reaction. In Tokyo 200 journalists crowded into a press conference to hear him take questions on the movie and, as quite often happens, overseas interest was considerably more intelligent in its coverage than his home country. He had made no secret of his belief that there had been mistakes in the initial marketing of the film and the way the promotion of it as a love story had given audiences a totally wrong perception. In the wake of the huge publicity he began to consider that the film could be re-released into American cinemas, much as he had done with *Bonnie and Clyde*. Such a possibility for a film of this size was unheard of and unprecedented. He went as far as hiring the services of Michael Mahern, a man with a considerable reputation for movie hype.

They met for lunch, which extended on into dinner. Mahern was interested in Beatty's thoughts, that the movie had been wrongly positioned in the marketplace, wrongly sold to the public. He believed audiences were intelligent enough to be told up-front that John Reed was a man who has a place in both American and Russian political history, and that Louise Bryant was among the first most liberated women of this century, and went along with Reed not merely because she was in love with him, but also to satisfy her own quest for experience of history in the making.

Mahern arranged for some test sampling to try out the audience reaction to such thoughts. He ran into an immediate problem. Unlike *Bonnie and Clyde*, which the critics had attempted to bury and had almost succeeded in doing so before Beatty saved it, *Reds* had already been out in the provincial cinemas. It was too well known; the audiences knew it was Warren Beatty's film, that he had won an Oscar and that it was a love story. One other thing the research showed was that the story of Beatty and Keaton's romance, which had been featured as a massive overlay to *Reds* in the popular press and magazines, was more attractive to the public than Reed and Bryant.

The fame of Beatty and his lover was almost as important as the movie, and sadly, Mahern reported, the whole notion of the historical importance of *Reds* was simply not a great mover of opinion. Mahern therefore had to recommend that he did not believe he could successfully relaunch *Reds*. He believed it could have been better handled at the outset, but the moment had passed. It was too late.

Beatty hung on to the belief that he had made, as Nicholson put it, 'a hell of a good picture', and the measure of its importance to him was to be seen much later, in 1985, when Paramount began negotiations to sell *Reds* to ABC Television for $6.5 million. Beatty approved the sale, but pointed out that he still retained the final cut, and his lawyers said he would not permit any breach of contract in this respect. ABC said it wanted to slice ten minutes out of the movie so that it could conveniently fit into evening schedules. This effectively halted the sale of the television rights, because although the television company was able to cut the film to conform with regulations on the showing of scenes which included violence, sex or bad language, it was not able to cut it simply because they felt it was too long – not without Beatty's say-so, and he wasn't saying so. It became a matter of principle as a court case loomed.

With Charlie Bludhorn having recently died and Barry Diller having moved to 20th Century-Fox, there were few people at Paramount involved from the outset of the project who could sit down with him and discuss it. It probably would not have mattered anyway. Beatty was adamant that he was not going to allow his film to be cut, and he gave as an example of his feelings the time he saw *Bonnie and Clyde* on television. 'I knew every gunshot; they were there for a reason

– and then they were gone. I knew every cut.'

All directors try to protect the final cut, so that their influence on the film's final appearance is total, and in Beatty's case this was usually doubly important. His position could be said to be comparable with that of an artist who lends a canvas to a gallery and then discovers upon its return that a couple of trees in the landscape have been painted out. Beatty admitted it seemed trivial arguing over nine minutes of film. 'Then you remember,' he said, 'what you were doing at a location for those nine minutes, trying to get it right. And then you object to letting it go down the tube so that they can start the local news bulletin at eleven p.m. It is bad enough having the movie interrupted by people selling Roto-Rooter. It became, as always, a question of art form, or are movies just made for distraction? We have got to keep our dignity.'

For ABC Television it presented an insurmountable problem. They called off the deal, and Paramount did not get its $6.5 million. Was that sensible? Beatty described it as a victory for artistic principle; but *Reds* deserved to be seen by a wider audience. For Beatty, the important of *Reds* in all its respects would remain a significant segment of his career, and his life, which no one, regardless of critical opinion, could take away.

He had to move on, find something different, less intense to bring him back. It was a slow, laborious process and it looked, for a time, if he was going to become bogged down by another obsessive work, a movie about Howard Hughes. 'His interest went back a long way,' explained Leslie Caron, and almost as far back as his crystallising thoughts about John Reed. 'When we were living at the Beverly Wilshire, Howard Hughes had a penthouse there. Warren used to try to discover when Hughes was in residence and would go looking for him. But everybody was sworn to secrecy – even for Warren Beatty. I don't think he ever saw him.'

Towards the end of 1982, he arranged a meeting with lawyers representing the estate of Howard Hughes concerning the rights to the use of his name. Hughes, like Reed, was another figure of intrigue for Beatty. He was, by then, already working on a draft script dealing with Hughes' early years in the aircraft industry and his arrival in Hollywood.

To outsiders who wanted to know why he was pursuing the Howard Hughes story, he would answer enigmatically that it had something to do 'with becoming victim of your own accumulated power.' This phrase could invoke almost as much intrigue and investigation as the subject itself – Hughes and Beatty were very similar in too many ways; mannerisms, shyness, charm and reclusiveness, whose careers ran roughly parallel with some magnificent successes and occasional failures. A victim of his own power? That was Hughes. Beatty was a victim of his own fame.

It offered the potential for the most tantalising and commercial screen portrayal he had yet undertaken because it centred around a modern character, one of the great genius eccentrics, and womanisers, of American society. But, like John Reed, Howard Hughes became a quagmire of interest in which he became bogged down, revisited and – at the time of writing in 1992 – had not been defined in any tangible form. There is still hope.

Two other projects on which he first began working in this post-*Reds* period of confusing signals included a screen version of the comic strip hero Dick Tracy, which many said would never come to fruition, and a screenplay he was having written on the life and times of Benjamin 'Bugsy' Siegel, the mob figure who created Las Vegas. Both were projects that would remain ahead of him for some years to come.

Beatty was apparently not ready to go back to work, not work as in directing Hollywood movies. According to Kathy Bushkin, press secretary for Senator Gary Hart, Beatty was engaged on 'what he hoped would be the greatest movie he had ever produced . . . a true-life one about the President of the United States.' The politics and the power had become another important diversion which in part explained his distraction over choosing a new movie.

It began in the autumn of 1982, when his friend from the McGovern days, Gary Hart, decided he would run for the Democratic nomination for the 1984 presidential race.

Initially, Beatty was a shadowy though persistent figure,

who was more likely to be discovered giving advice or making calls to senior party figures on the telephone late at night than appearing in person at the campaign meetings. Even Gary Hart, himself a stickler for secrecy and surprise, nicknamed him the Phantom because for most of the time he was barely visible but his influence pervaded much of the campaign strategy.

For Gary Hart, Beatty's involvement was important in his bid for the White House. No other presidential candidate since John F. Kennedy was more suited to the archetypal vision of a successful, modern politician nor had benefited more strongly from the support and activity of Hollywood celebrities. Even the reigning President, Ronald Reagan, whose 'home town' it had become, would have been envious. Beatty was a prime mover at every level, and according to one observer was Hart's 'most significant Hollywood resource.'

Hart slipped easily into the role that Hollywood demanded. He was young and darkly handsome, like Beatty himself. He was also artistically minded, having written novels, and was quietly anti-establishment. Hollywood-based fund-raising helped Hart launch his bid for the 1984 candidacy, and his association with the celebrities lifted him out of the mundane battleground of politics into the glitzy arena of Tinsel Town.

He was provided with an aura, enjoyed the celebrity attention and did not seem averse even to the gaudiness of the film capital, although some doubted the advisability of this. Theodore Sorensen, an old hand from the Kennedy days who became chairman of Hart's 1984 campaign, believed he was in awe of the people who were giving him most support. He was excited by the glamour of Hollywood life, and was struck by the mythology of the place, that it offered unlimited personal freedoms to its élite, which of course was never true, as Beatty well knew.

Beatty tried to ensure that Hart's involvement with Hollywood was kept at a practical and political level, unaffected and even untainted by the diamond-studded, sexually orientated world. It was by then common knowledge that John Kennedy's flirtation with the stars descended much deeper, into the most insidious, ill-judged pursuit of personal pleasure and sexual gratification with the likes of Marilyn Monroe.

Hart's very being there, among the dream-pedlars, ensured that media interest would be through a wide-angled lens. Ironically, the friendship with Warren Beatty provided his opposers in the Republican movement with a dubious focal point. This in itself helped encourage a close scrutiny of Hart. It may well have been because he recognised the dangers that lay within the Hollywood flirtation which had so bedazzled Kennedy that Beatty kept his own significance in the Hart organisation almost to underground status.

During the early months of the campaign, from the autumn of 1982 through to the summer of 1983, he stayed pretty much apart from Hart's main body of supporters. He refused to attend parties and events, did not join the spectacular star line-ups at functions to raise money and promote Hart's candidacy. He even declined an offer to join the candidate's Media Advisory Group, which might well have benefited from his personal experience. He wanted nothing to do with the bandwagon at all, at least not publicly. He was a quietly confident figure at the epicentre of the campaign, but removed from it by design. He kept in contact with managers and officials by telephone and his meetings with the top echelons and Hart himself were more clandestine, for he realised that his own reputation might drag Hart into a media maelstrom.

Meanwhile, his efforts would be based largely on what Hart believed was his personal brilliance in assessing public mood, and how this would affect and influence feelings about politics and issues. Many of his ideas were impossibly naïve, but the injection of fresh, unconventional thinking helped transform Hart from a political nonentity into a serious challenger for the next two presidential elections, 1984 and 1988.

Insiders noticed that one of the most important aspects of Beatty's influence was in Hart's oratorial abilities. Beatty talked him into ditching rhetoric on policy issues and going straight for the realities that faced the voting public. Beatty's telephone conversations within the group acted as a kind of unofficial bush telegraph, enabling each section of the Hart campaign machine to discover and appreciate the needs and feelings of the other. Beatty would describe his work as modest – 'I tried to be a good friend and I tried to help in any way that I could. I did whatever I could.'

Hart, on the other hand, felt comfortable with having a confident and influential aide, even if a lot of his ideas were off the wall. 'He always wanted to paint with bold strokes,' Hart remembered. Through the winter of 1983–4 Beatty had largely restricted his role in Hart's campaign to that of being on hand for friendship and support whenever needed, but as the race hotted up he was allowed a strong voice in the fundamental strategy of the final months.

Hart had secured some stunning success in the New England states, then his campaign faltered and only then did observers become aware of the importance of Beatty's presence in the Hart organisation. It was at this point that Beatty stepped up his personal involvement to a virtual twenty-four hour commitment. As the vital New York primary approached, Raymond D. Strother, Hart's public relations man, Pat Caddell, his opinion poll adviser, and Beatty persuaded him to make a thirty-minute television broadcast to bolster his support. On the night when the telecast was to be recorded a blizzard raged off the east coast and delayed Hart's arrival at the studio. The only copy of his planned speech was in the briefcase of Pat Caddell, who arrived even after the candidate.

Only then was it discovered that the speech overran the allotted time by half as much again. With the studio deadline fast approaching, Beatty – like a film director working on a movie script – joined them and began cutting and rewriting the speech to a more manageable length, and continued rewriting even as Hart recorded the first pages.

Hart, however, did not fare as well as they had hoped. Over the next few weeks, his percentages began to decline. Beatty asserted his role in the campaign with even greater authority and berated himself for not having done so earlier. He became one of the most influential figures, and often Beatty was the only person Hart would talk to. 'He trusted Warren implicitly,' said Caddell. 'He was comfortable with him, much more so than with the rest of us.'

As the Hart campaign stumbled further, Beatty attempted to pull victory out of the chaos. This was best demonstrated when Pat Caddell had a falling-out with the candidate over tactics and they were not talking to each other. One evening after the New York primary, there was a campaign meeting

271

at which Caddell hardly said a word. Beatty, normally a softly spoken man who could at times be inaudible, beckoned Caddell outside and, in the pollster's words, 'ripped the shit out of me and then told me to get the hell back in there and do something.'

Beatty's high-level involvement in the campaign, in which his contribution ranged across the whole strata of American political issues of the day, posed an interesting possibility for the future. Beatty's position in public life could have been transformed. He had spoken in the disappointing aftermath of *Reds* about giving up movies. He was at a personal crossroads in his life which might have been resolved with a significant role in the Hart administration, had it come about.

In the end, the situation did not arise. His efforts were to no avail. Mondale won the Democratic nomination but lost the election to Reagan's second term. Mondale was a spent force, but Hart lived to fight another day, and Beatty would be back in the forefront when he came out for what proved to be the final disastrous chapter four years later.

19

A Song and Dance

Diane Keaton had gone the way of his past loves. There were some words of disappointment and regret, especially from him, and there would be times in the immediate future when they were in the same room together and barely acknowledged each other's presence. In spite of having been together during one of the most intensely pressurised periods of Beatty's life they had had little contact with each other for some time, although Nicholson took her out to dinner often enough until Al Pacino began seeing her. By then Warren Beatty was on the move again, looking and travelling and telephoning.

He was discussing deals but could be firm about none. The most likely contender for his immediate attention was a script outline written by his friend Elaine May, called *Ishtar*, a contemporary road movie on the lines of the Crosby and Hope series with Dorothy Lamour. The central characters were down-on-their-luck singer-songwriters who have gone to Morocco to work in a night-club and get caught up in foreign intrigue involving terrorist groups and the CIA. But the plot of *Ishtar* bore no comparison to the mystery and intrigue that would surround the making of the film itself. *Ishtar* was destined to become a Hollywood saga, the product and the epitome of all that was going on in that highly precious city of movie-makers and creative artists – a story of friendship and squabbles, of loyalty and treachery, and of a very great deal of money going down the tubes.

Ishtar was neither intellectually nor professionally demanding but it was funny, and in 1985 Beatty decided he would like to do it, for no other reason than his loyalty and regard for Elaine May, then fifty-four, who also wanted to direct her work. She had not directed a picture since *Mikey and Nicky* almost a decade earlier, when she had taken two years to edit her ill-fated movie, and she had had difficulty in finding work as a director ever since. The word around the trade was that Beatty's support for *Ishtar* was for May's sake, and they both knew that if it flopped, it might be her last picture as a director.

He said he liked the idea and decided to put together a package with himself as producer and co-star, with Dustin Hoffman, if he would agree, in the other top role. Hoffman, who was by no means a close friend of Beatty's until they began work on the picture – but then, who was? – also liked the sound of it, and the whole project was costed and sent off to Guy McElwaine, Beatty's former press agent from years back who had recently become head of Columbia Studios. 'After I read the script,' said Hoffman, 'and talked on the phone to Warren, we found a commonality of taste and we just got on from there.'

In the spring of 1985, Beatty and May were invited to McElwaine's Burbank office, which was at the far end of a long second-floor corridor whose walls were lined with huge blow-ups of past Columbia hits. McElwaine's room assaulted the eyes of all who entered. It was wholly decorated in a deep maroon, floor to ceiling and wall to wall, and heavily smoked glass in the Columbia building ensured that this gloom was not penetrated by one ray of sunlight. There were four very large sofas over which were laid skin rugs. Everyone sat around talking about the script. McElwaine, too, liked the idea, but negotiations were protracted. The budget was big, with initial estimates at over $25 million, perhaps more, and Columbia, whose 1984–5 grosses had not been up to expectations, hummed and hahed – not least because of Elaine May's well-known artistry in directing movies, which was translated in the trade as a reputation for being 'difficult'.

Beatty himself was a known perfectionist when directing and Hoffman, too, had a similar reputation which had been widely reported over the years, and of late when he was said to have had several squabbles with director Sydney Pollack while they were making *Tootsie*. The three of them together did not inspire the unswerving commitment of the money men, who run scared of words like art and perfection and interpretation. They preferred descriptions which unashamedly included the prefix 'blockbuster'. Columbia had just had one, *Ghostbusters*, but in 1985, when *Ishtar* was being finalised, initial returns from the Columbia output of movies, which included *Jagged Edge*, *Silverado* and *Fright Night*, had been fairly disappointing, if not disastrous. Others, like *New Kids*, *Sylvester* and *The Slugger's Wife* were worse. The word around Columbia was that changes at the top were imminent.

However, discussions went on and Beatty and May tinkered with the script and waited for movement. Guy McElwaine recommended that Columbia went ahead, and did so largely on the basis of Beatty's track record, notwithstanding his misgivings about Miss May's past difficulties in completing a picture. 'You had to be very careful of saying no to something of Warren's,' said McElwaine, 'because at that time his record as a producer-star was about a thousand per cent in terms of what has been recouped from his pictures, cost to gross.'

Also in those early months of 1985, writer James Toback was being pressed by Beatty to complete a screenplay on Bugsy Siegel and Beatty also showed more than a flicker of interest in producing another Toback script called *The Pick-up Artist*. Toback, who urgently needed a financial boost, was hopeful of a positive response, but the discussions over the script and who were the right actors for key roles went on for weeks, then months and then faded altogether. Nothing was achieved and Toback began to look elsewhere for a producer.

The idea of a Dick Tracy movie also returned to the drawing-board at the beginning of 1985 and Beatty talked to Martin Scorsese about directing. He himself intended to produce and star, and co-write the script. Scorsese, better known for stark movies like *Taxi Driver*, which brilliantly personified the bitter realism of the seventies with his story of a Vietnam War veteran, was amused by the idea of bringing the thirties comic strip hero to life.

Beatty had visions of a big, colourful, fun production with

musical numbers and larger-than-life characterisations. He and Scorsese talked around it, and discussed the script. Talk was one thing, commitment another; they circled each other for weeks and slowly, the project was moulded into a fairly definite form, though Beatty had made no deal with any studio and the costs of transferring these ideas to the screen looked menacingly high.

They met intermittently and they talked some more. The final cut, which was a sore point with Beatty after the attempts to slice some footage from *Reds* for television, was equally important to the director. Finally, they made some sort of agreement and Scorsese put his signature to some paperwork, but heard nothing more. In the meantime, he got married and went off on his honeymoon to Venice, where he received a telephone call. It was Beatty, offering his congratulations, but no commitment in terms of *Dick Tracy*. So it went on the back burner, and Scorsese heard nothing more of it until, a few years later, he learned Warren that was going to produce, direct and star in the picture himself.

Beatty had not made a movie since 1980 and there was still no definite project ahead by May of 1985, although *Ishtar* now seemed a real possibility. He'd had long meetings at Columbia, right at the top with Francis 'Fay' Vincent, the chairman of Columbia's parent company, and studio head Guy McElwaine. The costings were a nightmare. Was the script for a comedy really strong enough to support two major stars and a budget of that size? Eventually McElwaine announced that he had won approval on the basis of a budget of $27.5 million, which included $5.5 million for each of the two stars, with Beatty having an additional $500,000 for being producer as well.

Beatty and Hoffman as a double act looked exceedingly promising. Even so, it would mean Beatty would not be seen back on the silver screen for at least another year, possibly two. What other modern actor would dare go that long without risk to his future?'

Tension was running high, as happened when he was building up to a movie start. Also, now that Keaton was no longer around, a flurry of female companions had been mentioned

in the previous few months. One newcomer was more persist-
ently present than the others which, if the past pattern was
to be adhered to, would suggest that Beatty's comeback to the
movies was imminent. It was Isabelle Adjani, the third co-
star in *Ishtar*. Beatty and Isabelle were together long before
she was cast. The German-born actress was twenty-nine years
old and had appeared in a small collection of small movies.
Beatty first met her when she was cast by Roman Polanski for
his 1976 French-based movie *The Tenant*, co-starring Polanski
himself, Shelley Winters and Melvyn Douglas. Since then she
had appeared in other low-key movies, including two made in
Europe, *Quartet* and *One Deadly Summer*, although to the
movie-going public Adjani was relatively unknown.

She possessed a classic oval face and features which looked
stunning even without make-up. Beatty was soon to describe
her as 'the most gifted person for the screen I have ever
known,' which was a truly grand statement, considering the
number he had known. Their affair lingered in Paris for a
while and a French magazine said Beatty was going to marry
her. That was truly good sign. If past form was followed, it
meant that he was into a new relationship, which meant a
new film was now about to take off – and as for wedding
bells, only fools would put money on it.

The prospect was hardly worth discussing now, and readers
may wish to refer to notes on past encounters to refresh their
memories on the course these matters usually took: a strong
wooing, lots of charm etc., etc.; a film is made and there is
publicity. The newspapers continued to have this penchant
for marrying people off – anyone and everyone from Jack
Nicholson and Anjelica Huston (which never happened) to
Prince Andrew and Koo Stark, and then Beatty and who
knows who? Who knows when? Not even he, or them. How
silly it all seems, looking back. And what was the point? By
the mid-eighties, marriages were falling like machine-gunned
Nazis in a John Wayne war film.

Ishtar finally came to life one Sunday afternoon in Los
Angeles when Beatty and Elaine May brought a group of
friends and actors together at his home on Mulholland Drive,
which he now used in preference to the Los Angeles hotel
suites, though not exclusively. In the living-room, Beatty

associates were assembled like the characters in the final scene of an Agatha Christie novel. Their purpose was a brainstorming session, to hear the readings from the script and give their opinions.

There were a couple of writers, Peter Feibleman, who was the executor of Lillian Hellman's estate, and Herb Gardner, whose play *I'm Not Rappaport* had just opened on Broadway; Dustin Hoffman, who also had great admiration for May after she worked on the script of his film *Tootsie*; actor Charles Grodin, who had worked with both Beatty and May in the past, and other friends. Once everyone was settled, May handed out copies of the script and assigned parts to some of the assembled, and they began a reading.

Ishtar, it emerges, has a plot of routine comedy, slipping into comic intrigue. The first part of the action is in New York, where the Hoffman character is dying a death as a comedian and Beatty, similarly unsuccessful, talks him out of a suicide bid from the ledge of an apartment block. The two singer-songwriters are by no means God's gift to the music industry, either, and when their agent (to be played by Jack Weston) gets them work in a Moroccan night-club, they gladly accept. Once in the Middle East, they become embroiled in an intrigue, marooned in the mythical Kingdom of Ishtar, where leftist terrorists are planning to overthrow the local Emir. Beatty is recruited by one side when romanced by Isabelle Adjani, while Hoffman is recruited by the CIA, and they are innocently working against each other.

The reading went on for a couple of hours. The jokes were often very funny, there were some set-pieces – such as one farcical incident involving a blind camel – and there were to be some song and dance routines for the two leading men. Beatty and Elaine May took the temperature of those present. Everyone thought it was terrific and that overworked phrase 'great potential' was mentioned. Some present offered individual words of advice on changing this and that, and they were all pretty well agreed that it was going to be expensive. That was the key issue – but did anyone really challenge the fact that this might turn out to be the most expensive comedy ever made in Hollywood? What was the justification for it?

There were no undercurrents or epic situations in what was

after all no more than a modernisation of the old Crosby-Hope routines. It was a relatively lightweight story, enlivened by Elaine May's intelligent humour with a host of one-liners and gags which, on a good day, would get any audience laughing. Was it really sufficient to exploit the very creative, but expensive, talents of the star pairing?

They pressed on.

In the long, hot summer of 1985, with *Ishtar* subject to final pre-production work, Beatty momentarily ducked back into politics as a major fund-raiser and platform speaker for Californian Supreme Court Chief Justice Rose Bird, who was facing a re-election challenge. He gave a momentous, rousing speech in San Francisco, which was interrupted by hefty applause during his references to the 'descendants of Joe McCarthy' who were trying to oust Rose Bird from her job. A standing ovation from a crowd of supporters was not mirrored in hostile sections of the press, who accused him of being outrageous and unfair, and of being the high-profile poodle of back-room manipulators. He winced but seemed unperturbed, and once again rejected notions that he himself might stand for public office, for which he only had to say the word for a nomination.

Ishtar was announced as a definite starter against all the predictions of those allegedly in the know. Filming was scheduled to begin in August, with eight weeks in Morocco and six weeks in New York.

August came and went and the movie hadn't started. By September, it was still not underway, in spite of a production schedule that dictated an August start and a January finish, enabling editing and post-production to take place in late spring to achieve a final cut version for viewing in August and a November 1986 release, just in time for consideration for that year's Oscars. These strictures had been more precise than usual, given Elaine May's last experience as a director.

By October, there were more script conferences, and new actors had to be found for some of the minor roles because the delay had meant some of the original cast were now unavailable. Some production people were in the same difficulty and had to leave because of other contracts. It certainly seemed from the outset as if the movie had one of those jinxes that makes little things go wrong, but only those little things that cost a lot to put right, and everything began to take a little longer and cost more than had been planned. The location proved a problem. Production designer Paul Sylbert had been dispatched to North Africa to find some desert with undulating sand dunes, close to some decent hotels, that would not involve the cast trekking too far for their scenes. Sylbert found the ideal spot in the Moroccan Sahara, with two very classy hotels right alongside.

When the unit arrived, however, there were problems. Elaine May decided she would now prefer a flat desert, not one with big dunes. 'But I thought you wanted dunes,' Sylbert queried.

'No,' said May, 'flat . . .'

'Oh well, flat desert it is, then,' said the ever-pleasant Sylbert, and hired a small army of local labour and machinery to bulldoze the Sahara. 'Right there in the middle of the dunes,' he recalled, 'I built Elaine a flat desert.'

There were other difficulties arising almost daily, as they do in far-off locations. A small example: something little but vital broke off one of the cameras when they were filming in Morocco, and a replacement could not be found locally. A man had to buy the piece in New York and fly it hastily to Marrakech. They could not risk the part being lost or held up in customs. Next some camels were wanted; one camel in particular was required to look blind on screen, and there had to be a couple of back-ups in case the first one dropped down dead or ran off. Beatty and May anticipated there would be no problem locating such camels in Morocco. But it was neither easy nor cheap.

The *Ishtar* set was surrounded by secrecy and was placed out of bounds to showbusiness reporters anxious to get an update on the working of this triumvirate of volatile, temperamental and creative people. *Ishtar* remained a remote and unwelcoming set to visitors, even friendly ones sent by Columbia's publicity people anxious to drum up some advance hype on this expensive desert song and dance act.

Word leaked out, however, that there were some temperamental tensions. Beatty and Hoffman were well-behaved, but even they began to tire of Elaine May's insistence on 'getting it right', which sometimes entailed retaking some scenes twenty times or more, sometimes with three cameras running.

The shooting schedules were out of the window – eight weeks in Morocco and eventually nine weeks in New York – and by February there was a further major hold-up when the climactic musical numbers for Beatty and Hoffman were not ready. Production actually shut down for a couple of days while the songs were rewritten and the scenes rehearsed and played by Beatty and Hoffman. As one technician reported, 'The whole set was buzzing with rumours about the picture and about Columbia Studios itself. Something was up, and no one knew what was going on – there was even talk of the movie being shut down completely because it had gone way over the top, moneywise.' Columbia's production manager, Mac Brown, said it was one of those productions where no one appeared to be overspending wildly or irresponsibly. 'It seemed to me that money was of secondary importance to creativity – that was the main issue,' he said.

Back in New York, where the final scenes were being shot, May actually called a wrap at 10.12 p.m. on the night the Academy awards were being staged in Los Angeles – 24 March 1986, three months behind the original schedule and well over budget. Later, Columbia would confirm that the true cost had escalated to more than $40 million and there would be intense speculation as to the viability of such a film, needing as it would gross takings in excess of $100 million to break even.

Elaine May assembled her team of editors and technicians in a suite at the Brill Building and began her task of cutting the 104 hours of filmed footage into 105 minutes of running time. The trade press, champing at the bit because they had been unable to get a vision of *Ishtar*, was still expecting her to deliver her final print in time for an end-of-year showing. But already some kind of campaign was underway – known in Hollywood as 'bad mouthing' – months before anyone had even clapped eyes on it. This was just one of Beatty's problems. An explosion of temperaments and personalities was waiting to happen.

Unbeknown to Beatty and Hoffman, a man they both considered to be one of their arch-enemies was about to enter the scenario: David Puttnam, the British director. The very mention of his name aroused bitter memories from their past and they both talked about him with some venom.

The arrival of Puttnam in the midst of Hollywood and in one of the top mogul jobs, as head of Columbia Studios, came right out of the blue. In the late spring of 1986 Puttnam was approached by Fay Vincent to replace Guy McElwaine as chairman of Columbia Pictures and senior executive vice-president and director of the parent Columbian Pictures Industries, of which Vincent was head. The ultimate owner was the entertainments division of Coca-Cola, which had instigated the head-hunting of the man who was considered to be the great white hope of the British film industry.

Vincent and his deputy flew to London to secure his services. Puttnam would be wooed, although he laid down some stringent demands for total autonomy in the job. They hammered out pretty well all the points that might cause disagreement, and Puttnam knew enough about the set-up at Columbia to raise an important question. He went straight to a key issue: Beatty and Hoffman. 'You realise that we don't get along,' he said to Vincent.

'Why should that affect this situation?' Vincent replied.

'Ishtar.'

'But it's as good as done. We only have post-production to complete.'

Vincent agreed that it had gone way over budget and that the bills were coming in. Vincent later admitted that really wasn't the point of Puttnam's raising the issue – he just did not understand the 'enormity of the hatred' that existed against the British director. Puttnam explained the situation in detail and was quite candid about the fact that he believed that Beatty and Hoffman might even try to stop him being hired. Vincent listened and said at once that he realised that both men could well be exceedingly negative about Puttnam's appointment but he assured Puttnam that he had personally been involved with the production of *Ishtar* and would continue to resolve any problems that arose – thus more or less avoiding any need for contact between them.

The very fact that the conversation was taking place demonstrated the joint force of Beatty and Hoffman, though in reality it was barely feasible that even they could have stopped Coca-Cola hiring the man of their choice. *Ishtar* was, after all, only one of many films involving many stars and directors and their tough-dealing agents which Puttnam would be inheriting from McElwaine. But the appointment of the head of studio was virtually resting on Vincent being able to assure Puttnam that he could resolve any problem with Beatty and Hoffman.

There was little doubt that the two stars would consider Puttnam to be an enemy, and that feeling was soon voiced when they heard that Puttnam was en route. But as Puttnam well knew, he would face some fairly widespread abuse from Hollywood in general, many of whose inmates considered him to be no great figure, an insignificant Brit with no US track record, apart from *Midnight Express* and *Chariots of Fire*. His other major movies, *The Killing Fields*, *Local Hero* and *The Mission* had made money but not been particularly successful. In Britain, the reactions ranged from accusations of treachery for walking out on what remained of the film industry to expressions of delight for this superb opportunity.

Hollywood waited, and knives were being sharpened. Beatty made it plain that he did not want to deal with the man, and Hoffman said he would not even speak to him. 'He's going to torpedo my picture and will do everything to kill off *Ishtar* – I know it,' Beatty told Vincent in an irate telephone conversation.

So what was the cause of the resentment?

In Hoffman's case, the story went back to 1978, when Puttnam was producing a movie called *Agatha*, the story of Agatha Christie's mysterious disappearance in 1926, when she went to Harrogate under an assumed name, apparently intent on committing suicide. Vanessa Redgrave was in the leading role and all was proceeding when Puttnam lost the backing of Rank, who discovered that Colonel Christie, from whom Agatha had been fleeing at the time of her mental distress, had been a director of Rank.

Late one afternoon Puttnam received a telephone call from Hoffman's then manager Jarvis Astaire who was in Los Angeles. He said Hoffman would really like to become involved in the movie and he could bring finance from First Artists, to whom he was contracted for one more picture. Hoffman had read the screenplay and wanted a part in it. It would also suit him personally at the time to be in England. They talked about some minor changes which would accommodate Hoffman's role. However, according to Puttnam, Hoffman arrived in London with a scriptwriter and was intent on rewriting the entire screenplay.

To cut a long story short, Puttnam soon accused Hoffman of trying to take over the picture, a claim that was backed up by Vanessa Redgrave, who apparently refused to speak to Hoffman other than when saying her lines. There was, by all accounts, a bit of a to-do and Puttnam had his name removed from the credits and left the film in Hoffman's hands. Hoffman blamed Puttnam for commencing filming before the new script – which Hoffman had initiated – was completed.

There were more rows and delays and Hoffman and First Artists ended up in court. First Artists took the picture away from Hoffman; he sued for an injunction to stop them distributing it and lost. 'I got the shit kicked out of me from all sides,' was his now famous assessment of the situation.

Hoffman was apparently even more put out, though, a couple of years later when Puttnam gave a magazine interview. 'I described Hoffman as a bit of a pest – he wasn't too happy about that and that's when animosity really became intense,' Puttnam said.

From that day, Puttnam remained high on Hoffman's list of most hated men. In this he was joined by Beatty who reckoned Puttnam had done him a great disservice. His story went back to the 1981 Oscar nominations when Puttnam's *Chariots of Fire* and Beatty's *Reds* were in competition for the awards, especially for best picture. Beatty believed that Puttnam had been saying some pretty uncomplimentary things about his film during the run-up to awards night, and he had never forgiven him.

As Puttnam explained, 'I had never actually met Warren Beatty, although I had been on a platform with him with five or six other people. So we had had no conversation about this at all. In fact, what had happened in the run-up to the Oscars was that I was simply fighting my corner for my little film *Chariots of Fire* and stressing the David and Goliath thing which is really all you can do in that highly competitive scenario. That's what got up his nose – he was touchy about *Reds* and I think once again, he was being slugged about the cost of his picture. When I arrived on his scene at Columbia at the time of *Ishtar*, I think there was something of an echo going back to that time – my film versus his.'

When the June announcement of Puttnam's appointment was made, *Ishtar* was still far away from being ready for release, which was why Beatty was worried. He had a meeting with Vincent, who assured him once again that Puttnam would not be involved in any way with *Ishtar*. Puttnam was not due to start the job until 1 September, to give him a chance to read up on the paperwork of his new undertaking. Even so, Beatty remained unconvinced that Puttnam would not bring down some 'very negative attitudes towards my picture' in the months ahead.

With the trade press already querying the delays in even nominating a release date, this would not have been difficult; *Ishtar* was being talked into becoming a disaster. Talk in the trade was rife and was merely fuelled in August when Columbia took a full-page advertisement in the *Hollywood Reporter* which simply said, '*Ishtar*: National Release 22 May 1987.'

Later, *Parade* magazine, read by thirty-one million Americans, ran an article that infuriated both Beatty and Hoffman, alleging that the movie was so disappointing that Columbia was keeping it under wraps until more work had been completed. Columbia strongly denied this was the case, and in answer to repeated inquiries to the studio about the fate of the picture issued the same response: 'It is still in post-production preparation.'

The truth was that Elaine May had not finished her post-production work, and was weeks away from producing a final version. The pressure of media attention had a depressing effect on the participants, and especially the media-shy May. One day a writer she knew wandered into her editing room and discovered her hunched over the console. 'Hi . . . what are you doing in town?' she asked.

'A story on *Ishtar* . . .'

'*Et tu, Brute!*' she said, without looking up from her screen.

It was no secret by then that there was no love lost between

Puttnam and Beatty. Puttnam, having reviewed all the pictures in progress, canned several and scrapped plans for a few others he had inherited from McElwaine. But he kept his hands off *Ishtar*. Vincent continued to deal with Beatty and Hoffman, as agreed, although there were two areas in which Puttnam felt he had a right to make his opinions known to Vincent: costs and resources. He had observed that the post-production bills were still coming in. The costs of the picture had ballooned worryingly, to which Beatty allegedly responded: 'Who gives a fuck what he thinks – just tell him to sign the cheques!'

More important to Puttnam, however, were the demands the *Ishtar* production was making on studio resources, particularly the PR and advertising departments. Puttnam said that Beatty kept changing his mind or rewriting the promotion material so that Shelley Hochran, who was in charge of the promotion, made literally dozens of presentations before obtaining his final approval. 'This,' said Puttnam, 'put demands on our resources which were needed with equal urgency elsewhere.'

Beatty and Hoffman felt that they had been let down by the studio, and that they could no longer trust Vincent. Even promotional people, over whom Beatty had a contractual veto, were being questioned because he thought they were 'loyal to David, and not to me.'

Ishtar was not Puttnam's problem but he could not dismiss it because it was his overall task to put Columbia on a profitable footing. He was having a similar running battle with Bill Cosby over *Leonard Part VI*, which eventually bombed; he had Dan Aykroyd leaving the production of *Vibes* and assorted other battles with a fair cross-section of Hollywood's finest talent, intermingled with a good few prima donnas and piranhas who were lining up against the new boss. Beatty and Hoffman were important to Beatty and Hoffman; to Puttnam they were two more people with problems, although as he quite understood, very sharp and powerful ones.

Finally, *Ishtar* was ready for release, twelve months after the final film footage was exposed. It opened at three major New York houses and then at 1,142 cinemas across the country. In view of all the discussion that the movie had engendered in the media, everyone was waiting to see what all the fuss was about.

It was not about much at all – except the money, and everyone retained that as their focus. Critical reaction was often complimentary, never ecstatic and sometimes downright hurtful. Although *Time* listed it as close to Elaine May's best work, the *Hollywood Reporter*, which had kept its readers abreast of the *Ishtar* developments as they happened, cruelly denounced the movie as 'colossally dunderheaded'. There were several poison arrows aimed at the triumvirate, and especially Beatty, who was fifty that year. *Village Voice* scowled: 'He's a bit long in the tooth to engage in the adolescent skittishness about sex, hetero and homo, that adds a dose of painful infantilism to the massive ineptitude of the movie as a whole.'

That summed up the movie. It was hilarious in places, but there was nothing else to say. It did not hold up a $40 million budget and this was quickly proved at the box office, where it faced general public apathy and averaged only very modest business on the opening weekend. It was pulled out very quickly and, with *Ishtar*, Beatty lost some of his shine.

Before the bad news became so apparent, Beatty and Hoffman held a dinner party for some of their friends from *Ishtar*, which writer Brad Darrach joined. He was discussing the film with Hoffman, who was furious because he believed that the critics had reviewed the budget and not the film. 'It is impossible now to make a movie with two big stars for under $35 million – and that's without Morocco,' he said. At that point, Beatty's sinewy hand clapped over Hoffman's mouth. 'We're not talking money, are we?'

But money was the bottom line, as always, and there was an ever-decreasing tolerance for financial failure, regardless of the art and the creativity of it all. Puttnam decided that for him personally it was a 'no-win' situation and he did not even see the movie.

Ishtar was one of a string of failures from the Columbia studio, and little more than a year later, Coca-Cola announced a reshuffling of their feature films division. Fay Vincent moved to the main Coke division, and later left the company to return to law practice. David Puttnam assessed that his own contract had been broken and headed home to Britain with a bucketful of compensatory dollars.

Beatty, meanwhile, pocketed his $6 million fee which may or may not have been sufficient to ease the pain of what was his most disastrous movie. It had jolted him and his reputation like nothing else had and taken his power-rating down several notches.

20

Dick and Madonna

For a man of fifty who had a home which was now a superb monument to his affluence but little else, and who was possessed by an apparent continuing wanderlust involving women and travel; a man fast of foot who is glimpsed in passing or is momentarily the centre of attention before he moves on, the only anchor was his occasional movies, when he was engrossed in the making of them. Thereafter, he seemed to be moving through a kind of social vacuum in which there was no kind of foothold. He was like the shadowy figure in a *noir* movie, emerging and disappearing at will, with no one quite sure where he was, what he was doing or why he was doing it, or with whom.

A man who has lived half a century and has accumulated a considerable fortune has also usually gathered around him an entourage or a circle of close friends and relations. A man of that age has usually put down some roots. Beatty appeared not to have done this to any large degree, and even his 'family', such as it was, tended to be other people's. He had a habit of using the temporary family he would acquire while in the process of making a movie, which consisted of his actors and actresses and crew on the film. Not much had changed since Leslie Caron's description of his behaviour years earlier. He was like a father and a brother, and occasionally a lover, and sometimes he sought warmth and love in other people's homes and surroundings.

This was noticed by Dustin Hoffman. Beatty would be there, joining the family group. Hoffman told the writer Brad Darrach: 'Lisa and I both like him, but he makes us sad and we don't quite know why. There's an essential loneliness in him. I'm not surprised he is considering a movie about Howard Hughes. I mean, I see him dying alone with nobody there to love him or hold his hand. It hurts to think about that.'

Men of fifty begin to react to those kind of thoughts, and then, if they are so disposed, put them out of their minds by reaffirming their prowess and their abilities as a lover and their attraction to younger women. Beatty was remarkably well-preserved, though there were flecks of grey hair, and laughter lines and crows' feet that make-up could hardly cover. Fifty, as one reviewer had pointed out, was no age for continuing adolescence, but that did not apply to Beatty, or at least he thought it did not. There was an inherent loneliness in the life that he had led for so many years, yet he did not appear to want to change it; alternatively he might have been subconsciously trying to compensate for it.

Politics was by then back on the agenda. Beatty was still in the throes of promotional activity for the ill-fated *Ishtar* when his pal Gary Hart announced he would run for the 1988 Democratic nomination for President. The preamble and the build-up had begun months before and Beatty was dashing between the editing suite in New York and meetings in Washington and elsewhere to help Hart get his campaign on the move. Much of his contact, though, was by telephone, direct to Gary Hart or to one of the senior campaign leaders.

That summer Beatty reportedly lent the senator $265,000 to buy 135 acres around his home at what would prove to be an aptly named address, Troublesome Gulch. It was still early days in the campaign and he was heavily engaged on his picture. But he was still very close to the hub of the campaign, especially in the area of mustering financial support and particularly in giving counsel to Hart.

Pat Caddell was again a central figure in the campaign and became a Beatty point of contact. As Hart began his journey in a more positive way, Beatty once again joined the inner circle as one of the most powerful men in the Hart camp. They enjoyed each other's company and this very fact allowed Hart's enemies – and even some of his own Party supporters

— to draw the conclusion that Hart also shared Beatty's love of women. The many occasions he stayed at Beatty's house on Mulholland Drive, where he would also meet Jack Nicholson, would be duly noted, and the fact that he often stayed there even when Beatty was not in Los Angeles raised queries as to the reason why he was using this legendary and impregnable palace of variety.

The association of Beatty, fabled stud, and Hart, the politician who enjoyed female company, was but one step away from disturbing rumours. Aware that this undercurrent of gossip was gathering momentum as Hart set out on his second bid for the presidency, some of the closer members of his staff tried to steer him away from staying in Los Angeles but Hart rejected their advice. Long afterwards, when he had time to reflect, he admitted, 'If people wanted to say there were orgies going on up there and I was chasing starlets, there was nothing I could do about that.' Hart refused to say he would not stay at Beatty's again, because he reckoned if he gave way on one simple issue like that, he would be expected to give way all down the line.

He said he and Beatty had that discussion and Hart had dismissed it because it was an innocent situation. True, Beatty had people staying there from time to time, but that was 'his business and not mine,' said Hart, and with that he pointedly refused to turn his back on Beatty, whom he counted as one of his closest friends and advisers. As Pat Caddell confirmed, Beatty could speak to and advise Hart in a manner no other member of the team was able to do — and he usually got results.

However, some of his previous supporters in Hollywood, like Robert Redford, were already distancing themselves from him. Redford made no secret of his view that although he had supported Hart in two senatorial campaigns, he did not think he had the ability for the highest office in the land. He also told one interviewer that Hart's biggest mistake was getting mixed up 'with the Hollywood set . . . because he ended up thinking he was invisible.'

These misgivings, rumbling like a grumbling appendix as Hart prepared to announce his candidacy, caused him some acute financial problems. Support in Hollywood, where he had been given the initial impetus for the 1984 campaign, was somewhat grudging, even lacking. Hart was becoming noticeably hesitant about running and had a long talk with Beatty in April 1987. What was discussed between the two men is known only to them, but on 13 April Hart announced he would run and set off for Los Angeles to stump up some cash with a series of $1,000 a head fund-raisers, spoiled only by some embarrassingly persistent marshals armed with debt notices relating to some unpaid bills from Hart's 1984 campaign.

If that was an embarrassment, what happened next was a disaster. The *Miami Herald*, which like many other newspapers was trying to substantiate the long-standing rumours of Hart's alleged infidelity, trailed him to a liaison with a model, Donna Rice, whom he had met at a New Year's Day party in Aspen. Soon it would be revealed that Hart had taken Rice on a cruise to Bimini with another colleague and another girl, and had even allowed himself to be photographed with Donna sitting on his lap. That, more than anything, angered Beatty, and for once he questioned Hart's suitability for high office. It was doubly ironic, as Patrick Caddell pointed out, that no journalist, no newspaper had been able to get any kind of story of Hart womanising in Beatty's circle.

Influential backers in Hollywood were stunned by the breaking news and several turned against him, bitter that he had shown poor judgement and dismayed by his behaviour. Beatty was no stranger to such disclosures on his own front, but then, he wasn't married and he wasn't running for President. As Hart flew home to Denver to consider his next move, Beatty was in constant touch. All that day, he was on the telephone to Hart and his advisers. Pat Caddell, who was in Los Angeles, went to Beatty's house for a brainstorming meeting and stayed for dinner.

Beatty knew the limits of the way publicity could be controlled and his advice to Hart was as concise as it could be. He said he should stay and fight. He should admit that he had had an affair, get his wife to say that she was standing by him and then refuse to talk about it any further.

Beatty stayed up through the night, making and taking endless telephone calls prior to Hart's decision to meet the press the following morning to make his announcement. Before he finally took to his bed that morning, he knew it was over. One further devastating piece of news heightened the drama. Word filtered out that the *Washington Post* was planning to publish more damning evidence of Hart's alleged infidelity. True or not, it did not matter by then. What happened to Hart in terms of media scrutiny into the private life of a current politician was virtually unprecedented, but after years of mounting and searing revelations of Jack Kennedy's affairs, it really came as no surprise.

Politicians, especially those running for high office, could in future expect total and absolute investigation into every corner of their lives. Gary Hart's recklessness would ensure it. Hart's campaign was dead in the water, and by 8 May 1987, he knew it. He went to his press conference, defiant but bowed. He declared that though he passionately believed that politics should not be decided upon in such a manner, he had decided to withdraw.

The story did not end immediately. In the months ahead, Hart's indiscretions became a focus for analysis and conjecture. What was disappointing from Beatty's point of view was that Hart was an idealistic theorist with a deep appreciation of national feelings and mood. Whether his style and vision for America and the Western world was right, at that particular moment, to succeed eight years of Reagan extremism was another matter. Beatty refused to be drawn on the topic, although he could hardly suppress his anger at the way the media had gone for Hart.

Few thought they would hear the name again, but seven months later, at the beginning of December, Hart astonished the political world by announcing he was re-entering the race for President. He said the public had all the information about him that they needed, and the only people who were pressing for absolute disclosure were the newsmen. Beatty believed it ought to be possible to separate private lives from political ambition. On the steps of the New Hampshire statehouse where Hart paid his $1,000 fee to register for the state's lead-off primary for February 1988, he announced defiantly, 'Let the people decide . . . the voters are not dumb. They know . . .' His wife Lee, at his side, added, 'We are ready for anything.'

The *New York Post* reported that Beatty had been a key figure in persuading Hart to try again. The move was treated with widespread derision, especially among the Republicans. George Bush's adviser, Richard Bond, came up with anticipated invective: 'Gary Hart is not fit to be President. It shows the sorry state the Democratic Party is in.'

Hart failed to muster the support he needed. Very shortly afterwards, he pulled out of the campaign a second time and ended his journey which, it had once seemed, could possibly have ended up in the White House. If Beatty had ambitions to tag along with Hart if and when he became President, he never voiced them, and indeed went as far as to refuse questions about his motivations for giving so much time and energy to Hart's cause. If the outcome had been different, as it could so easily have been but for that boat trip with Donna Rice, Beatty might have been in line for some attachment to the President's office.

He was certainly bitter and angry at the way it had all turned out. He gave tentative support to the eventual Democratic nomination, Michael Dukakis. But the latter did not court, or even want, the more active support that Beatty had lent to previous campaigns.

From a personal point of view, Beatty had taken two big knocks in a row: Hart preceded by *Ishtar*, which was being talked of in the same breath as *Heaven's Gate* as being among Hollywood's biggest financial disasters of recent times. For the first time in years, his status and power were under threat. That old Hollywood edict that you are only as successful as your last picture was never more applicable, and once the political distractions had gone from his life he turned instantly to the thought of re-establishing his position. He would not have put it in those terms himself. He was still a powerful man, but his ability to dictate terms to any studio would be far less emphatic.

Beatty needed a big one; he needed it right and he needed it to be a success. He had three contenders on the back burner, *Dick Tracy*, which was well advanced in terms of script and demographics, *Bugsy Siegel*, and finally his other great obsession after *Reds*, the life story of Howard Hughes, which had the three Ps at the fore of Beatty's mythical escutcheon – politics, power and pussy.

The selection of *Dick Tracy* as the one to bring him back was finalised only after much Beatty-type procrastination. Developments elsewhere helped push him along. Jack Nicholson, who had completed seven pictures since the turn of the decade, compared to Beatty's two, including *The Shining* and *Terms of Endearment*, for which he won an Oscar, received an unusual offer. It was at 4.00 a.m. one morning, when he was working on the set of *The Witches of Eastwick*, which was destined to be another Nicholson box-office hit, that Jack was approached by the producers of the upcoming blockbuster *Batman* with the idea of his playing the Joker.

'I wouldn't do that if you paid me fifty mill,' he said to the burgeoning whizzkid duo of Peter Guber and Jon Peters, who were also co-producers of *The Witches of Eastwick*. As it turned out, fifty mill was not such an outlandish idea. Guber and Peters flew him to England to see the sets, which were being built at Pinewood Studios. Jack read the script, liked what he saw and agreed to do it, for a $6 million fee and a percentage of the profits from the movie, the videos and the massive merchandising operation that was being planned.

The trade press announcement that marked the beginning of the hype around *Batman* came as Beatty was finalising his own thoughts for *Dick Tracy*, and once again he had given himself the most challenging of all possible alternatives – to be producer, director and star. The two pictures, coming so close together, would be seen as being in competition and *Batman*, which was planned for a 1989 release date almost a year earlier than *Dick Tracy*, would set the mark to beat in terms of box-office grosses.

They were two totally different pictures, though many observers had expected them to be similar in approach simply because they were both based upon comic characters. With Nicholson bearing down on his in competition, Beatty took his project to Walt Disney Studios, renowned for their caution and penny-pinching attitude towards producers and their budgets. Disney chairman Jeffrey Katzenberg, well aware of the *Ishtar* débâcle, spelled out to Beatty in no uncertain terms that the $23 million budget should not be exceeded and reportedly warned that any excess would have to come from Beatty's own pocket. The total budget of direct costs, which would include post-production work and promotion, was set at a maximum of $35 million.

Beatty was nervous. This feeling of needing one to show that he could still do it was only exacerbated by a survey in the influential magazine *Premiere* which showed that Beatty's rating in the list of Hollywood's most powerful people had slumped alarmingly to forty-fifth out of a hundred, way behind fellow actors like Nicholson, Sylvester Stallone, Michael Douglas, Robert Redford, Arnold Schwarzenegger, Tom Cruise and even little Danny De Vito.

This poll was also a good guide to Beatty's own bankability as a star. His record as an actor, director and producer had been worthy of acclaim through the achievement of just four of his own major films, *Bonnie and Clyde*, *Shampoo*, *Heaven Can Wait* and *Reds*. This respect, however, came largely from 'within the trade' – from his peers and studio bosses or movie buffs. As far as the public was concerned, Beatty was not perceived as a great star, and he was certainly not a guaranteed crowd-puller.

The name Beatty was more likely to attract a smirk. His talent no longer moved the modern generation of women as it had in the seventies and, to a lesser degree, in the eighties and his acting, that Stella Adler-inspired staccato, stuttering delivery of underplayed lines which had been his trademark, could often sound dated. His pictures on bedroom walls had long ago been replaced by wallpaper that matched the curtains. He had never won the hearts of the cinema-going public like some of his contemporaries who came to stardom around the same time as himself – Paul Newman, Robert Redford and even Sean Connery. And as an actor – which is how the public see him, and not as a director or producer – he was overshadowed by the modern box-office rages, like Nicholson, Michael Douglas and Arnold Schwarzenegger. He was a big star in Hollywood but not so big outside.

In that respect, he had much more to prove with *Dick Tracy* than, say, Nicholson, whose name at the top of the credits on *Batman* took the producers halfway to box-office success. By then, *The Witches of Eastwick* had also taken $125 million, and had made a fortune for its backers, not to mention Nicholson himself.

As the star of *Dick Tracy*, which meant he would be the dominant screen presence throughout, Beatty had surely recognised that the movie would eventually have to stand on its own merit. The appeal, the modern appeal, to an audience to which Dick Tracy was some distant childhood memory, or perhaps even none at all, would have to be caught by ingenious casting and meticulous promotion. There would have to be a certain public re-education about Tracy, especially in overseas markets, where he was less remembered, unlike Batman, which was re-running in the television version all around the world.

He began the setting up in the early months of 1988. The whole thing just took him over. The key was to make *Dick Tracy* surprising as well as appealing. He saw Al Pacino, whom he wanted as the notorious crime boss, Big Boy Caprice, but who would be unrecognisable behind the layers of latex. He tried the trick that he used to get Nicholson to play Eugene O'Neill, explaining the role to Pacino and then asking, 'Who do you think I should get for it?'

'Cut the crap, Warren,' said Pacino. 'If you want me to play it, then just ask. And, by the way, the answer's yes.'

Pacino was joined by other friends like Dustin Hoffman, whose face would be similarly and hideously distorted as Mumbles, James Caan as Spaldoni, Michael J. Pollard as Bug Bailey, Paul Sorvino as Lips Mandis, Dick Van Dyke as D.A. Fletcher, Charles Durning as Chief Brandon... it was a superb line-up of American character talent, which was bought in at considerably less than the going rate by doing deals on percentages. This all-star cast would have normally cost any other producer $20 million or more up-front, not counting the remaining actors and technicians, which would have left him short of funds to make the picture.

The two female leads presented something more of a problem. He had it in his mind to bring someone spectacular to the role of Breathless Mahoney – he had mentioned Kathleen Turner, Kim Basinger or Michelle Pfeiffer, but all would have been too expensive. The lesser female role of Tess Trueheart went initially to Sean Young, but he was still stuck on finding a suitable Breathless at the right money.

Out of the blue, he got a call from Madonna Louise Veronica Ciccone, the singing star of considerable note, who had read about *Dick Tracy* and had decided she wanted to play Beatty's leading lady. 'Warren,' she declared, 'I want this part. Right?'

Beatty said he would get back to her. He had known Madonna and her husband Sean Penn for a long time – he and Sean were good friends, though Sean and Madonna were not. Their marriage had hit trouble, not least because of her inability to take time off work and the constant worldwide tours to start a family. Beatty had long been intrigued by her acting talent. Madonna never knew that in 1984, he used to call in to see the daily rushes of *Desperately Seeking Susan*, in which Madonna co-starred and which Susan Seidelman was editing. Seidelman said: 'Watching his face watching hers, I knew he wanted her. From that day on, I had a premonition that some day they would be together.'

In the summer of 1988 Madonna was attempting to force the issue but surprisingly Beatty was not keen. Shooting was due to start early in the New Year and he had completed most of his cast list with the exception of Breathless. Beatty was holding back on Madonna. He was probably in awe of her, even a little afraid. He knew she was volatile and that her range of expletives was comparable to that of any man he knew. She was not the sort to be charmed by sweet nothings in the left ear.

She had made so much money from her music that she was beholden to no one. She could buy and sell Beatty. There was another less obvious aspect to his reluctance. Katzenberg at Disney had casting approval, and Madonna hardly fitted the wholesome Disney image that would be laid over this movie: Dick Tracy, the hero who beats the crime bosses. No sex, drugs or rock'n'roll – a glossy tale of good versus evil, with a nice little romance as the sub-plot, all wrapped up to get a rating of PG12 and the widest possible focus for family viewing.

That's the way its stayed until Beatty had worked his way down his list, and Madonna called again to say: 'I'll work for a scale fee . . . $1,440 a week plus a percentage.'

At that price, she was a bargain in anybody's language, and Beatty was virtually forced to sell her to Katzenberg. There was still the problem of her notoriety, which Disney believed might keep some film-goers away. This was outweighed by the reasoning that Madonna would cover another age gap: those Americans under thirty who would neither remember Dick Tracy nor react to Beatty would certainly flock in for Madonna.

'You're hired,' said Beatty in a call to Madonna that autumn, and she was presented with a contract and assigned a bungalow on the Universal Studios lot, where *Dick Tracy* was to be filmed. Fears that Madonna might attract the wrong kind of publicity for their movie were justified. Just before Christmas Sean Penn turned up and demanded to know if Madonna was going ahead with *Dick Tracy*, because she had promised him they would start a family no later than 1989. She said it was all sealed; she was playing Breathless and that was that.

A volley of obscenities were exchanged and Penn stormed off; she did not see him again until after Christmas when he turned up at their Malibu home seriously drunk. A scene of loud and horrific domestic argument proceeded for some hours until Madonna ran screaming from the house and called the local sheriff's department. A small posse arrived and surrounded the house, calling to Penn over a loudhailer to come out with his hands up. He was handcuffed and taken to the local police station, but was later released after Madonna said she would not press charges. However, she did file for divorce, and went off to meet Beatty to start work on *Dick*.

By then, what had been an intriguing fascination for Madonna's work had developed into something more serious, even before they had really begun working together. If there truly existed a Plan A in the Beatty *modus operandi* of getting the picture and the girl and intertwining the whole into a passionate package of love and romance and mega-publicity, then Plan A was back in operation ... but this time, he had run into someone completely different, a woman of considerable sexual prowess herself, a woman of considerable strength who traded upon her sexuality and her raucousness and her wholly uncensored stage act of sexual simulation, and whose current reputation put his own well into the shade.

Madonna, in her few years at the top, was more famous than Beatty had ever been, and that must have been slightly intimidating for him, although the reverse was the case for Madonna – she admitted to being in awe of him herself. He was twenty-two years her senior and old enough to be her father. He was like a father figure initially, putting a protective arm around her which she often intuitively shrugged off. No one puts their arm around Madonna. They became lovers well before the cameras began to roll. Madonna knew there were many who had been there before her and she would find herself thinking about that: 'I would be saying to myself, "This guy's been with the most glamorous women in the world" and I'd go "Oh my God! O my God!" Then I'd think, "What the hell . . . I'm better than all of them." '

Beatty found her work disciplines incredible. She would stand for his sixteen- or eighteen-hour working days without a quibble, but on the other hand, if she thought he was 'pissing around' with too many takes she would say so, which actually helped him, because sometimes he would forget that he was on a strict eighteen-week schedule, with no delays or extra charges. So she would goad him . . . 'Warren, for Christ's sake come o-n-n-n.'

'OK, OK baby. Please take your mark . . .'

'I'm on my fucking mark . . . right here. OK?'

There were occasional flare-ups when he insisted on retakes, and the language was hot. 'Hey Beatty,' she yelled in one enforced interlude while he contemplated his angles, 'are you going to shoot this fucking scene or not, you asshole?'

Those on the set who had worked with Beatty previously, like Estelle Parsons and Michael J. Pollard, looked at each other and rolled their eyes.

As the movie scenes wore on, so did the Beatty-Madonna romance, accompanied by some attentive publicity. On the set they embraced and petted openly, and soon they were being seen around town at all the fashionable night-spots and dining-rooms, like Spago, holding hands and staying close in the most public of tables. They were being seen and wanted to be seen. It was all part and parcel of the promotion and advance hype for *Dick Tracy*, now completed after nineteen weeks' filming, for which Madonna tendered her account for $27,360. That, she told Beatty, was the cheapest she had worked since she was a nobody. He said he was sure *Dick Tracy* would hit the spot, and she would get a good payday later.

Beatty ducked out of sight for the editing and post-production work on *Dick Tracy*, and Madonna went back to New York to begin work on her new stage concept for which she was searching for ideas by touring sex shows and dance houses. The craze of vogueing had arrived and she had a whole show staged by a freestyle dance group who were so brilliant, she said, 'I didn't know where to look.' So she advertised in *Daily Variety* for seven fierce male dancers to back the Material Girl, and 'wimps and wannabes' need not apply.

Between times, the phone lines between them were busy, and whatever was going on between Beatty and Madonna had some lifespan left yet . . .

21

Madonna Takes All

There was a lot of talk about Beatty and Madonna, and whether their affair was just a stunt to promote *Dick Tracy*. It was and it wasn't. Aides in the Madonna camp would report a continuing and steamy relationship. But the intent of the hype was deep and calculated, and the extent of it – especially on Madonna's part – would only emerge in the months leading up to the release of the movie. It was extraordinary.

Madonna threw herself into a sensational worldwide orgy of self-expression that left Beatty himself breathless. It was a slow-burn build-up that began in the dying weeks of 1989 and gathered pace early in the new year, when gossip writers were analysing their relationship. They were a curious pairing. Madonna was always frank and loud and controversial about her men. She admitted to looking at the bulge in their pants before wasting any time on potential lovers and she liked them strong and butch, young and virile. Beatty's adventurous love making was hardly in the S and M category that Madonna flirted with in her stage acts. She, on the other hand, was the absolute bumping and grinding opposite to some of the women who had populated his life, who were genteel in comparison.

Neither did Beatty seem put off by the regular presence of Madonna's closest friend, Sandra Bernhard, who was always somewhere close, and often travelled with her. They used to taunt him by disappearing into the powder room and returning having swapped clothes.

It was a disjointed romance; he was still engaged on the

editing of *Dick Tracy*, working day and night through the early
months of 1990 to prepare for a June release, while she was
putting the final touches to plans for her Blond Ambition
world tour. In the weeks before she left, they made a point of
being seen around Hollywood and New York.

The affair was no stunt, but that did not stop them from
turning it into one. The hype was all that mattered, and
they pursued that aim as if the whole relationship had been
carefully and meticulously planned for the purpose. Some
nights they would dine in two places, taking a main course
in one and a dessert in another. Actress, author and television
presenter Elisa Celli, wife of Hollywood-based British producer Trevor Wallace, said: 'They were the talk of the town
for weeks. It seemed everywhere you went Warren and
Madonna were there – Spago, Adriano's, La Scala, the Citrus
– and they weren't slinking away in some dark corner. They
were there for all to see.'

And everyone saw. Beatty and Madonna made sure of that.
She attracted attention with her sexy clothes, adorned with
lots of black lace and high skirts, and her playful teasing,
sitting on Beatty's lap. Then they would dash off to one of
the Sunset Boulevard night-spots, where they might find Jack
Nicholson nightclubbing while Rebecca Broussard was at
home waiting for the birth of their baby, which arrived in
April.

Jack was languishing in the success of *Batman*, which
brought him personally upwards of $50 million. Nicholson,
who had achieved massive publicity and acclaim for his portrayal of the Joker, was a hard act to follow. *Dick Tracy* was
a different kind of film, but it was still being viewed as in
the same mould, and would be judged as such.

Beatty knew better than anyone by now that if he hadn't
got it right, then *Dick Tracy* could face a massacre by the
critics and he personally would be crucified. *Batman*, which
Disney executives had taken a great interest in as a precursor
to their own movie, was a stunning commercial success. It
quickly zoomed into the realms of blockbuster status, taking
$200 million in domestic grosses in the first four weeks alone,
and the merchandising operation round the world was being
talked of in terms of producing a $1 billion bonanza, from

which Nicholson would benefit by tens of millions.

So he could justifiably smile that killer smile when he saw Beatty at the Roxberry night-spot – it was a grin that said, 'Hey, Warren, follow that!' They gathered some companionship and retired for a party at Jack's place. But Jack knew that Warren had a secret weapon in his armoury of promotional activity for *Dick Tracy*. It was Madonna herself, at her most sexy, shockingly outrageous best (or worst). Beatty had seen a preview of the new stage act for her world tour and he was amazed by it. He had seen her final rehearsal in Los Angeles for the Blond Ambition show, which was to open in Tokyo on 13 April, the first leg of the sell-out world tour. Nine concerts in Japan alone secured ticket sales in excess of $4 million, without the merchandising that was part of the circus.

At the first gig, 35,000 screaming, shouting, ecstatic fans gave a foretaste of what was to follow. Newsreels picked up on her stage performance in Tokyo as she burst on to the stage in her ivory corset with its gold conical breasts and dangling suspender belt and performed an act which simulated every sexual possibility. She tantalised her audiences with references to sado-masochism, with lines like 'When I hurt people, I feel better – know what I mean?' and following her rendition of the *Dick Tracy* number 'Hanky Panky' she added, 'You all know the pleasures of a good spanking.'

The promotion of *Dick Tracy* was a built-in facet of the tour. She performed three numbers from the movie, which was also linked to her new album, entitled 'I'm Breathless'. Beatty was there in spirit, if not in person, when she performed a duet with a tape of his voice in the number 'Now I'm Following You', and her team of male dancers were adorned in Dick Tracy-style yellow overcoats. A specially prepared movie trailer was flashed on to big screens in the auditorium and the audience went into raptures when they heard her reciting the gems, 'Dick . . . that's an interesting name' and 'My body hurts just thinking about it.'

Around the world and back again, Madonna was promoting the movie. At her first concert in America, on 4 May, at the Summit Arena, in Houston, Texas, Beatty should have been in the wings. Madonna had even sent a private jet to collect him. When start time came and he hadn't arrived, she was

305

pacing around, angry and screaming at anyone who got in her way. 'Jeez, where's that motherfucker? Where is he?' She delayed the start for twenty minutes before going on.

He telephoned afterwards and apologised. He explained he was busy with the final arrangements for the release of *Dick Tracy*. There were a thousand last-minute details to attend to, and he hoped she was not angry. Madonna hung up and let out a loud scream. She made only a brief visit to a party thrown in her honour and then went back to her hotel room, locked herself in and refused all calls.

She ploughed on with the tour, city after city, until Beatty finally caught up with her on the opening night in Los Angeles. She was still angry. 'Motherfuckers!' she bawled as she came off after the first set. 'Who put those assholes in the front rows? All I've got is three rows of fat fuckers leering up at me.' She was moaning that the front seats appeared to have been commandeered for some corporate outing of ageing, balding, ogling males.

Then she spotted Beatty, who was standing at the back of the wings and she yelled, 'Don't stand back there, Warren. Come over here. See this, this crap... can you believe it, what I have to do every fucking night of my life? Are you going to be nicer to me now, Warren?'

Who was she doing it for? It was principally for Madonna. Beatty's movie was a vehicle for her. She badly wanted a success in a major movie, but it was just a small part of one massive commercial operation which was now swamping Beatty's own position. Her spin-offs were immense. The world tour was netting millions of dollars; the album 'I'm Breathless' which had been acclaimed as the best she had produced, had been kept out of the deal she struck with Beatty and Disney studios. She had the songs produced on her own label for Time Warner, and the album stood to make her well in excess of $12 million. She had also hammered a tight percentages deal with Disney on box-office receipts, merchandising and video sales. Even before the picture came out, she was looking at potentially $20 million. It was little wonder she had agreed to make the picture for union scale of $1,440 a week.

On her own admission, she was hyping the movie for all she was worth, and she was doing it of her own volition. In her usual frank style, she said, 'Disney did not ask me to market the movie. Let's say I'm killing twelve birds with one stone ... it's a two-way street. I'm pushing everything. Sure. I have to. Most people don't associate me with movies but then, I also have a much bigger following than Warren does. A lot of my audience have never heard of him.'

A touch of bitterness was evident, and Madonna, tired and exhausted from the continuing roadshow that still had another month to go, seemed to be taking a few sideswipes at Warren. It happened again when she appeared on the top-rated Arsenio Hall talk show, which was an event in itself. She rarely appeared on chat shows and did not bother to temper her language, either.

Arsenio prodded her with some personal questions, and her back went up, not least when he talked about Beatty. 'What does Warren Beatty have that we don't have?' Hall asked.

'About a billion dollars.'

'Joan Collins said he was sexually insatiable.'

'He was twenty at the time. Aren't all twenty-year-olds insatiable?'

'Does the name Joan Collins make you jealous?'

'No. I mean, have you seen her lately?'

Madonna was everywhere. By the early summer of 1990, when *Dick Tracy* finally opened in New York, she had been featured in just about every major glossy magazine and colour supplement around the world, and writers from around the world were queuing to interview her as her tour progressed through ten countries and was seen live by audiences of two million. Her own video and album, featuring some of the *Dick Tracy* musical numbers, completely dominated the record scene.

A trade survey in Hollywood produced a most remarkable result, that a hundred per cent of those interviewed were aware of *Dick Tracy* before it opened. And since Disney was about to unleash its own $10 million promotional and marketing campaign, the movie could hardly fail to attract attention.

Prompted by his own need to talk about the picture – and the absolute certainty of being overshadowed by Madonna – Beatty came out of his shell for the first time in almost a decade. Apart from a few modest interviews he gave for *Ishtar* before retreating back into his self-imposed seclusion, Beatty had said nothing of note to the press since the late 1980s. In May, while Madonna was attracting huge publicity from the tour, he went on the *Barbara Walters Show*. It was classic Beatty – apparently shy, and blinking without his glasses, he was slow in answering and often gave the air of mystery.

Next, he agreed to one of those long and searching *Rolling Stone* interviews which had been compared variously by subjects to having teeth pulled or spending half a day on a psychiatrist's couch. It would be virtually impossible for him to stick to his normal routine of saying nothing in particular. In fact writer Bill Zehme admitted in his preamble to the piece that to 'interview Warren Beatty is to want to kill him.'

The long pauses between his monosyllabic replies were recorded and it was easy to imagine the interviewer shuffling in his seat waiting for the reply to come . . . or was it Beatty who was shuffling?

Zehme: OK, you and Madonna . . . the truth?

Beatty: Art is truth.

Zehme: That's all. You want to go with that?

Beatty: OK by me.

Zehme: Describe the qualities she possesses that convinced you to cast her as the sexpot temptress Breathless Mahoney. How does she qualify?

Beatty: Madonna is (twenty-one-second pause) simultaneously touching and more fun than a barrel of monkeys (eleven seconds). She's funny and she's (twenty-one seconds) gifted in so many areas and has a kind of energy as a performer that can't help but make you engaged.

Zehme: You mean sexual energy?

Beatty: (Forty-seven-second pause) Um, she has it all.

But the man from *Rolling Stone* had heard that it was over between Beatty and Madonna. Beatty would not answer on the record. He had retained the right to go off the record when he felt so inclined. It was a favourite trick that he had injected into newspaper interviews years ago to get out of answering questions of a personal nature. This was one of them, and the question of his continuing relationship with Madonna was fudged, though the interviewer drew the conclusion that it was still on.

The launch of *Dick Tracy*, after all the hype, was something of an anti-climax. The danger of such a build-up is always that the product – in this case a movie, but it could have been anything – might not stand the critical test of public opinion. Reviewers were already wary of what Lawrence J. Quirk described in *Quirk's Review* as 'The hype overkill and oppressive advance hoopla', and went to the opening prepared to dislike *Dick Tracy*.

By and large reviewers enjoyed the film, although several tempered their comments with the observations that Beatty had turned in a sweet-natured picture that gave his Dick Tracy an aesthetic look and which low-keyed Madonna to the extent that none of her electrifying stage presence came across. Such comments were wholly deserved. It was an excellent movie technically, with the superb photography and set designs of two Beatty stalwarts, Vittorio Storaro and Dick Sylbert respectively. The music was excellent, the whole presentation was rich in colour and ideas, but the dead hand of Disney-fication lay over it, so that there was a serious lack of excitement.

It needed darker undertones of the type achieved by the director of *Batman* with his characterisation, especially from Nicholson as the Joker. The trouble with Beatty's comic strip characters was that they were exactly that – comical. It was a good movie, but it could have been so much better. There was simply nothing to get hold of except the artistry, and art isn't commercial. It was, as Beatty admitted, a picture of innocence and purity. But by most measures, *Dick Tracy* was a success. It very quickly notched up domestic grosses of $110 million against direct costs which came in at a good deal less than $40 million.

The merchandising and all the other spin-offs would make *Dick Tracy* a very profitable movie indeed, and one which ought to have put Beatty personally back in the driving seat. After all, he had done exactly what Disney had asked by producing a very profitable movie for under $40 million. It had cost half as much as some of the modern blockbusters of the same period, such as *Days of Thunder, Die Hard 2* and *The Godfather Part III*.

There were, however, still rumours of dissatisfaction at

Disney, especially as *Dick Tracy* had not outgrossed *Batman*. Developments in the aftermath spotlighted the inflated values and expectations of Hollywood, and gave some insight into the whole back-room scenario of movie high finance. A leaked confidential internal memo written by Katzenberg stated: '*Dick Tracy* made demands on our time, talent and treasury that . . . may not have been worth it.'

Beatty was furious that he should be so publicly humiliated. Katzenberg knew it hurt and had not intended the memo for public dissemination. He did not recant, but said the memo had been misunderstood. He sent Beatty an olive tree and a chocolate dartboard with his own face on it and two white doves in a golden cage.

Beatty let his feelings be known through the influential film magazine *Premiere*. He said he found it fascinating that a man could have a picture that was as profitable as *Dick Tracy* and then put 'a negative spin on it' because it did not do as well as *Batman*. 'Dick Tracy was a fragile little movie,' said Beatty. 'I was stunned that it did as well as it did. And they should be so lucky . . . I mean, they got the costs back on cassette sales alone.'

He said the whole Disney-fication of the picture, the wish for it to be the biggest blockbuster of all time, and the attempt to balloon it into a different kind of movie might have been miscalculated. Their expectations were too high. 'What must they feel when they have a picture which is unprofitable?' Beatty wondered. 'At the time I thought [Katzenberg] might be the most capable manager I had ever known in Hollywood. He treated me very well. Perhaps too well . . . it could be that there was something basically frustrating in that he had to put up with someone who had complete artistic control in his contract. They don't ordinarily have to deal with gorillas like me . . . but I still don't understand it.'

Dick Tracy was a huge success, despite the after-hours wrangling. Yet it still left a bitter taste.

Madonna, too, had moved on after some heated exchanges. She found a new boyfriend, whom she met at her birthday party, given by her brother in mid-July, and had a row with Beatty over his seeing other women but he not expecting her to see other men. Bang! The phone went down and so did her relationship. When the movie was over, so was the single most important bond. Love? There surely was none. As one of her close associates described it, Madonna 'screwed his brains out' and left.

She did not want maturity in a man, and made that abundantly clear when she went public with her new man, a handsome male model named Tony Ward, five years her junior, who had appeared in pin-up poses in male gay magazines. The message to Beatty was as effective as a punch in the face.

Also, her own sharp business acumen had creamed off millions from the whole *Dick Tracy* exercise, which she had wrapped up and incorporated into her own worldwide marketing operation of concerts, videos and albums. Madonna danced off into the sunset, ready to make her next killing, which would include the release of her own documentary of exhibitionism, initially titled *Truth or Dare: On the Road, Behind the Scenes and in Bed with Madonna*, which was filmed during her Blond Ambition tour.

When Beatty heard that the movie included some taped telephone conversations between the singer and himself, in which he was heard telling her he loved her, he insisted that they should be removed. He said they were done without his knowledge, and he wanted them out. Madonna reluctantly agreed. 'I don't think he ever respected what I was attempting to do,' she moaned. 'He just thought I was fucking around with some kind of a home movie.' He was well out of it.

If there was a watershed, a dawning of realisations about his life and work, it probably came then, at the end of the *Dick Tracy* episode and all that went with it. He had just passed his fifty-third birthday – almost too late for a mid-life crisis, but the arrows pointed towards it. The nation expects... Warren Beatty to go on fulfilling the role of national stud. He was an institution. The media would be bereft without it. But how much longer could he go on like this, flitting from one voluptuary to another, falling in love, having a fling, making a movie and then being alone again? Age and social changes were running against him, but it surely went deeper. Advice from friends and relatives was decidedly outspoken.

Sachi Parker, Beatty's niece, declared that autumn, 'I feel his loneliness. I don't know if it's true, but I feel he's living in this big house at the top of a hill with no one to share it, or his life.' And Dustin Hoffman, father of six, continued to berate him with friendly persuasion: 'I'm begging him, before his testosterone level drops . . . I'm begging him to get married and have children.'

Even his sister, Shirley MacLaine, had identified her brother's 'psychological dilemma' but admitted that it was something she could not resolve with simple advice. If he had listened to her, he would have married Julie Christie years ago.

Where would it have led? In the sparse discussion he has allowed himself on the women in his past, their importance appeared always to be attached to his work as much as his personal relationships. It may have been deeper, but he has remained so secretive and unapproachable on his 'private life' that it becomes difficult to assess his true feelings for any one of them.

He was in love with them all, undoubtedly, and love has different meanings at various stages of a particular relationship. He has spoken of most – with the possible exception of Madonna – with an enduring fondness: 'I loved Diane Keaton . . . she made me laugh and made me cry.' And then he adds the rider that pins his affections to his work: 'If she had not made *Reds*, I do not know what I would have done.' And he loved Julie Christie, but then says, 'I don't know that I could have functioned without Julie in *Heaven Can Wait*.'

Only Norman Mailer, himself a veteran of relationships past, has managed to get him to unwind a little of his thoughts in that direction. It was his philosophy that a lover on such a scale could not survive without a philosophy and Beatty, before the interview was done, would confirm that premise.

In a conversation with the author taped for *Vanity Fair* Mailer put it to Beatty that his idea of fidelity was to have one woman who was steady and anything else that came along. Beatty was now prepared to state that in his view anyone who did that was a failure.

He went further, adding that the highest level of sexual

excitement in his life had always been in a monogamous relationship. He grew up in Virginia thinking that he would marry the first woman he had sex with and would stay married for the rest of his life. This, of course, did not happen. But, he insisted he had never gone from being in love with one woman to being in love with another immediately. Thus, he suggested, in that context he had never been unfaithful.

Mailer found this analogy somewhat curious and questioned Beatty further, and particularly on the popular understanding that outside of his major relationships, there had been others in between, those interludes of sex, perhaps briefly snatched on a spur of the moment. Yes, Beatty admitted, there was fire where the smoke was coming from and it was not something he was proud of – nor ashamed. That did not, however, affect his overall premise and he insisted that to be in love with one woman and to find another one more interesting had never happened to him.

It was a surprising statement, yet in comparison to Nicholson, there was a certain charming politeness, even correctness, in which Beatty viewed the way he had conducted his affairs and, finally, explained his attitude towards them, and women. As Mailer said, it is one thing to be a legendary womaniser; it is another to be a generous, discreet and considerate womaniser.

Nicholson and Beatty were the two outstanding *boulevardiers* of their day but Beatty had avoided some of the more sensational publicity which had accompanied Jack's sexual exploits, most recently when a British model, Karen Mayo-Chandler, sold her kiss-and-tell story to *Playboy*, branding him as Spanking Jack, the ultimate sex machine. While Nicholson appeared to have given no quarter to monogamy, feminists, accusations of male chauvinism, advancing years, or even to his physical appearance, Beatty had become his opposite in many respects. Their intentions had always been the same – to fill their lives between work with the excitement of sex. At the end of it, where had it led them?

Nicholson was in a relationship which would soon result in a second child, and then a parting from Broussard, and then more women. He did have an advantage over Beatty. He had stayed in the limelight, year in year out, he had cut across generations and become the biggest male attraction in Hollywood. He could still command the attention of women through all age groups; wherever in the world he might land, women fell at his feet.

Beatty, in the years between movies, had often disappeared from view. And in those months after Madonna, when he had no relationship, he had to face an advancing truth – the field of operation was narrowing, and it was further cooled by the threat of AIDS, the modern scourge of the promiscuous. If the Madonna experience had shown him one thing, it was that he should recognise his age, and act accordingly.

If he needed reminders, they were all around him. Joan Collins (three marriages later and alone again) and Leslie Caron were both hitting sixty. Natalie Wood was already dead, from a tragic and mysterious drowning; Julie Christie had taken to her country hideaway in England, locked the door and refused to come out . . . he could pick any name from that long list, but could he visualise himself alongside any of them, there in the dying days of the first year of a new decade?

An interesting thought, but also a doubtful one.

22
Bugsy and Bening

The black Mercedes convertible drove slowly past a house in Linden Street, Beverly Hills. It would be seen time and again in the coming months and anyone noticing its reappearance every now and again might also have recognised the driver, who thought he was invisible behind his dark shades. It was Warren Beatty. The house that was the focus of his attention was number 810, a large while building which was of sufficient character that one might imagine a drama to have been played out there, as indeed it had.

This house was once the rented home of Virginia Hill, a Hollywood starlet and goodtime girl whose moment of fame arrived on 20 June 1947, when her boyfriend, Benjamin 'Bugsy' Siegel, was shot three times in the head by Mafia hitmen and lay dying on her front lawn.

Bugsy Siegel was the man who founded Las Vegas and mingled with stars of stage and screen upon whom he modelled himself, with his nifty clothes, his hand-made silk shirts and his women. He was actually a likeable man, and a romantic who took elocution lessons to rid himself of his Brooklyn accent. He was also a very dangerous, ruthless and brutal gangster who killed strangers on a whim, once plotted to assassinate Mussolini and who liked to humiliate his enemies by making them crawl on the floor, barking like a dog.

In the twenties and thirties, he was a close associate of the supreme Mafia leadership on the east coast and ran with fabled crime characters like Lucky Luciano, Frank Costello and Meyer Lansky. They sent him to California in 1935 to seize control of the west coast rackets and develop the Mafia business interests in gambling, protection, drugs and prostitution. This he did with some style and panache, and used some of the proceeds to invest in the odd movie and to build the Flamingo Hotel in Las Vegas, which was previously a small cattle town of no particular merit. He got a gaming licence at a time when casino gambling was banned in the rest of America and Las Vegas began to flourish.

In the meantime, he became a well-known figure in Hollywood. He used to dine at Ciro's and made many friends, including George Raft, later a front-man and greeter for Mafia casinos in the Caribbean and London, Gary Cooper and Cary Grant, who reportedly based his portrayal of Mr Lucky on Bugsy. Siegel's flirtation with Hollywood even led him to take a screen test himself, but he was no actor; it was mere narcissistic fantasy. Instead, he went on with his dream of building his hotel in the desert.

Unfortunately, Siegel owed the mob a very large amount of money for which they were pressing. When he had not paid by the final due date of 20 June, a hitman called at Virginia Hill's place and let him have it. That night Meyer Lanksy and his brother Jake took over the Flamingo Hotel and Bugsy Siegel was no more.

Although Bugsy had been portrayed several times on screen – he was the thinly disguised character of Moe Green, shot through the eye in *The Godfather* – no one had ever told his story, which had more than its share of classic elements of the life and times of a gangster. As we have seen, Warren Beatty had been toying with it for five years and saw it first and foremost as the story of a relationship, between Siegel and Virginia Hill, weaving his web around those two central characters just as he had done in *Bonnie and Clyde*, *Reds* and *Heaven Can Wait*. He also saw humour and black comedy, romanticism and violence, and this was what he had been telling the screenwriter James Toback for months – it was not a gangster movie or even a movie specifically about a gangster; it was about a relationship. The rest, the humour and the violence, would fall in around it.

The first draft of the script had long been completed, and altered and tinkered with in Beatty's usual style; *Bugsy* would have the Beatty stamp all over it, tackling the serious through the comic and the lighthearted, addressing troubling and dangerous questions without losing sight of the fact that this was entertainment.

It becomes ever more tempting at this point in the proceedings – and especially in this final chapter – to examine Beatty's manoeuvrability and to discover how his characters and his plot constructions are built around himself, and contain in part elements of him personally and his life. And when we look closely it is possible to see, now, that across his whole body of work there are points of reference which are autobiographical. Not literally, of course; but as you wander through the characters he has created for his audiences you can see that they are portraits of human behaviour in a variety of circumstances, and in each one he has buried parts of himself, perhaps subconsciously, just as they send time capsules into space, waiting for them to be discovered.

Apart from a couple of cast-offs, failures, it is possible to visualise his concept of progression through exactly three decades of economical movie-making so that the whole set is broadly speaking a portrait of himself, and that is why almost without exception they involve a woman, usually a different woman from the time before. He moved on, and on and on – until he came to Bugsy, who is also like Beatty in some particular ways, or at least is made to seem similar. Even the violence of Bugsy and previously Clyde have a place in his psyche, because violence comes on many levels – observed, imagined, fantasised. There is even violent love. All are present. That is important in the presentation of his work; disbelief *has* to be suspended.

Now, here is a clue to forthcoming developments. He was explaining the romance of Bugsy Siegel to director Barry Levinson, long before the picture was ready to be made, long before he selected his co-star. He said, 'The thing about Siegel . . . he was very promiscuous throughout his life, until he met Virginia Hill. That's what makes this story so vital. When they got together, he never went after another woman.' And later Beatty said that the relationship between Siegel and Hill was his key to the movie, that Bugsy had 'found someone who knew him and accepted him for what he was.'

317

This statement was profound and must surely have been set aside in Beatty's subconscious, to be acted out on screen and then, finally and naturally, in real life, just as everything he has ever done in life has in some way been transferred from the movie characters he has played and vice versa.

The package was put up to TriStar, who made him a very good offer. Beatty would be producer, star and co-writer. He said he definitely did not want to direct this time; he was now convinced that the difference between directing oneself in a movie and being directed was the difference between masturbating and making love.

He connected with Barry Levinson, who he had admired since *Diner*, which he regarded as a small masterpiece. Levinson and Toback hit it off, too, and the groundwork was tackled. Once the *Dick Tracy* promotional effort had been completed, towards the end of 1990, Beatty began in earnest on *Bugsy*. By then, of course, Madonna was history in his life and he in hers.

At that point, in the autumn of 1990, came the moment when he began his search for his Virginia Hill. On his list were half a dozen names but he had already decided who he wanted. She would not be immediately familiar to many but she had done some good work. Her name was Annette Bening, she was new and she had been attracting attention for a series of exceptional performances on screen. Beatty had been especially impressed by her role as the young, dimpled and perpetually smiling girl in Milos Forman's *Valmont*. And Pauline Kael described her in Stephen Frears' *The Grifters*, in which she played the bubbly con artist Myra Langtry, as 'a stunning actress and superb wiggler.'

Beatty had a high regard for Pauline Kael's opinion, and he made contact with Bening. They had their first meeting in the unglamorous surroundings of a pizza parlour in a shopping mall. He said afterwards that at the time, he was looking for someone to make him feel good and 'When I met her, I felt relief.'

Beatty was extravagant with his praise for Bening's professional abilities. He said it was clear to anyone that this was the most formidable young actress in movies today. Readers will recall that he has made such grandiose statements in the past – about Madonna, about Isabelle, about . . . well, quite a few. He was always genuinely lavish with his praise, and usually he meant it. He said he had heard about Bening long before he actually saw her because of what he'd picked up on the jungle telegraph. 'It's like a drumbeat,' he explained. 'Someone has a tone in their voice when they speak about somebody. Real talent and real intelligence and wit, the best voice in the world, the best body, the best face, and the best appreciation of a joke . . . I defy anyone to leave the room when she's laughing. How can anyone be so gifted?'

So that is Beatty and Bening, set for something more than just a co-starring team in a new movie. This sounded extremely serious. Mike Nichols, who directed Bening opposite Harrison Ford in *Regarding Henry*, confirmed this great ovation of Beatty's: 'She's confusing because she's so perfect. Her kindness is perfect, her technique is perfect, her relaxation is perfect.'

In searching for a portrayal of Virginia Hill, the woman who stopped the gangster Bugsy Siegel in his tracks, he found Annette Bening, who did exactly the same for Beatty. Here was an actress, then thirty-three years old, who appeared to be free of stress and anxiety and any of those other insecurities and neuroses that send young actresses into the daily care of therapists. She oozed calm and charm, displayed a noticeable consideration for the feelings of others and, in that Hollywood world of clashing egos and temperaments, she was incredibly unpretentious.

Where did she come from, this Miss Perfect who was about to change Beatty's life? She was not especially famous, had never attracted much media attention in thirteen years as an actress, yet her coming importance, after all that has gone before in this life of Beatty, is deserving of a closer look.

Annette Bening was born in 1958, the fourth child of a couple from Iowa, who moved to Topeka, then Wichita, Kansas, and on to San Diego, by which time Annette was seven. Her father was the manager of an insurance company and her mother was a paid soloist in church. Annette was above average at school and, like most young girls of aspiring middle-class families, took up ballet as a youngster and lost interest when she became a teenager.

However, she did adopt a healthy interest in school drama and then went to private classes in San Diego. She graduated from high school early and spent a year working as a cook on a boat that took fishing parties out from San Diego, so that she could scuba dive.

Later, she went to San Francisco State, studied acting and won a place at the American Conservatory Theatre, where she was selected as one of four students to go to New York to perform a presentation of work for agents and producers. However, she refused all offers, deciding that she wasn't yet ready for the great wide world, and returned to ACT to broaden her experience for a further three years with roles such as Lady Macbeth, Juliet, and Emily in *Our Town*. She was self-assured and noted particularly for her work on voice production, an aspect upon which she lectured ACT students when she returned there as an 'old girl' when she was working and successful a few years later. Ed Hastings, one of her directors at ACT, reckoned she had an uncanny ability to zero in on the special ingredient a particular role might aspire to.

She met and fell in love with Steven White, an actor and director at ACT, and began to live with him in 1981, although her parents were not aware that her room-mate was also her boyfriend. They were married in conventional style, she wearing her mother's long white wedding dress, in San Diego in 1984.

In 1985, they moved to work with the Colorado Shakespeare Festival at Denver. Her marriage ran into trouble that year, too, and in 1986 she moved to New York and began scouring Broadway for parts. She had ambitions but was remarkably sensible about what the future might hold. Show her a play, and she would act – and that's what she imagined she might do for the rest of her life, appearing in regional theatre with highlights on Broadway.

She appeared in some successful work, and was given a rapturous reception in *Coastal Disturbances* and then in Michael Weller's play *Spoils of War*. Movies quickly followed – *The Grifters*, in which she performed a memorable and intense nude scene, *Valmont, Postcards from the Edge,*

Regarding Henry – and then *Bugsy*, and Beatty.

Why was he doing it, this film about a once-famous but now half-forgotten gangster? Period pieces and gangster movies aren't box office any more. *The Godfather Part III* and *Billy Bathgate* proved that. He knew he was taking a risk, but then, with the exception of *Ishtar*, he has always startled conventional wisdom. Like the film and the story of Bugsy that he had Toback write, Beatty was once again tackling some of America's social ambiguities and hypocrisies in which infamy can be interpreted as fame – as in the case of Siegel himself, or Al Capone or even Charlie Manson – and the violence that is part of it somehow becomes unimportant.

There were still plenty of people around Hollywood who remembered Bugsy Siegel, and from his research Beatty would discover that his subject hated the nickname. He preferred to be called Ben. There would be a dramatic moment in the picture when one of his associates almost gets killed for calling him Bugsy. Beatty, as Siegel, rampages: 'A bug is nothing. A bug does not exist ... the word has no meaning. It is used only out of ignorance or malice ... insects include a wide variety of creatures that fly and crawl but none of them can be called a bug.'

Beatty also discovered that Siegel had two distinct sides to him, two personalities. One was a mild, well-mannered, polite person; the other was a sadistic killer. In the chasm between those two extremes, there were some deep psychological traits that Beatty drew upon in what was to become a meticulous characterisation, much on the lines of his study of Clyde Barrow and John Reed. He would later admit, too, that it was impossible not to draw on his own personal experiences, those billions of minuscule events from real life that are locked away in the subconscious.

James Toback best summed up Beatty's performance: 'It is revolutionary for Warren in the sense that the character taps into dark feelings that he has held in check throughout his own life. In Bugsy, he shows sexual frenzy, homicidal violence and psychopathy encased in a very elegant, stylised veneer.'

As in *Bonnie and Clyde*, Beatty was insistent on the level of perceived humour to counteract the violence and he expected – but did not get, in these violent nineties – some kind of moral backlash over his almost sympathetic portrayal of a psychopath, seen in this movie as a visionary who has foreseen the future of Las Vegas and built its first gambling palace on a pile of Mafia debt. It was a dubious thought, attempting to include Bugsy Siegel on the list of American dreamers who have sacrificed themselves for their cause, and he could see that critics might say that *Bugsy*, like *Bonnie and Clyde*, made the reprehensible palatable. This, he explained, was not the point of the movie. Sometimes, to listen to Beatty, or to analyse the scripts in which he has had a hand, he seems to be as far away from real life as it is possible to be. Only he could underscore the creation of the screen Bugsy with the explanation that it was not a story about a gangster, or Las Vegas, but a story of a passionate man who takes an idea and transforms it into something tangible and real, and for which he knows, at the end, that the price to be paid is death.

The attention to detail, as in *Reds*, was abundant and James Toback's dialogue for *Bugsy* was sharp, realistic and full of wit. His injections of light relief were deliberate and carefully timed, as when his Bugsy was trying to improve his diction, and divest himself of his accent, by reciting the phrase, 'Twenty dwarfs took turns doing handstands on the carpet.'

Beatty's killer is also seen attempting to improve his looks with sessions under a sunlamp, and lying on a day bed in a hair net, a face mask and with cucumber slices over his eyes. The very picture of it in the mind's eye takes some of the heat out of what might otherwise easily have degenerated into an overbearing, occasionally harrowing portrait of gangsterism, to which the British actor Ben Kingsley added his own blend of the sinister as Siegel's mentor, Meyer Lansky.

And then, finally, there is the relationship with Bening's Virginia Hill, a wild and tempestuous woman who took no bullshit from Bugsy and who liked to break glass objects during their many rows. In fact, apart from two or three erotic scenes, the relationship is shown as a tumultuous one, fired by Siegel's jealousy of Hill's affairs with various attractive men of the moment, from Gene Krupa to a Spanish bullfighter.

Barry Levinson secured superb work from Bening, too, and doubtless this was due in part to the fact that she and Beatty were involved off screen, which as we know from the past, was almost a prerequisite for some of his best performances with his leading ladies.

His views on this subject had been voiced years ago, but he had given up repeating them because they were always taken out of context. He believed that once an actor had been introduced to an actress he might be playing opposite, then that relationship should be allowed to develop in its own space so that the two of them actually feel and discover they have become the centre of the universe. Whether they end up being emotionally or sexually involved, or merely thrown together for the benefit of the camera, was a matter of some importance because it ultimately affected the performance. He apparently did not see this as in any way cynical or manipulative, or even deliberate. As he has himself pointed out, quite often he has become involved with an actress *before* a film was in view (as with Collins, Caron and Christie).

Conversely, Bening has said that from the outset, she knew Beatty liked to create the chemistry between himself and his co-star, but she went into the picture with the resolution that she would not get involved with him privately. Beatty had other ideas. He admitted to having been smitten from the moment of their first meeting in the pizza place, and although the gossip columnists very quickly assigned space to a developing attachment between them as off-screen lovers, director Barry Levinson swears that he never saw any indication of it as they performed their daily acting tasks during the filming of *Bugsy*.

Her performance was remarkable, and she maintained the difficult proposition that a kept woman, as Virginia Hill was, could also be a liberated one.

Their affair was conducted with great secrecy, which is not easy on an open set, and not a hint of their closeness escaped to confirm idle speculation. This in itself was a complete change of pattern from the past. When the news finally leaked out, Beatty said, 'We did not want to place a burden on the people we were working with.' The news was sufficient for even the serious organs of news digest like *Time* magazine to record the passing of an era, under the headline 'A Playboy

Meets Miss Right', which marked the moment of truth for Hollywood's 'ideal bachelor'. For the revelation was not merely that Mr Beatty and Ms Bening were together, but that some time during the filming of the Siegel-Hill romance, i.e. in the first six months of 1991, they had conceived a child.

The baby, a daughter they named Kathlyn, arrived in the new year, along with the PR announcement of the marriage of her parents, Warren and Annette – made, incidentally, on 12 March 1992, which was the same day that members of the American Academy received their ballot papers for voting on that year's Oscars. So much was happening to Beatty and Bening in terms of their private life and the promotion of *Bugsy* that it was difficult to disentangle the publicity opportunities staged for the film from the coincidence of real events.

The Beatty-Bening baby became the centre of every tabloid's attention, the most celebrated birth since goodness knows when, and it was surrounded by headlines of a kind more lately reserved for British royalty, especially since it came around the time of the birth of Jack Nicholson's second child with Rebecca Broussard. There was much to be written about the two men in Hollywood who, above all others, have made a career out of their sexuality. Nicholson could have been speaking for both of them when he said of his new-found domesticity: 'I've had to bury a lot of psychological demons to get to this point.'

Compared to Nicholson, however, Beatty became positively monk-like. That was obvious when Nicholson telephoned him a couple of months after his marriage. They hadn't spoken for some time, not since Beatty had called from the hospital where he had watched Annette being delivered of their baby daughter.

'Hey babe,' said Nicholson, 'what's going on?'

'I gotta tell you,' said Beatty, 'this daughter of mine . . .'

Here were the two of the hottest lovers of Sunset Boulevard, and a thousand other more exotic settings, whose accumulated cast of conquests could pass for a crowd scene in *Cleopatra*, discussing most unfamiliar matters. The conversation which once would have centred on some of the finer points of life was almost entirely taken up with a surprising topic. As Nicholson described it, they had an in-depth discussion about parenthood. Nicholson joked that his former fellow *boulevard-ier* might never do anything else again. 'It's the age thing,' said Nicholson. 'We are starting to recognise our mortality and it's frightening.' Beatty sounded exceedingly proud and definitely monogamous.

Nicholson knew the feeling; he had started the current craze of fatherhood for the over-fifties in Hollywood, and since Rebecca Broussard had presented him with the first of two children, Lorraine, in April 1990, new dads had been sprouting on every block. When new fatherhood arrives at a certain age it is naturally a culture shock, especially for men stricken by the curse of hyperactive libidos. It provided a new focus of media attention upon Beatty in his new role as a father.

All of this was a stunning bonus for the advancement of their movie, *Bugsy*. As one journalistic wag wrote, Beatty could not have hoped for a greater avalanche of publicity had it been planned which, of course, it hadn't. The movie opened in New York in December 1991 to excellent reviews. *USA Today* described it as a movie in which he and Bening 'are more incendiary than anything between Lauren Bacall and Humphrey Bogart, or between Clark Gable and Vivien Leigh.' Richard Schickel, in *Time*, said it was an elegantly made, wickedly perverse and very smart new movie in which the producer-star, Beatty, 'is on to all the implications of the story, including its metaphors for moderns, and so are his creative associates. The picture belongs . . . in every sense of the word to Beatty. It is impossible to say whether, as an actor, he is performing or behaving, though he obviously sees something of Bugsy in himself.'

It went deeper. *Bugsy* had all the written-in elements that finally fired him to show his audiences a new Warren Beatty, a powerful actor. Even his most ardent fans have complained about his weaknesses in that area over the years, that he had played around too long with soft, meaningful characters, that he had clung too rigidly to the old techniques acquired during his training when the Method was all the rage.

In *Bugsy* it was different. Beatty pushed himself beyond all previous limits and ditched the Stanislavski lesson passed on all those years ago by Stella Adler – that if you have eighty per cent show only fifty. He gave the lot.

He discovered in Bugsy Siegel a character that would allow him to throw out all these inhibitions and all the familiar Beatty trademarks of awkwardness, the impaired delivery of his lines, the softness of his voice, that came with his past portrayals of men whom he had chosen because they were life's dreamers, passive and often shy. Beatty's Bugsy is an explosion of rages that made his audiences actually feel the heat, and cringe. He displayed terrible jealousy and managed to reach down into the untapped darkness in his soul, the kind that James Dean used to find when he rolled around on the floor in a foetal position moaning and groaning until he had psyched himself into the right state of mind.

Beatty observers would be left with the feeling that he ought to have done it years ago. The triumph was recognised with very good box-office receipts and, once again, by the film community itself, which awarded his movie ten Oscar nominations in all the major categories. The results were disappointing; they converted two of the nominations into Oscars, for costume design and art direction. But he had notched a unique record unrivalled anywhere in the history of Hollywood – his films had now acquired more than three dozen Academy award nominations.

Bugsy has cleared the air in many ways. It has provided him with a wife and a family and these have, indirectly, provided him with freedom, the greatest freedom he will ever have experienced. No longer will he have to face what was becoming a tormenting pressure to retain his reputation as a superstud and a leading Don Juan; in that respect the media can now leave him alone. He was already seen to be relaxing. In the wake of *Bugsy* and the round-the-world promotional effort, which took him and Annette on a whistle-stop tour of Europe and the Far East, he gave almost as many interviews as he has given in total in the previous twenty years.

He was still monosyllabic, but Annette was helping him to open up. She was also opening up the house, and inviting writers into the eyrie at the top of Mulholland Drive, the luxurious house set in thirty-seven acres of plantation which he has been tinkering with, like a script, for fifteen years. Its very presence in his life was more of a token than a symbol until Bening moved in. The success, the stardom, and the enduring fame seemed to be meaningless, too fluid.

The virtues she has brought to the Beatty house comple-
ment his mercurial intellect and charm. She too is charming,
but completely relaxed, and those who have observed them
at close hand report that oddly enough, Warren Beatty's
house, which he bought in the seventies, has the feel of having
been made for them. There was even a nursery, built off the
master bedroom – and it had been installed in readiness
during the early stages of the remodelling work fifteen years
earlier, and never used until now. It proves, he says, that
fatherhood was always on the agenda.

There is a topical coincidence to be recalled. The house was
once the home of the opera singer Lauritz Melchior, and
Bugsy Siegel also bought his house from an opera singer,
Lawrence Tibbett. Melchior's Art Deco house has been Beatty's only major concession to stardom while all around him
have built their huge mansions and filled their drives with
imported cars and every conceivable symbol of Hollywood's
inflationary age.

His is not a conspicuous house nor in any way ostentatious.
The oval swimming pool is but a pond compared with some
in the aerial shots of his neighbourhood. The pool is shel-
tered in part by an arch of drooping trees through which the
sunset on the Pacific horizon is always visible. His vistas
and his framing of garden features are as meticulous as his
film shots.

In the remodelling he built suites at opposite ends of the
house so that there could be space and privacy for those who
wanted it. The living-room is the one containing a vast
expanse of windows looking out over the variable landscape
of the San Fernando Valley, which is a breathtaking view
from this high perch when the smog clears.

The room itself gives the impression of space, freedom and
lightness and even the furniture is light coloured, in white
velvet chenille, and the two tables are glass. In the far area
to the back of the room is a grand piano, atop of which stands
a bronze statuette of a dancer. Unlike Nicholson's house,
where the walls are filled with his art collection of Matisse,
Picasso and other masters, Beatty's walls are bare, but there
are books all around which are reference works to his life,

such as *The Collected Letters and Speeches of John Reed*.
The filming of *Bugsy* saw a circle completed.

There was, whether he agreed with the assessment or not, a
new Beatty emerging in almost every major respect when one
reviews the key factors that have provided his motivation
and inspiration throughout the years, both personally and
professionally. He has anchored himself, finally, to the domesticity enforced by the presence of a wife and daughter, and
by all accounts enjoys the experience immensely. The house
has become a home, with the woman's touch apparent to all
who visit. Annette Bening's influence on his whole persona is
probably greater than any woman has previously achieved.

The time was right – because time was running out. He
was edging perilously closer to not being able to enjoy these
experiences at all, and he was in danger of proving the prediction of one of his past lovers – that he would die in his
own arms.

Bening took time to recover from the overwhelming position
of having become Warren Beatty's wife. Being a public person
was very new, but she quickly discovered how to handle it
and has opened him up, and straightened him out. While it is
impossible to forecast the permanency of the situation in that
world in which they live, Warren Beatty appears at the time
of writing to have settled, to have come to terms with at
least some of the conventions that he has been ignoring these
past years.

Annette was more forthcoming in her media interviews in
the months after their marriage than he has ever been about
his personal life. She confirmed that he was 'very happy, and
is a great father who helps with everything, including changing diapers.' She too believed he had reached a point in his
life when he had decided to settle down, and though he had
taken a long time to reach that decision, once he had, he was
totally committed to the idea.

His work may well benefit, too, and as we bring this account
of the life and times of Warren Beatty to a close for the time
being, it is clear that he is going to push ahead with his
career from a different standpoint. The Howard Hughes story,
which Beatty was, in some respects, becoming close to emulat-

ing, is still a back-burner project that may spring to life with a new vision. He and Annette were discussing a new film together, possibly a remake of the Cary Grant and Deborah Kerr classic *An Affair to Remember*. And there is his continuing interest in politics, which may rear again in his personal ambitions. He and Annette were high-profile guests at the inauguration party for President Bill Clinton in January 1993, and political or public office, which he has always shunned, could prove to be an appealing diversion as he approaches the autumnal years. The one factor which he always worried might rebound upon him in headlines, as with Gary Hart, was his private life. In a way, Bill Clinton showed how to dispose of similar attacks and allegations, though perhaps it does not matter any more.

Affairs past are no longer relevant, other than in a retrospective of his life. The new image of him as the family man provides a certain respectability that, while not eclipsing his reputation, will help to put it behind him if he so chooses. This has been a story of sex, lust and unbridled ambition interlaced with elements of power and politics; there have been some magnificent highs, which have provided him with considerable wealth, incredible movement, passion and emotion. And yet, overall, the picture is one of a man whose career, like his acting, has been curiously restrained; he could have been a much busier actor, even a better actor. As noted at the outset of this story, sex, glamour and acting would not hold the crux of the story, nor will it. It could never be all that there is in Beatty's life, as it has been for some of his contemporaries, and Warren Beatty has some surprises in store yet. Of that, there is no doubt.

Filmography

Splendor in the Grass Produced and directed by Elia Kazan.
Screenplay William Inge; *photography* Boris Kaufman; *music* David Amram; *production design* Richard Sylbert; *associate producers* William Inge and Charles H. McGuire. *Cast* Natalie Wood, Warren Beatty, Pat Hingle, Audrey Christie, Barbara Loden, Fred Stewart, Zohra Lampert, Joanna Roos, Jan Norris, Gary Lockwood, Sandy Dennis, John McGovern, Sean Garrison, William Inge.
Warner Bros, 124 minutes, opened 10 October 1961.

The Roman Spring of Mrs Stone Produced by Louis de Rochemont. Directed by José Quintero.
Screenplay Gavin Lambert (based on the novel by Tennessee Williams); *photography* Harry Waxman; *music* Richard Addinsell; *production design* Roger Furse; *art direction* Herbert Smith; *lyrics* sung by Cleo Laine. *Cast* Vivien Leigh, Warren Beatty, Lotte Lenya, Coral Browne, Jill St John, Jeremy Spenser, Stella Bonheur, Josephine Brown, Peter Dyneley, Carl Jaffe, Harold Kasket, Viola Keats, Bessie Love, Warren Mitchell, Ernest Thesiger, Sarah Miles.
Warner Bros, 104 minutes, opened 28 December 1961.

All Fall Down Produced by John Houseman. Directed by John Frankenheimer.
Screenplay William Inge (based on the novel by James Leo Herlihy); *photography* Lionel Lindon; *music* Alex North; *art*

direction George W. Davis and Preston Ames. *Cast* Warren Beatty, Eva Marie Saint, Karl Malden, Angela Lansbury, Brandon De Wilde, Constance Ford, Barbara Baxley, Evans Evans, Jennifer Howard.
MGM, 111 minutes, opened 11 April 1962.

Lilith Produced and directed by Robert Rossen, who also wrote the screenplay (based on the novel by J.R. Salamanca). *Photography* Eugen Shufftan; *music* Kenyon Hopkins; *production design* Richard Sylbert. *Cast* Warren Beatty, Jean Seberg, Peter Fonda, Kim Hunter, Anne Meacham, James Patterson, Jessica Walter, Gene Hackman.
Columbia, 114 minutes, opened 20 September 1964.

Mickey One Produced and directed by Arthur Penn.
Screenplay Alan Surgal; *photography* Ghislain Cloquet; *music* Eddie Sauter with Stan Getz; *production design* George Jenkins. *Cast* Warren Beatty, Alexandra Stewart, Franchot Tone, Hurd Hatfield, Teddy Hart, Jeff Corey, Kamatari Fujiwara, Donne Michelle.
Columbia, 93 minutes, opened 27 September 1965.

Promise Her Anything Produced by Stanley Rubin. Directed by Arthur Hiller.
Screenplay William Peter Blatty (based on a story by Arne Sultan and Marvin Worth); *photography* Douglas Slocombe; *music* Lynn Murray, *title song* by Burt Bacharach and Hal David; *art direction* Wilfrid Shingleton. *Cast* Warren Beatty, Leslie Caron, Bob Cummings, Hermione Gingold, Lionel Stander, Asa Maynor, Keenan Wynn, Cathleen Nesbitt, Michael Bradley, Bessie Love, Mavis Villiers, Warren Mitchell, Sydney Tafler.
Warner Bros, 98 minutes, opened 22 February 1966.

Kaleidoscope Produced by Elliott Kastner. Directed by Jack Smight.
Screenplay Robert and Jane Howard-Carrington (from their original story); *photography* Christopher Challis; *music* Stanley Myers; *art direction* Maurice Carter. *Cast* Warren Beatty, Susannah York, Clive Revill, Eric Porter, Murray Melvin,

George Sewell, Stanley Meadows, John Junkin, Larry Taylor, Yootha Joyce, Jane Birkin, George Murcell, Anthony Newlands.
Warner Bros, 103 minutes, opened 22 September 1966.

Bonnie and Clyde Produced by Warren Beatty. Directed by Arthur Penn.
Screenplay David Newman and Robert Benton; *consultant* Robert Towne; *photography* Burnett Guffey; *music* Charles Strouse; *art direction* Dean Tavoularis; *costumes* Theadora Van Runkle. *Cast* Warren Beatty, Faye Dunaway, Michael J. Pollard, Gene Hackman, Estelle Parsons, Denver Pyle, Dub Taylor, Evans Evans, Gene Wilder, James Stiver.
Warner Bros, 111 minutes, opened 13 August 1967.

The Only Game in Town Produced by Fred Kohlmar. Directed by George Stevens.
Screenplay Frank D. Gilroy (from his own play); *photography* Henri Decaë; *music* Maurice Jarre; *art direction* Herman Blumenthal and Auguste Capelier. *Cast* Elizabeth Taylor, Warren Beatty, Charles Braswell, Hank Henry.
20th Century-Fox, 113 minutes, opened 4 March 1970.

McCabe and Mrs Miller Produced by David Foster and Mitchell Brower. Directed by Robert Altman.
Screenplay Brian McKay and Robert Altman (based on the novel *McCabe* by Edmund Naughton); *photography* Vilmos Zsigmond; *lyrics* Leonard Cohen; *production design* Leon Ericksen. *Cast* Warren Beatty, Julie Christie, Rene Auberjonois, John Schuck, Bert Remsen, Keith Carradine, William Devane, Corey Fischer, Shelley Duvall, Michael Murphy, Anthony Holland, Hugh Millais, Manfred Schulz, Jace Vander Veen.
Warner Bros, 120 minutes, opened 24 June 1971.

$ (Dollars) Produced by Mike Frankovich. Directed and written by Richard Brooks.
Photography Petrus Schloemp; *music* Quincy Jones; *songs* 'Money is' and 'Do it to it' sung by Little Richard and 'When You're Smiling' by Roberta Flack; *art direction* Guy Sheppard

and Olaf Ivens. *Cast* Warren Beatty, Goldie Hawn, Gert Frobe, Robert Webber, Scott Brady, Arthur Brauss, Robert Stiles, Wolfgang Kieling, Robert Herron, Christiane Maybach, Hans Hutter, Monica Stender.
Columbia, 119 minutes, opened 15 December 1971.

The Parallax View Produced and directed by Alan J. Pakula.
Screenplay David Giler and Lorenzo Semple Jr (based on the novel by Loren Singer); *photography* Gordon Willis; *music* Michael Small; *production design* George Jenkins. *Cast* Warren Beatty, Hume Cronyn, William Daniels, Paula Prentiss, Kelly Thordsen, Earl Hindman, Kenneth Mars, Walter McGinn, Jim Davis, Bill Joyce, Bill McKinney, William Jordan, Stacy Keach, Ford Rainey.
Paramount, 102 minutes, opened 19 June 1974.

Shampoo Produced by Warren Beatty. Directed by Hal Ashby.
Screenplay Warren Beatty and Robert Towne; *photography* Laszlo Kovacs; *music* Paul Simon; *production design* Richard Sylbert. *Cast* Warren Beatty, Julie Christie, Goldie Hawn, Lee Grant, Jack Warden, Tony Bill, Carrie Fisher, Jay Robinson, George Furth, Brad Dexter, William Castle.
Columbia, 112 minutes, opened 11 February 1975.

The Fortune Produced by Mike Nichols and Don Devlin. Directed by Mike Nichols.
Screenplay Adrien Joyce; *photography* John Alonzo; *music* David Shire; *production design* Richard Sylbert. *Cast* Warren Beatty, Jack Nicholson, Stockard Channing, Florence Stanley, Richard B. Shull, Tom Newman, John Fiedler, Scatman Crothers, Dub Taylor, Ian Wolfe, Rose Michtom, Brian Avery, Christopher Guest, Kathryn Grody, Jim Antonio.
Columbia, 88 minutes, opened 20 May 1975.

Heaven Can Wait Produced by Warren Beatty. Directed by Warren Beatty and Buck Henry.
Screenplay Warren Beatty and Elaine May; *photography* William A. Fraker; *music* Dave Grusin; *production design* Paul Sylbert. *Cast* Warren Beatty, Julie Christie, James

Mason, Jack Warden, Charles Grodin, Dyan Cannon, Buck Henry, Vincent Gardenia, Joseph Maher, Dolph Sweet, R.G. Armstrong, John Randolph, William Sylvester.
Paramount, 101 minutes, opened 28 June 1978.

Reds Produced and directed by Warren Beatty.
Executive producers Simon Relph and Dede Allen; *associate producer* David MacLeod; *screenplay* Warren Beatty and Trevor Griffiths; *photography* Vittorio Storaro; *music* Stephen Sondheim and Dave Grusin; *production design* Richard Sylbert. *Cast* Warren Beatty, Diane Keaton, Jack Nicholson, Edward Herrmann, Jerzy Kosinski, Paul Sorvino, Maureen Stapleton, Nicolas Coster, M. Emmet Walsh, Ian Wolfe, Bessie Love, MacIntyre Dixon, Pat Starr, Eleanor D. Wilson, Max Wright, George Plimpton, Harry Ditson, Leigh Curran, Kathryn Grody, Brenda Currin, Nancy Dulguid, Norman Chancer, Dolph Sweet, Ramon Bieri, Jack O'Leary, Gene Hackman, William Daniels, Gerald Hiken, Dave King, Joseph Buloff, Stefan Gryff, Roger Sloman, Stuart Richman.
Paramount, 199 minutes, opened 3 December 1981.

Ishtar Produced by Warren Beatty. Written and directed by Elaine May.
Associate producer David MacLeod; *photography* Vittorio Storaro; *music* Dave Grusin; *production design* Paul Sylbert; *songs* Paul Williams. *Cast* Warren Beatty, Dustin Hoffman, Isabelle Adjani, Charles Grodin, Carol Kane, Tess Harper, Jack Weston.
Columbia, about 145 minutes, opened 14 May 1987.

Dick Tracy Produced and directed by Warren Beatty. Co-producer Jon Landau.
Screenplay Jim Cash and Jack Epps Jr (based on the characters created by Chester Gould); *photography* Vittorio Storaro; *music* Danny Elfman; *songs* Stephen Sondheim; *production design* Richard Sylbert; *art direction* Harold Michelson. *Cast* Warren Beatty, Madonna, Glenne Headley, Al Pacino, Dustin Hoffman, Charlie Korsmo, Charles Durning, Mandy Patinkin, James Caan, Paul Sorvino, Kathy Bates, Dick Van Dyke, Estelle Parsons, Mary Warnov, Lawrence Steven Meyers,

William Forsythe, Chuck Hicks, R.G. Armstrong, Henry Silva, Michael J. Pollard.
Disney, 105 minutes, opened 15 June 1990.

Bugsy Produced by Warren Beatty, Barry Levinson and Mark Johnson. Directed by Barry Levinson.
Screenplay James Toback; *photography* Allen Daviau; *music* Ennio Morricone; *production design* Dennis Gassner. *Cast* Warren Beatty, Annette Bening, Ben Kingsley, Harvey Keitel, Joe Mantega.
TriStar, 131 minutes, opened 13 December 1991

Select Bibliography

Andersen, Christopher, *Madonna Unauthorised*, Bantam. Doubleday, New York, 1991.

Bragg, Melvyn, *Rich, The Biography of Richard Burton*, Hodder and Stoughton, London, 1988.

Brownstein, Ronald, *The Power and the Glitter*, Pantheon, New York, 1990.

Collins, Joan, *Past Imperfect*, W.H. Allen, London, 1978.

Ekland, Britt, *True Britt*, Sphere Books, London, 1980.

Kazan, Elia, *A Life*, Andre Deutsch, London, 1988.

Lax, Edward, *Woody Allen, A Biography*, Jonathan Cape, London, 1991.

MacLaine, Shirley, *Don't Fall Off The Mountain*, Norton, New York, 1970.

Morley, Sheridan and Payne, Graham (eds), *The Noel Coward Diaries*, Little, Brown, New York, 1982.

Parker, John, *Five for Hollywood*, Macmillan, London, 1989.

Parker, John, *The Joker's Wild: The Biography of Jack Nicholson*, Anaya, London, 1991.

Polanski, Roman, *Roman, an Autobiography*, Morrow, New York, 1984.

Quirk, Laurence J., *The Films of Warren Beatty*, Citadel Press, New York, 1990.

Rader, Dotson, *Tennessee Williams: Cry of the Heart*, Doubleday, New York, 1985.

Strasberg, Susan, *Bittersweet*, Putnam, New York, 1980.

Thomson, David, *Warren Beatty, A Life and A Story*, Secker and Warburg, London, 1987.

Wood, Lana, *Natalie, A Memoir of Natalie Wood*, Putnam, New York, 1984.

Yule, Andrew, *Enigma, David Puttnam, The Story So Far*, Mainstream Publishing, Edinburgh, 1988.

Index

Academy awards *see* Oscars
Actors Studio 26, 32, 40, 46, 97–8, 108
Adjani, Isabelle 277, 278
Adler, Stella 2, 29–32, 34, 35
Agatha 283–4
All About Eve 264
All Fall Down 75, 76, 82, 86
All the Fine Young Cannibals 57
All the King's Men 99
Allen, Woody 9, 72, 237–8, 248, 251
Altman, Robert 175, 179, 182, 183
Andrews, Julie 124–5, 151
Annie Hall 237–8
anti-war demonstration 188–9
Arlington 14, 16–17
Ashby, Hal 200, 201, 204, 207, 217
Attenborough, Richard 104

'B' movies 33
Baez, Joan 216
Bardot, Brigitte 145
Barrow, Clyde *see Bonnie and Clyde*
Bates, Alan 176, 177
Batman 295, 296, 304–5, 309, 310
Beaton, Cecil 103
Beatty, Kathlyn (daughter) 324
Beatty, Warren
  business skills 121–2, 129–31
  casting, relations with women and
    238–40, *see also* Beatty, Warren,
    affairs
  celebrity status achieved 69–70
  childhood 11–17
  choosiness 34–5, 88–91, 99
  commitment, feelings on 175
  'discovered' 35
  as drop-out 21–2
  education 17–22
  family, relations with 15–16
  as father 324, 328
  fees 81
  at feminist meeting 222–5
  on fidelity 312–13
  aged fifty 289–90
  film critics on 61–2
  first dramatic role 46–7, 48–9
  first film offer 58
  and friendship 211–13
  health 34, 89, 257
  household 326–8
  interviews 9–10, 78–80, 91, 164–5,
    193–4, 307–8, 312–13
  marriage plans 61
  menial work done by 18–19, 34
  military service 64
  as 'Mr Clean' 166, 219
  as musician 14–15, 44
  and politics 89, 153–5, 166–7, 187–95,
    279
    see also Hart; McGovern; *Reds*;
      Reed, John; Russia
  and retakes 7, 133, 233–4, 255
  rootlessness 113–14
  scripts rejected by 88–90, 99
  self-identification in films 317
  and sport 17–18, 19–20, 233
  status under threat 294, 296
  surname 11, 70
  and the telephone 211–12
  television roles 35
  and travel 174

Beatty, Warren, affairs *see* Adjani;
    Bening; Carne; Caron; Christie;
    Collins; Ekland; Keaton; Madonna;
    Phillips; Strasberg, Susan; Wood,
    Lana; Wood, Natalie
Beaty, *see also* Beatty
Beaty, Henry Warren *see* Beatty,
    Warren
Beaty, Ira Owens (father) 12–14, 18, 22,
    49
Beaty, Kathlyn (mother) 12–14, 49
Beaty, Shirley *see* MacLaine, Shirley
Bening, Annette 9, 318–21, 323
    and Warren Beatty 323–9
Benton, Robert 117–18, 119–20, 128–9,
    139, 143
Bessant, Don 150, 152
Billy Liar 150
Bludhorn, Charlie 250–51, 260, 266
Bogarde, Dirk 150–1
Bogart, Humphrey 130
Bogdanovich, Peter 232
Bonnie and Clyde 3, 117–42, 170, 321
    casting 122–5
    financing 128–31, 133
    release 133–4
    re-release 139–40
    reviews 134–7
    takings 141
    Warren Beatty's involvement level
        141
Booth, Shirley 46, 47
Brando, Marlon 2, 26–7, 32, 39, 43, 48,
    63, 98
Brooks, Richard 184, 253
Broussard, Rebecca 221, 304, 313, 324,
    325
Bryant, Louise 241, 242
Bugsy 316–19, 321–23, 325–6
Burton, Richard 81, 82–3, 157–62, 164
    spending spree 158
Butch Cassidy and the Sundance Kid
    152
Butterfield 8: 42, 54

Caddell, Patrick 271–2, 290–92, 292
Callas, Maria 162
Cannon, Dyan 233, 235
'caper' movies 116, 184
Capote, Truman 3, 119
Carnal Knowledge 180–82
Carne, Judy 138, 146–9
Caron, Leslie 1–4, 102–3, 238

Bonnie and Clyde 117–19
Promise Her Anything 111–13, 115
theatre roles 104
and Warren Beatty 4, 95, 105–7,
    112–16, 119, 138, 142
Carter, Jimmy 247, 259
Cassavetes, John 145, 230
Cat on a Hot Tin Roof 254
Catholic church 168, 208
Chaplin, Oona 263
Chaplin, Sidney 43
Chariots of Fire 264, 284–5
Chinatown 210
Christie, Julie 3, 146, 149–52, 188, 202,
    205–6, 238, 314
    on infidelity 183–4
    and media 176–7
    and Warren Beatty 151–2, 154–5, 163,
        164–6, 173, 174–80, 182–4, 220,
        233, 312
CIA 188, 244
Cilento, Diane 100–101
cinemas
    chains 33
    projectionists 234
Citizen Kane 236
Cleopatra 38, 42, 54–5, 64, 161, 80, 158
Clift, Montgomery 2, 19, 26–7, 32, 39,
    45, 98, 116, 160
Clockwork Orange, The 200
close-ups, use of 160
Cold War, effects 25–6
Collins, Joan 38, 43–5, 49–50, 54, 60–61,
    64, 74–5, 314
    aims for *Cleopatra* 54–5, 64–5
    engaged to Warren Beatty 58–9, 61,
        64, 66–8, 74, 85–6
    pregnant 58–9
    studio suspends 50
Columbia Pictures 71, 108, 204–5,
    204–6, 226, 274–6, 280–82, 285,
    287
Come Back Little Sheba 46–7
commercial viability, films 201
communism *see* Reed, John; Russia
Connery, Sean 112, 137
Cornfeld, Bernie 6
Country Wife, The 203
Couples 204
Coward, Noel 66
Crist, Judith 110, 115, 134
Crowley, Mart 123–4
Crowther, Bosley 61, 75–6, 87, 110, 135

INDEX

Darling 150–51
Davis, Sally Ogle 5–6
Dean, James 2, 12, 21, 26, 27–9, 32, 39, 48, 56, 63, 86
desert, adjusted 280
Dick Tracy 268, 275–6, 294–301, 303–7, 309–11
Diller, Barry 232, 250, 252, 256–8, 260–61, 266
Disney studios 295, 298, 309–10
divorce procedure, pre-permissive 106, 107
Doctor Zhivago 151
Dollars 184–5
Donahue, Troy 55, 70
Donen, Stanley 82, 159
Drive He Said 180–1
drugs culture 166–7, 170
Dunaway, Faye 124, 131, 139–40

Eagleton, Thomas 193
East of Eden 28, 32, 39
Eastman, Carol *alias* 'Adrien Joyce' 209
Easy Rider 10, 140, 163, 164, 180, 181, 215
Ekland, Britt 7–8, 178–8
Esther and the King 59, 61
Evans, Robert 152, 232
explicitness in films 199–201

Faber, Steven 168
Fahrenheit 451: 3, 117, 118, 151
FBI 188, 244
fees, film stars' 81, 82, 94, 123, 128, 157–8, 164, 298
Feiffer, Jules 180
Feldman, Charlie 87–8
feminism 181, 222–5
Field, Betty 47, 49
First Artists 284
Fisher, Eddie 42, 44, 54, 81, 161
Fonda, Henry 94, 264
Fonda, Jane 37–8, 88, 124, 188, 196, 236
Fonda, Peter 100, 101, 163
Fortune, The 209–10
Freud 4, 115

Gable, Clark 42
Gigi 103, 104
Gilliatt, Penelope 136
Go-Between, The 176
Godfather, The 152–3, 170, 200, 237
Goldwyn, Sam 173

gossip columnists 44, 54, 60, 74, 78, 90–91, 125, 139, 219
Griffiths, Trevor 246, 264
Group Theater 29–30, 32, 40
gun control 154–5, 158, 195
Gypsy 76–7

Hackman, Gene 110, 124, 139–40
Hair 203–4, 237
Hall, Arsenio 307
Hall, Peter 103, 104, 104–6, 112–13
Hardcore 226
Harris, Richard 124–5
Harrison, Rex 158, 161, 164
Hart, Gary 190, 268–72
  scandal 290–4
Harvey, Laurence 150–51
Haskell, Molly 223–5, 234–5
Hawn, Goldie 184, 205–6
Hayes, Helen 19
Hayworth, Rita 40–41
Heaven Can Wait 18, 231–5
Heinz, Mr and Mrs H.J. 244
Hellman, Lillian 212–13, 241, 243, 247, 278
Henry, Buck 232, 234
Hepburn, Katharine 139, 264
Here Comes Mr Jordan 227, 231
Herlihy, Leo 75–6
Herrmann, Edward 252–3
Heston, Charlton 31, 33–4, 150, 188
Heyman, John 176
'high concept' 201
Hill, Virginia 315, 316, 322, 323
Hoffman, Dustin 1, 28, 69, 163, 274–5, 276, 278, 281, 283–4, 286–7, 289–90, 297, 312
Hollywood
  blacklists 188
  in throes of change 53–4, 80, 99, 127–8
Hopper, Dennis 163, 215–17
'Horace Whigham', identity of 249–50
Howard, Trevor 50, 105
Hughes, Howard 231, 267–8, 328
Humphrey, Hubert 193
Huston, Angelica 218, 221, 277
Huston, John 4, 115
Hyams, Joe 79

In Cold Blood 3–4, 119
Inge, William 2, 6, 33, 36, 45–7, 49, 50–51, 53, 59, 75, 79, 81, 98, 108

and Warren Beatty 35, 38–9, 45–7, 55, 75, 85–6
Ishtar 273–5, 276–83, 285–7
budget 281

James Bond films 112, 137
Jules et Jim 118

Kael, Pauline 137, 182, 318
'Kafkaesque' films, see *Mickey One*
Kaleidoscope 115–17
Katzenberg, Jeffrey 295, 298, 310
Kauffman, Stanley 208, 230
Kazan, Elia 19, 27, 28, 30, 39–40, 57–8, 61, 88–9, 97, 98, 108, 114
and James Dean 27–8
on Natalie Wood 57, 70
Keaton, Diane 236–8, 255, 262, 264
and Warren Beatty 236, 238–41, 247, 248, 273, 312
and Woody Allen 237–8
Kennedy, Jacqueline 162
Kennedy, John F. 88–90, 153, 196, 269
Kennedy, Senator Robert 153–4, 196
Kerr, Walter 32–3
King, Carole 191
Kingsley, Ben 322
'kitchen-sink' drama 87
Knife in the Water 144
Kosinski, Jerzy 251, 257

L-Shaped Room, The 1, 3, 95, 104
Las Vegas 268, 315, 316, 322
Last Detail, The 200
Last Tango in Paris 195, 201
Leigh, Vivien 62–6, 68, 147, 240
Lemmon, Jack 36
Lennon, John 188
Lenya, Lotte 65
Levinson, Barry 317–18, 323
Lewis, Bobby 30, 31, 32
Lilith 99–100
Loew, Arthur, Jr 43–4, 94–5
Logan, Joshua 35–6, 37, 38
London, 'swinging' 111–12, 204
Loren, Sophia 81
Loss of Roses, A 46–7, 48–9, 55
Love with a Proper Stranger 94
Lownes, Victor 144, 169

*M*A*S*H* 175
McCabe and Mrs Miller 176–80, 182–3
McCarthy, Senator Joseph 99, 188, 243

McElwaine, Guy 274–6, 282
McGovern, George 155, 167, 189–95
MacLaine, Shirley (sister) 95, 190, 192, 236, 312
early days 13–17, 18
first roles 22
McQueen, Steve 88, 94, 98
Madonna 298–301, 303–12
roadshow 305–8
and Warren Beatty 300–301, 303–11, 312
Mafia 315–16
Mahern, Michael 265–6
Mailer, Norman 312–13
Manchurian Candidate, The 196
Mann, Bernice 204–5
Mann, Daniel 46–7
Manson, Charles 170, 321
Marshall, Marion 82–3, 92
maternal influences 12–14
May, Elaine 192, 229–35, 250, 273–5, 277–81, 285–7
Mayer, Louis B. 187
Method acting 2, 26, 29–33, 325–6
principles 30–31
and rest of cast 47–8
training *see* Adler; Strasberg, Lee
MGM 41–3, 75, 128, 217
Mickey One 102, 105, 107–10
Mikey and Nicky 229–30
Miller, Arthur 33, 46, 86
Mirsch, Walter 71
Monroe, Marilyn 26, 30, 36, 46, 269
Moreau, Jeanne 222–6
Morgenstern, Joseph 136, 137
Myra Breckenridge 204

New York 28–31, 33, 34, 35–6, 54, 108, 191
Newley, Anthony 74–5
Newman, David 117–18, 139, 143
Newman, Paul 57, 98, 99, 116, 139, 153, 264
Nichols, Mike 181, 191, 200, 209, 229, 246, 264, 319
Nicholson, Jack 10, 98, 122, 140, 163, 173, 180–82, 200, 210–12, 217, 264, 295, 313–14, 324–5, 327
origins 14
Batman 295, 296, 304–5, 309
as father 304, 313, 324
and marriage 221
Reds 251, 254–6, 262–3

INDEX

The Fortune 209–10
  on Warren Beatty 210–11
1950s film stars: 27, 42
Nixon, Richard 189, 192, 193, 203, 204, 205
Novak, Kim 36, 46
nudity in entertainment 200, 203–4, 237

Odets, Clifford 30, 40–41, 98, 99
Olivier, Laurence 32, 62–3, 66, 112, 236, 254
On Golden Pond 263–4
O'Neill, Eugene 14, 30, 241–2
Only Game in Town, The 157, 159–64, 168
Osborne, John 87
Oscars
  and nominations 1, 10, 36, 42, 46, 54, 76, 81, 86, 95, 99, 103, 139–40, 151, 152, 166, 184, 195, 196, 210, 231, 235–6, 251, 262–3, 264, 284, 295, 326

Pacino, Al 273, 297
'packaging', film 201
Pakula, Alan J. 195–6
Parallax View, The 195–7, 203
Paramount movies 152, 230, 232, 250, 252–3, 256–7, 260–61, 266–7
Paris, social life 162–3
Parker, Bonnie, *see Bonnie and Clyde*
Parrish 37–8, 70–71
Penn, Arthur 4, 98, 107–8, 122, 131, 134–5, 139, 222, 223–4
Penn, Sean 298, 299
Phillips, John 215–17
Phillips, Michelle 215–20, 238
  and Warren Beatty 215, 218–20
Place in the Sun, A 160
Playboy Organisation 249
Plimpton, George 249–50, 251–2
Polanski, Roman 143–4, 146, 168–71, 210, 251, 277
Pollard, Michael J. 125, 139–40
Power, Debbie 44, 94
Preminger, Otto 101, 124
Priggen, Norman 176
Promise Her Anything 3, 111–15
PT 109: 88–90
Puttnam, David 264–5, 282–6, 288

Raft, George 316
Raphael, Frederic 150–1

ratings, film 168, 181, 199–200, 208
Reagan, Ronald 56–7, 188, 194, 247, 260, 293
realism in films 40, 87
Rebel Without A Cause 28–9, 48, 56
Redford, Robert 88, 123, 153, 192, 195, 291
Redgrave, Vanessa 283–4
Reds 174, 239, 241–67, 284–5
  budget 256
  casting 247, 249–52
  marketing 265–6
  reviewed 261–2
  settings 253
  and world political climate 259
Reed, John 174, 187, 241–3, 245–6
  see also Reds
Reed, Rex 234, 262
Remick, Lee 55, 57
Renoir, Jean 41, 104, 204
Rice, Donna 292
Road to Hong Kong 68, 74
Robbins, Jerome 70, 70–71, 72
rock concerts 191–2
Roman Spring of Mrs Stone, The 62–4, 65, 68, 76, 86
Rosemary's Baby 145, 168
Rossen, Robert 99, 99–102
Russia 25–6, 242–8
  see also Reds; Reed, John

Saint Joan 101
St John, Jill 66
sales, film prop 128
Schlesinger, John 150–51, 163
Schrader, Paul 226
Scorsese, Martin 275–6
Scott, George C. 99, 152, 226–7
Seberg, Jean 100–102, 188
Sellers, Peter 178
Shakespeare, William 2, 104, 112, 150
Shampoo 195, 201–8
  lawsuit 204–5
Siegel, Benjamin 'Bugsy' 268, 315–17, 321
Simon and Garfunkel 191
Sinatra, Frank 157, 192
Skouras, Spyros 64
Smight, Jack 116
social conscience and art 41, 153–4
Sons and Lovers 49–50
Sorensen, Theodore 269
Southern traditions 13

Splendor in the Grass 55, 57–8, 59–62, 76, 81, 86
Springer, John 78, 143
Staircase 157–9, 168
Stanislavski *see* Method
Stapleton, Maureen 6–7, 26, 45–6, 51, 251, 253–4, 264
  on actors' training 31–2
  on Marlon Brando 48
  on travelling to England 254
Stevens, George 11, 26, 157, 159–60
Strasberg, Lee 2, 30–32, 97
Strasberg, Susan 67, 147
Streetcar Named Desire, A 26–7, 62–3
Streisand, Barbra 191, 195
strike of extras 258
studio system 27, 33–4
Sukarno, Mme Dewi 145

Tate, Sharon 144, 145, 168–9
  murdered 169–70
Taylor, Elizabeth 12, 26, 42, 43–4, 54, 82, 128, 164
  and *Cleopatra* 38, 54–5, 64–5, 74, 81
  and Richard Burton 81, 82–3
  The Only Game in Town 157–63
  and Warren Beatty 161–2
television 33–5, 266–7
Ten Days That Shook the World 174, 242
Thompson, Tommy 92, 93
Thoroughly Modern Millie 135, 137
Time magazine 70, 136, 137, 170
Toback, James 275, 321–2
Todd, Mike 42, 44
Tone, Franchot 108, 109
Towne, Robert 101, 122, 131–2, 200, 201, 203–5, 208, 210, 250
Tracy, Spencer 3, 71, 139
Tristar 318
Truffaut, Francis 3, 117–18, 151
20th Century-Fox 38, 43, 49–50, 64–5, 71, 80, 144, 158–9, 163–4, 266
Tynan, Kenneth 49

USA, social changes 25–6

Valley of the Dolls 168

Vietnam *see* anti-war demonstration
Vincent, Francis 'Fay' 276, 282–3, 286–8
Visconti, Luchino 67, 88
Voight, Jon 163, 166, 236

Wagner, Robert 55–6, 59–61, 71–2, 74–5, 77, 82–3, 88, 92, 254
Wanger, Walter 43
Warden, Jack 206, 233, 235
Warner Brothers 28, 37, 89, 116, 136, 140
Warner, Jack 38, 55, 56, 57, 70, 93, 129–31, 133, 187
  character 129–31
Watergate 194, 203
Welles, Orson 232, 235–6
West Side Story 70, 71, 76, 81
'What's new, pussycat?' 72
Whitcomb, John 79
White, Steven 320
Who's Afraid of Virginia Woolf? 181, 264
Wild One, The 27
Williams, Tennessee 2, 33, 46, 47, 50–51, 62–4, 86
Wise, Robert 71, 72–3
Witches of Eastwick, The 295, 296–7
Wood, Lana 61, 92, 202–3
Wood, Natalie 12, 28, 58, 59, 70–71, 76–7, 94–5, 163, 238, 314
  and analyst 123–4
  and *Bonnie and Clyde* 122–3
  operated on 71
  and Robert Wagner 55–6, 73–4, 77, 82, 83, 254
  and *Splendor in the Grass* 58–60, 61–2, 70, 76
  and Warren Beatty 72–8, 81–3, 88, 91–3
  and *West Side Story* 70–73

Yevtushenko, Yevgeny 244–5
York, Susannah 4–5, 39, 115–16
youth culture 25–8, 166–7, 167–8, 170

Zanuck, Darryl F. 157–60, 163, 164
Zimmerman, Paul 196
Zinoviev, Gregory 251